The AEF in Print

The AEF
in Print

An Anthology of American

Journalism in World War I

Edited by Chris Dubbs and
John-Daniel Kelley

University of North Texas Press
Denton, Texas

10 9 8 7 6 5 4 3 2 1

Permissions:
University of North Texas Press
1155 Union Circle #311336
Denton, TX 76203-5017

The paper used in this book meets the minimum requirements of the American
National Standard for Permanence of Paper for Printed Library Materials,
z39.48.1984. Binding materials have been chosen for durability.

Library of Congress Cataloging-in-Publication Data
Dubbs, Chris (Military historian), editor. | Kelley, John-Daniel, 1991- editor.
      The AEF in print : an anthology of American journalism in World War I /
edited by Chris Dubbs and John-Daniel Kelley.
      pages cm.
Includes bibliographical references and index.
      ISBN-13 978-1-57441-713-5 (cloth : alk. paper)
      ISBN-13 978-1-57441-721-0 (ebook)
1. United States. Army. American Expeditionary Forces—Press coverage—
History. 2. World War, 1914–1918—Press coverage—United States. 3. World War,
1914–1918—Campaigns—Western Front. 4. Journalism—United States—History—
20th century. 5. United States—History, Military—20th century.

D632 .A34 2018
070.4/4994041273–dc23
2018003000

The electronic edition of this book was made possible
by the support of the Vick Family Foundation.
Typeset by vPrompt eServices.

Contents

List of Illustrations

Introduction

New York Times correspondent Wythe Williams described the daunting task facing America when it entered the war as "the biggest, hardest and greatest work ever attempted by a people since mankind flocked into nations at Babel." That bit of journalistic hyperbole hit fairly close to the mark. Not only did the country have to transform its fledgling army—experienced at fighting Indians, doddering colonial empires, and Mexican bandits—into a million-man, modern fighting force, but it had to project and sustain that power 3,000 miles away, across a U-boat-infested ocean.

By the time the United States entered the war in April 1917, Americans knew well the gruesome nature of this conflict. American reporters had been actively covering the war since it began in August 1914. In fact, as representatives of the neutral United States, those journalists got access to every army, in every war zone. They struggled through an initial period of suffocating military secrecy and harassment, and then learned to function with strict censorship, wartime propaganda, and official efforts to manage the news.

Despite the hurdles, American newspapers overflowed with news of the war. Urban newspapers often had their own correspondent in the war zone. Smaller papers subscribed to one of the news services, such as United Press, Associated Press, and the International News Service, that fed a constant flow of breaking news. Magazines sent famous journalists, novelists, and military experts to the war zone to write feature stories that gave a fuller picture of events. In the early years of the war, American readers were often better informed about developments in the conflict than people in any of the warring countries.

Once the United States took the long-delayed step of entering the war, the nature of reporting changed. Now that the country was sending its own boys to fight, American readers sought to understand and be reassured about their participation. How were boys just off the farm or plucked from the streets of small towns and big cities transformed into soldiers and sailors? How did a troop ship avoid lurking U-boats? How did the doughboys get on with our French and British allies? What abominations awaited them in the trenches? How well did they fight? How was their sacrifice honored?

From the declaration of war, through mobilization, the triumphal arrival of the first U.S. troops in France, training, the slow introduction to the fighting, the string of battles, and the Armistice, reporters covered every step of the journey. No other nation took so deliberate a plunge into the war, and thus none made so complete a public chronicle of the experience.

Like every other military, the U.S. Army recognized the need to balance the public's appetite for war news with the need to safeguard military activities. The American Expeditionary Forces followed the lead of its allies by credentialing a small pool of reporters to its army. Credentialed correspondents wore an army uniform, without insignia of rank, and were subject to military regulations. Only credentialed correspondents received AEF briefings, took conducted war zone tours, and were permitted to witness battles. The military initially thought that fifteen correspondents would be sufficient to cover the American army, but that number quickly doubled and then tripled.

Additionally, the AEF created the position of "Visiting Correspondent," a reporter who was attached to an individual division and responsible for writing the news of only that division's activities. Frank Sibley of the *Boston Globe* became the first Visiting Correspondent, serving with the Twenty-sixth Division, composed largely of men from New England. Following the Twenty-sixth through training and their first experiences with combat, Sibley was able to send regular news stories so that *Globe* readers could stay informed about their hometown boys.

Female journalists, very small in numbers prior to U.S. entry, appeared in greater numbers once America entered the fight. Two were credentialed as Visiting Correspondents—Elizabeth Frazier (*Saturday Evening Post*) and Cecile Dorrian (*Newark Evening News*), but others found ways to cover the war without AEF sanction. In Chapter 9, Shirley Putnam draws on her experience as a Red Cross nurse's aide to tell readers of the magazine *The Bellman* about caring for the wounded following the Battle of Château-Thierry. War reporting, providing eyewitness accounts on events so important to the American public, increased the professional stature of American women journalists.

World War I occurred during a pivotal period in the evolution of journalistic norms and military-press relations. The standards of ethics and objectivity in news reporting would not begin to take firm root until the decade after the war, when participants offered more sobering and critical accounts in their memoirs. There is also a marked contrast between the reporting done by American journalists before and after U.S. entry into the war. As observers from a neutral nation, reporters often gave more realistic portrayals of combat, military strategy, and the impact of war on the civilian population. Once America joined the conflict, they became promoters of the U.S. war effort. They might occasionally offer gritty details of fighting and sound a somber note on casualties, but that usually came with a positive spin.

To assure unwavering public support for the war, President Woodrow Wilson created the Committee on Public Information (CPI), directed by former journalist George Creel. The CPI promoted the war effort in many ways, including by reporting the news and attempting to control it. Although the CPI had no official powers of censorship, it implemented "voluntary guidelines" for the news media and helped to pass the Espionage Act of 1917 and the Sedition Act of 1918. The Espionage Act prohibited the expression of opinions that would interfere with the U.S. military efforts to defeat Germany. The Sedition Act criminalized the writing of anything critical of American involvement in the war. The impact of these laws and the CPI's influence meant that *every* news story was censored to some extent, somewhere along the line, either by the journalist who wrote it, the military censor who passed it, the government-controlled cables that transmitted it, or in newspaper and magazine offices, in accordance with the "voluntary" rules. Readers of *The AEF in Print* will pick up on the propagandistic tone in some of the articles in this collection.

The AEF in Print is a sampling of the journalistic record of the United States involvement in World War I, from mobilization through the Armistice. Although small contingents of American soldiers also served in Italy and Russia and vast civilian armies supported the war effort on the homefront, the selected articles focus primarily on the fighting men on the Western front and on the dangerous waters of the Atlantic.

This collection features some of the most memorable American reporting of the war: Floyd Gibbons (*Chicago Tribune*) writing about being shot at the Battle of Belleau Wood; Irvin Cobb describing for readers of the *Saturday Evening Post* the torpedoed troop ship *Tuscania* sinking beneath the waves, taking over two hundred soldiers to their death; and the article by George Pattullo (*Saturday Evening Post*) that enshrined Tennessee backwoodsman Alvin York as the most famous doughboy of the war.

But it is the other articles in *The AEF in Print* that fill out the story. Articles were selected to show the phases of American involvement in the war, from mobilization to the Armistice. They offer glimpses of Americans learning to be soldiers, being warmly embraced by beleaguered French troops, firing the first American shot of the war, facing their first gas attack, fighting as the newly constituted American army, suffering through wounds and fatalities, and celebrating the end of the war. They note the curious role of African-American fighters attached to the French Army and the part played by women as army nurses and "Hello Girls."

The AEF in Print is a cross section of America in World War I, as told through newspaper and magazine articles—precisely how the American public experienced the Great War.

Chris Dubbs & John-Daniel Kelley
April 6, 2017, the 100th anniversary of United States entry into World War I

✦

✦

✦

✦

✦

Chapter 1

Mobilization

Introduction

When America entered the war in April 1917, the contrast between the U.S. Army and those of the other belligerent nations was staggering to contemplate. The United States had a small standing army and National Guard force of some 200,000 men. Two months earlier, it had wrapped up its "Punitive Expedition, U.S. Army," in which General John J. Pershing led 10,000 troops into Mexico to deal with the paramilitary forces of revolutionary Francisco "Pancho" Villa that had killed U.S. citizens and raided across the border.

The army engaged in minor skirmishes for eleven months, but failed to capture Villa. Virtually the entire U.S. regular army and federalized National Guard troops were required to patrol the U.S. border to prevent further raids. The campaign resulted in twenty-four American casualties (fourteen military and ten civilian).

Over roughly that same period, French and German forces clashed in the epic ten-month Battle of Verdun. Both sides employed armies of over a million men, fired an estimated ten million artillery shells, and combined, suffered more than 700,000 casualties—just one battle in a war that routinely dealt in such titanic numbers. The statistics on the Eastern Front were even more stunning.

Nothing was clearer in the spring of 1917 than how ill-prepared the U.S. Army was to join the fighting on the Western Front. It had no experience in the kind of modern warfare being fought in Europe. It did not have enough men and officers, weapons and equipment, training facilities, or ships to transport troops across the Atlantic. Clearly, it would be a long time before America could do its share of the fighting.

Despite this sobering reality, Britain and France urged their new ally to quickly send to France a force—no matter how small— to bolster military and civilian morale. This request set U.S. war preparations moving in two parallel directions. As a small contingent hurried to the war zone to begin training with French veterans, mobilization moved into full swing at home.

To raise an army on the scale of those fighting in Europe, the United States implemented conscription for the first time since the Civil War. Ten million men registered for the draft, the order in which they would be inducted to be determined by a lottery. "The greatest lottery of all time enthroned the gods of fortune in a room at the Capitol today," began the dramatic front-page story in the *Washington Times* on July 20, 1917. Before a room of dignitaries, military officers, and reporters, Secretary of War Newton Baker, blindfolded, dipped his hand into a glass container to pick the first number. When the clerk announced the first number— 258—reporters in the room scribbled out the news and handed it to messenger boys, who rushed it to the telegraph in a nearby room. The telegraph clattered out the news to the waiting country that men holding draft cards numbered 258 would be the first called to the trenches in France.

Training camps sprouted around the country and quickly filled with raw recruits who had to be taught the basics of military discipline before they could learn the art of soldiering. The article "My First Six Weeks with the Colors" tells of one man's transformation from civilian to soldier.

One component of U.S. war preparation that was not lacking, however, was leadership. General John J. Pershing, the youngest of America's major generals, was appointed to lead the American Expeditionary Forces. Pershing already had as extensive a military resume as an American officer of that era could, having served in the Philippines, the Spanish-American War, and most recently

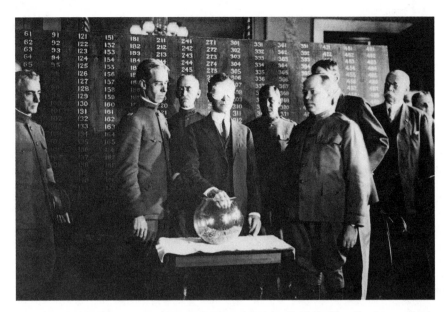

On 20 July 1917, Secretary of War Newton Baker, blindfolded, drew the first number in the draft lottery: Number 258. Those drafted were to serve in the American Expeditionary Forces (AEF) during World War I. *Source:* National Archives and Records Administration, 165-WW-420(P379). Wikimedia Commons.

in the Mexican expedition. He was widely respected both in the military and by the public, and quickly seized on the monumental task that faced him: preparing U.S. military forces for war.

While America began its war preparation, General Pershing sailed to France in early June. He was followed over the next few weeks by 14,000 American troops, some mustered from the regular army and others who were new recruits. They were America's first contingent of fighters. In the article "The First Contingent Sails for France," journalist Nelson Collins details the mood onboard the first troopship to sail for Europe. For many of these soldiers, who had never been far from their home town, the voyage represented the first dose of reality that they were embarking on a grand adventure. To the public, it felt like America was about to enter the war.

Although America was commended for its efforts to "catch up" to the other belligerent countries, a year would pass before the weight of American numbers made an impactful difference in the conflict. In that time, recruitment and training efforts gathered speed, and emergency calls went out for women to serve the cause as nurses and telephone operators. The article "Fighting Sisters of Fighting Men," explains how trained nurses answered the call to be ready for when America joined the fighting. The final selection in this chapter offers a glimpse of the "Hello Girls," a group of bi-lingual, female telephone operators just before it sailed for France to make its unique contribution to the war effort.

Allies Want U.S. Troops in France Immediately

"The American flag and the American uniform … would be the veritable signal of approaching deliverance."

"Send Army to France for Moral Effect"[1]
The Day Book (Chicago), April 21, 1917

London, April 21. Winston Churchill, former first lord of the admiralty, now himself in khaki, wants an American expeditionary force sent to France as soon as possible simply for the effect the presence of Americans would have on the allied forces.

"Of course, I can express only my personal opinion," he said to the United Press today, "but it seems to me certain that the presence of even a single American division on the battlefields of France or Flanders[2] this year would exercise influence and afford encouragement out of all proportion to the actual number of men employed.

"It was always represented to us that the timely arrival of even a small force of British troops in France would stimulate and cheer the heart of every French soldier.

"As it turned out, our small army achieved very great material results in addition to its moral effect. Perhaps it played a decisive part in the supreme events of the opening phase of the war. But now, when the terrible weight and burden of this struggle has pressed for nearly three years upon the French, British and Belgian troops, the arrival of the American flag and the American

1. News stories from the Associated Press typically ran without a byline; whereas those from the rival United Press usually gave the reporter's name. Some newspapers that used AP stories did not even identify them as such or referred to the story as being from their own war correspondent.
2. That region of northern Belgium that saw continuous fighting throughout the war, including the mammoth battles around the city of Ypres. Preparation for the 3rd Battle of Ypres (also known as Passchendaele) was underway when this article was written.

uniform on the actual line of battle would be the veritable signal of approaching deliverance and of victory and would kindle joy and enthusiasm in every heart."

In the War but not Ready for It

"We have lost a month; we have lost the best month of the war—the best because it was the first."

Editorial
"Our War Preparations Lagging"
The Literary Digest, May 19, 1917

Memories of disastrous unpreparedness in our former wars are recalled by some editors who survey the lack of actual accomplishment in our first thirty days of war. Their criticisms of the officials responsible are not euphemistic. We have been planning, not doing, it is said, and the *Boston Transcript* (Ind. Rep.) predicts an explosion in Washington the like of which the nation has not witnessed since the war with Spain. The sooner this explosion comes the better for the country, according to this journal. Of opposition journals, the *New York Tribune* (Rep.) is making the most exhaustive campaign perhaps toward wakefulness. As one of its correspondents in the capital says, this country is "at war but not in it," and he quotes one of the President's "most communicative advisers" as saying:

> Don't fool the American people. I am afraid there is an impression through the land that a very great deal has been accomplished. This is a time of all others when it is up to the newspapers to tell the truth, and by that I mean to convey no false impression by the way facts are stated. As a matter of truth, very little has been accomplished, especially in the Navy and War Departments. Our unpreparedness to strike a blow is literally appalling. The task we have ahead of us is prodigious. There is no use deluding ourselves.

The Tribune correspondent gives credit to the Council of National Defense[3] for heroic work, but he tells us "that there is

---

3. The Council of National Defense was an organization established in August 1916, eight months prior to U.S. entry into the war, charged with the coordination of industry and resources in support of the war effort. Its broad charges covered industry, transportation, farm production, finance, and public morale.

much lost motion." He pictures the Commission as confronted by the difficulties that confront any one endeavoring to do business with the United States Government. The way is impeded at every step by red tape, some of which is necessary but a good deal of which is not. Nevertheless, in spite of obstructions, the Advisory Commission is slowly making head way of a fundamental kind, and he tells us that in its civilian advisers "the Government has some of the best administrative brains of the country." Another Washington correspondent of *The Tribune* says that men in the Council of National Defense, familiar in the business world, look with dismay on a "vast mechanism that centers nowhere," and he adds:

> That is what is the matter. There is an organization for making war or for making ready for war; a vast organization that is growing daily with the creation of boards, but it is an organization that can not get things done. There is no direction given to its efforts. It is an organization without an effective head. It has many energetic members, but they have no definite and certain relation to each other. There are a variety of activities, many of them interesting and impressive, but they run along parallel lines and don't come together in any common center. The Government hasn't a program intelligently framed and executed from above, but it has a lot of parts of a program being pushed upward from below.

It is the realization of this condition, we are told further, that excites discussion of a war-cabinet.

Editorially, *The Tribune* asks whether "the old American democracy is to rival the new Russia[4] in ineptitude at the critical moment of the struggle between democracy and despotism." Taking as a standard of measurement the first thirty-three days after the beginning of our war and the first thirty-three days of the beginning of the conflict in Europe, this journal reminds us that the end of that period was the first day of the battle of the Marne. Before that date, Germany had mobilized 1,500,000 soldiers and had invaded Belgium, and the army of Kluck[5] had passed Paris and was many

4. "New Russia" refers to the republic created when the Russian Revolution forced the abdication of the Czar in March 1917. The Revolution followed heavy military setbacks and ushered in a period of chaos, during which Russia's Provisional Government was challenged by the more radical forces of Bolshevism. Mutinies, protests and strikes became common.

5. General Alexander von Kluck, commander of the German First Army in the opening days of the war.

miles to the southeast. Belgium had put 100,000 men into the field, Great Britain had mobilized her great fleet, and had transported an army larger than our whole available field force across the Channel. France had mobilized more than 1,000,000 men, suffered many defeats, and was just at the point of launching that great final counter-offensive which "won the battle of the Marne and saved Europe and civilization from German barbarism." The measure of the present situation, according to this critic, is the measure of time, and it is urged that we mistake not the situation, for within a few months the war may be lost and won, and we read:

> If it is lost by those who are fighting Germany in Europe it will be lost by us also, and upon us will come the burden of defending ourselves. And if the present chaos and confusion continue in this country the war will be lost and won despite our entrance. We shall be unable to aid our Allies to victory or save them from defeat. We have lost a month; we have lost the best month of the war—the best because it was the first. We are going on in a manner which will insure the loss of a second month. We are imitating the British method of muddling through, but without their advantage. France could and did hold Germany for two years while Britain got ready, but no one can hold Germany for two years while we get ready. If we are not ready to do something at once and much in the next few months, the issue of the war will be decided and we shall have to face the consequences.

General "Black Jack" Pershing to Command U.S. Troops

"The man who will lead the division to France fought
Apaches and Sioux Indians."

"Pershing Cool, Brave, Strong"
Aberdeen Herald (WA), June 8, 1917

For the first time in history the United States will send a force of troops for military purposes to Europe, and to "Black Jack" Pershing, youngest of the major generals, has fallen the distinction of commanding this expeditionary division. Through skirmishes with the Indians, battles against Spain, Filipino insurrections and

Major General John J. "Black Jack" Pershing was appointed to head of the American Expeditionary Forces in World War I. *Source:* George Grantham Bain Collection, Prints and Photographs Division, Library of Congress, LC-B2-4281-6.

clashes with the Mexicans Major General Pershing has won his way until now he receives the active command of the first Americans fighting under this flag who will come to grips with the Germans in the Armageddon. For thirty-one years Pershing has been a soldier, and during that time be has crowded into the chapters of his life action, troubles and laurels that make him a distinctive figure among the general officers of the regular army.

"Black Jack" Pershing, as the men of the rank and file know the commander of the department of the south and the successor to the late Frederick Funston,[6] is the type of the soldier whom Frederic Remington immortalized in his pictures of the Indian campaigns. Lean, but rugged, his six feet and better every inch bone and muscle, he typifies the ideal cavalry officer. He has been hardened by field service physically and has been broadened in executive service by several difficult posts in the Philippines. He cares little for swivel chairs and desks, but he dotes on boots and saddles, and in his Mexican expedition he took his troops ahead with such dash and efficiency that his command won the unstinted praise of foreign officers. One British subaltern, sent for observation purposes, called Pershing's command "the finest body of soldiers of its size in the world."

General Pershing is fifty-three years old, and his honors came with a rush during the last sixteen years. He was born in Laclede, Linn county, Mo. Pershing was appointed to West Point in 1882 and four years later was graduated as senior cadet captain, the highest honors which come to any undergraduate of the Military academy.

Won Fame Fighting Indians

The man who will lead the division to France fought Apaches and Sioux Indians until the militaristic Poor Lo[7] gave up the unequal fight and became pacific again. For seven years Lieutenant Pershing never knew a promotion, but in 1893 he was raised to the rank of first lieutenant. He was assigned to the Tenth cavalry, the crack negro command that afterward won fame at the San Juan blockhouse.[8] Because of the fact that he was appointed to the colored troop he earned the sobriquet of "Black Jack."

The young officer applied himself to a study of tactics, an application which has since resulted in the acknowledgment of Pershing as the best strategist in the regular army. Such became his reputation even then that he was assigned to West Point

---

6. Major General Frederick Funston was initially favored by President Woodrow Wilson to lead the American Expeditionary Forces. However, his untimely death on February 19, 1917, at the age of 51, opened the door for the appointment of General Pershing.

7. "Poor Lo" is a term once used to characterize the "vanishing Indian." It is a contracted form of "Lo, the poor Indian!" a line from Alexander Pope's poem "Essay on Man."

8. A Spanish fort captured during the Battle of San Juan Hill, a decisive battle of the Spanish-American War.

as an instructor on this subject. He did not remain above the Hudson long, for the war with Spain broke out, and Pershing applied instantly for a place with the negro Tenth. His command was shipped to Cuba among the first troops of that expedition-ary force, and he distinguished himself in the field. His colonel termed him "the bravest and coolest man he ever saw under fire," while at the battle of El Caney[9] Pershing was promoted to captain for signal gallantry in action.

Sent to the Philippines

When the war ended President McKinley exercised his executive right and gave Captain Pershing a berth as the head of the customs and insular affairs in the war department. But the life of the bureaucrat was like an opiate to the man of action. Pershing tired of the endless routine and was anxious to get back to the battle line again. So he asked to be sent to the Philippines, where the little brown men were cutting up rough with the nephews of their adopted Uncle Samuel. So to Mindanao Pershing went as adjutant general of that department. He familiarized himself with the Moro problem,[10] for the brown bandits were largely of that tribe, fighters, cruel and bloodthirsty too.

Active command of the expedition to subjugate these tribes-men was finally given to Captain Pershing, and after months of applied diplomacy and bullets he brought them to subjec-tion. He was made military governor of Mindanao and showed such executive foresight and prescience in his dealings with the natives that the Moros chose Pershing to be a datto, or ruler. This subjugation of a fighting race was accomplished with the loss of but two American lives.

Pershing is loved by his men and respected by his subordinates. "The best commander in the army," said a man who served in Mexico with Pershing. "A tactician and a strategist who will not shame American traditions," this same officer added.

----

9. A brief battle of the Spanish-American War that supported the main assault on San Juan Hill.

10. Moros were ethnic Muslims in the southern Philippines, who resisted U.S. take-over of the Philippines following the Spanish-American War. The Moro Rebellion ran from 1899–1913.

Training with the National Army

"For hour after hour we drilled."

By One of the Drafted Men
"My First Six Weeks with the Colors"
The Independent, November 3, 1917

When the list of the men drafted first for the new National Army[11] was published last July, a host of my friends telephoned or called to give sympathy and advice. Their ideas of military life were far from encouraging. They declared frankly that my constitution could not bear the strain of the work, which would be terrific. And there was my wife. By all means, urged several, I should urge exemption for her sake.

The prospect was not bright. For ten years I had been the traveling representative of an old and wealthy bond firm. I stopped always at the best hotels in the larger cities. Usually I would rise shortly after nine o'clock, call leisurely at several dignified offices, and the day's work was over. I never stinted myself on clothing and food, for my salary was not niggardly. Except for an occasional game of golf, I took no physical exercise, and I had grown fleshy and rather pale.

However, a few weeks later I left for the training camp. I accompanied recruits from every walk of life, mechanics, farmers, lawyers, business men, clerks, miners, doctors; but the greater number were young farmers.

At the railroad depot we were met by a detachment of officers and privates, who lined us up with military promptness and marched us to the receiving station. Within an hour the final physical examination was completed. We were conducted to the camp quartermaster warehouses to receive our clothing and bedding allowances. Each man was given two pairs of breeches, two olive drab flannel shirts, one blouse, one hat, two pairs of shoes, one pair of leggins, three pairs of underclothes and four pairs of socks; for his bunk, each received two olive drab blankets and a canvas bed-sack, to be filled with hay. We were told that overcoats would be issued later.

---

11. The National Army was created when the U.S. entered the war, by combining the regular U.S. Army with units of the National Guard, conscripts, and volunteers.

A train load of drafted men arriving at Camp Meade, near Middletown, PA, to begin their military training. Library of Congress. *Source:* Harris & Ewing Collection, Prints and Photographs Division, Library of Congress, LC-H261-9483.

That same day military life began in earnest. At the barracks (a substantial two-storied pine building, large enough to quarter two hundred and fifty men) our serious, athletic young captain informed us:

"A recruit kit, consisting of two face towels, soap, a hair brush, a tooth brush and a comb, will be issued to every man this afternoon. Your civilian toilet articles must be returned to your homes at once. You will wear the regulation clothing—no leather leggins or fancy hats. The Government wants each man to be outfitted alike."

I felt a pang of disappointment. I had provided myself with a tailor-made uniform, athletic shoes, leather leggins and an expensive military hat. My wife had given me twelve hand-embroidered towels and two pairs of linen sheets of the finest quality. And my suit-cases contained numerous toilet articles, soaps, oils and much else.

The captain taught us how to make up our bunks. The two blankets were at the head of the small iron bed, the folded edges to the left. Shoes were put under the edge of the bed below the blankets, the toes pointing evenly out ward. There was a particular spot for the smallest article. And the bunks must be kept in this order except between taps and reveille and during the hour for sweeping and scrubbing in the morning.

The occupant of the bunk next to mine was a man named Hicks, who, tho intelligent looking, wore a sullen, sour expression, which I instantly disliked. My bunk-mate on the other side was an overgrown, awkward farmer youth with powerful, grimy hands, brown teeth and dirty ears. His name was Blevins. His filthiness disgusted me.

Before noon a mess kit, containing a meat can, a knife, fork and spoon, a condiment can and a pan, was given to every man in the barracks. A few moments later the first sergeant yelled, "come and get it!" and we hurried down into the big mess hall for dinner. Out of tall, shining cans the cooks ladled boiled cabbage, roast beef, macaroni and cheese, boiled potatoes, stewed peaches and lemonade, filling each pan and cup as we filed past. This fare was a sample of the meals served to us during the next two weeks.

That afternoon we began work on the rudiments of drill. The hand salute, which, if given accurately is no simple performance, was carefully explained and practiced for an hour. Next we were divided into squads of eight men to learn to keep step properly. And neither is this an easy task for a raw recruit.

Back and forth, back and forth, we marched on the black strip of drill ground between the barracks. I had never walked so much in my life, and sweat rolled from every pore. My back ached dully; my feet burned. But the second lieutenant (a youth with a pale, thin fringe above his lip) continued commanding sharply, "one, two, three, four, one, two, three, four."

Suddenly he wheeled about and came up to me briskly.

"Get in step," he shouted, glaring at me. "You're not dead yet."

The muscles of my jaws twitched, and I breathed an oath of vengeance. But I fell in step and I kept up with the count. I began to feel ashamed of my weariness. About me men were striving with the enthusiasm and determination of candidates for a college football eleven. Deeply in earnest, they apparently enjoyed every moment. And they were learning remarkably fast—the officers frankly told us so. Before we fell out that afternoon, the captain said:

"We'll learn a song now, men. It's quite simple. Here it goes:

"We'll hang Kaiser William[12] to a sour
        apple tree,

12. Kaiser Wilhelm II, Emperor of Germany.

> We'll hang Kaiser William to a sour
>   apple tree,
> We'll hang Kaiser William to a sour
>   apple tree,
> As we go marching onward."

And as they sang, the whole meaning of our part in the war, the fine ideals and possessions we were to fight for, came to me with an overwhelming rush. I felt the keen thrill that I had known twelve years before on the side lines of a close varsity football match. I sang, too, more loudly and more wholeheartedly than any one near me. From that moment on I was an American soldier.

The next day the regular schedule of training went into effect. From 5:40 a.m. until noon we stood inspection of quarters and worked at calisthenics, dismounted artillery drill, guard duty, physical drill, semaphore signaling and artillery nomenclature. From 1:30 p.m. to 4:30 p.m. we studied camp sanitation, care of health, first-aid treatment, care of equipment and clothing, courtesies and customs of the military service, rules of war, rights of prisoners of war and Articles of War. Between 4:30 p.m. and supper at 6 p.m. we polished our shoes, bathed and shaved. The regulations permitted men to wear mustaches and beards, but they must be kept neatly trimmed. We were required to bathe twice a week and to wash our hands before each meal. Our under clothing was critically inspected at least twice each month.

Hicks, Blevins and I had nothing to do with one another. Hicks continued sullen and Blevins remained dirty until noon of the third day, when both strangely disappeared.

After passing the final physical examination, each of us had been vaccinated against small-pox and inoculated to prevent typhoid and paratyphoid. There were three inoculations, the last two following intervals of ten days. These precautions were to make us immune from the diseases for three years.

The physical standard of the recruits had proven excellent. Only two per cent of the arrivals had been rejected, and at the fifty infirmaries in the camp, very few men were reporting daily, altho the authorities insisted that the slightest ailments or injuries be treated by experts.

The work steadily grew harder. For hour after hour we drilled at to the right flank, to the left flank, to the rear, squads right and squads left. We became sore and stiff, but there was no let-up. Apparently I could never learn to hold a pivot, and I made an awkward mess of changing step. The comments of the young lieutenant with the fringe of mustache became sarcastic.

I had never seen a better behaved lot of men. Saloons and cafés were strictly forbidden to sell us liquor, and the regulations dealt severely with soldiers who gambled. At first I missed my occasional cocktail, but after a week I found I could live quite easily without it.

A remarkable change came over Hicks and Blevins. Because he had hesitated to obey an order, Hicks had been assigned to three days at kitchen police, which meant toiling over hot ranges and scouring huge pots. When he returned to regular work, he was no longer sullen, and he has never hesitated to carry out another order. A sergeant had taken Blevins in hand and bathed and shaved him until he was a new man. He had done extra duty, too. Now he needs no urging to keep himself clean.

Every evening after supper I walked over to one of the nine attractive Y.M.C.A.[13] buildings to write to my wife. But we received no letters, for the camp mail service was not yet working. During the brief rest periods, Hicks, Blevins and I lay on our bunks, reading or trying to sleep and growing more lonesome as time passed. Then one day the letters came, and we received several apiece. Overjoyed, I forgot myself and repeated to Hicks something my wife had written; a moment later Blevins was excitedly asking us to read a long letter from his sweetheart. Instantly the three of us became friends, and we have remained friends ever since.

After this incident our evenings were no longer lonesome. We formed a habit of attending the nightly concerts and performances given by experts at the big Y.M.C.A. auditorium, under the auspices of that generous organization. We are planning to enroll soon in one of the French classes which will be held in the Y.M.C.A. recreation halls. One Y.M.C.A. director has arranged an athletic program, during which amateur pugilists will box. Hicks and I are matched for five rounds.

13. Today, most human service needs of soldiers are handled by the military. However, in WWI, various nonprofit organizations served that need, including the YMCA, Red Cross, Salvation Army, and others.

The Government is doing all it can to provide well for us. Our quarters are better than those used by the Regular Army or the National Guard. The bath houses are furnished with equipment equal to that found in the best Gymnasiums in the country. The utmost care is taken in the preparation of the food, for mess inspectors, trained specialists, pass thru the kitchens daily, keenly alert for filth or improper cooking methods. Our mess sergeant is adding savings from his rations allowance, and soon we shall be eating delicacies, purchased from civilian merchants.

The harder I worked the more mistakes I seemed to make. But I was determined to succeed. One day my wife wrote that she was coming to the training camp for a day's visit. Much as I longed to see her, this news troubled me, for I pictured my dismay when the young lieutenant would criticize my awkwardness in her presence.

Our course we had scarcely begun. We were to study first the artillery drill regulations of the United States Army; then we were to take up the European fighting methods practiced today. Before the training period has ended, the infantry will have had experience in bomb-throwing, bomb-firing, bayonet fencing and trench charging. Trenches are being constructed on the wide target ranges. When we arrive in France, we shall require only a brief course of intensive special training before we are ready for the front.

The strict discipline has brought many excellent results. Men who knew little or nothing about sanitation, have learned to guard their health properly. Lazy men have acquired the habit of working ambitiously with regained self-respect. Drinking men have ceased to drink. There are very few who are not striving with body and soul to perfect a powerful military machine that will crush the menace of Germany for all time.

We have not learned when our training in the United States will end. Even the officers do not know this.

As the day for my wife to arrive drew near, I became almost sick. I dreaded being humiliated before her, for my letters frankly described me as a most promising soldier.

A few moments before the train came in, the lieutenant with the small mustache sent for me. In the orderly room he eyed me sternly.

LEWIS MACHINE GUN CREW, CAMP MILLS

Soldiers learning about the Lewis machine gun at Camp Mills, Long Island, NY, in July 1917. *Source:* George Grantham Bain Collection, Prints and Photographs Division, Library of Congress, LC-B2-4326-15.

"I've been watching you for some time," he began bluntly. "You have interested me, I confess. You certainly have worked hard enough, and there is no doubt of your good intentions.

"But you have made many mistakes—a great many, in fact, haven't you?"

I nodded, my mouth dry. Some new blunder, I guessed. I resolved again to get even when the war ended.

"I have had you promoted to be a corporal. The Army likes men with your ambition and energy; the Army also believes in a square deal. There may be a sergeant's place open soon. I advise you to keep working hard."

I must have almost fainted. Instead I ran with a bounding heart to the train to meet my wife. I was a corporal! And before long I might be a sergeant!

I shall never forget my wife's surprise when she saw me.

"Fred," she cried, after I had kissed her. "You look magnificent: All your fleshiness is gone. You're so tall and straight and brown. Your eyes are so clear and bright. Your arm is as hard as steel. You are a soldier, aren't you?"

"I am a corporal," I replied.

The First Contingent Sails for France

"These soldiers seemed to accept President Wilson's phrase 'making the world safe for democracy' at its full face-value."

Nelson Collins
"The First Convoy"
The Century Magazine, September 1917

On a day in June, sunny and muggy, with a thin mist over the harbor, the assembling of the ships began. From piers near the Battery and from piers near the foot of Twenty-third Street ships made their way across the North River to the piers in Hoboken used in times of peace by the Hamburg-American and North German Lloyd lines.[14] We moved out into the North River at eight-thirty. The bridge was still undressed, and workmen were busy about it as we backed out into the river. As we swung toward the Hoboken pier, another ship, coming up from the Battery, converged on our course, heading for the same dock. Another showed up just the other side of her. We were berthed by nine-thirty, three abreast in one dock. But ships kept coming until well past three in the afternoon, for the coastwise trade was swinging into the war.

Gradually in among us the freight barges, with men in olive-drab sprawled on their high-piled luggage, appeared, and lay for hours till we should be ready.

Scores of tugs pushed and pulled, puffed harshly, and became quickly silent as pressure relaxed. The derrick tugs hung about ready to lift the luggage aboard. A power-boat in the naval service darted through at thirty-five knots an hour. Meantime detachments

14. On April 6, 1917, the U.S. Army seized the ships belonging to these two German shipping companies that were in Hoboken, NJ and later converted them to troop transports.

of soldiers marched through the warehouses to the pier-heads and lounged there. Fine fellows they were. Fine even after one had seen the Anzacs,[15] the English, the Scotch, the Irish, and the French; too fine to be killed except in a cause even finer than they. They waved to the soldiers on the barges jammed in among the ships and tugs, glanced curiously up the sides of the ship, then set themselves to wait with the patience born of sentry-duty. They waited hours in the mist-threaded sunshine, and all the time more dun-colored ships, with names obscured, but not invisible, swung in for them.

It is a strange medley of authorities, military, naval, merchant marine, overlapping but not interfering, cordial not jealous, but involving unexpected quick adjustments of courtesies and responsibilities.

In old passenger days, our ship could carry seventeen hundred with her normal accommodations; but now we had built bunks of slightly sagging canvas across board supports, three deep, on the two upper decks of five hatchways. Wash-houses had been erected on the open deck.

The sun was beginning to drop behind the Hoboken warehouses when the last of the slate-colored ships made a berth. Railroad barge after railroad barge jammed with luggage massed about us. Tugs and excursion-steamers crowded with soldiers kept coming up from the Battery.

The embarkation lasted all night. By four in the morning we had soldiers of the regular army, medical reserve officers and men, and two hundred nurses aboard. They were aboard, but not all of them were stowed. The medical contingent to go abroad with us came about five in the afternoon. The officers were in uniform, but the men—medical students from Johns Hopkins, most of them, I was told, just finished with their third year of study—had not been uniformed yet. They were a good body of men, excellent material, as anybody could see; but not shaped up.

The embarking of the regulars started after six o'clock in the evening. They had been five days on a train, and had been confined all the muggy day in their cars at Jersey City on top of that. They toiled up the gangway with their load of equipment. "A good ship," one or two said appreciatively as they came over

---

15. ANZAC: Australian and New Zealand Army Corps.

the side. "Step light, and don't rock the boat," called one. "Do I go
up-stairs or downstairs?" asked one, pointing first to the ladder
up to the quarter-deck and then to an open hatchway. Most of
them said, "What time do we sail?" or said nothing at all. There
was naturally some confusion, but the whole thing was remarkably well ordered. Men with undoubtable cards assigning them to
identified bunks found said identified bunks already occupied,
and there was no instance recorded of the first occupant giving
up the place.

By two o'clock in the morning the tone of the ship had altered.
The men had "carried on" for six days, had sat stifled in cars all the
muggy day excepting for an hour on the platforms, and had been
cheerful on the piers. Sheer tiredness made everybody a little crabbed
during the dead hours before dawn came. One young private found a
highly original grievance for the hour and the occasion. "Ain't there
any place for a damned buck private to sit and read?" he demanded
after inspecting the second-cabin smoking-room, which had been
assigned to officers. By five there was deep, though not always silent,
peace all over the ship. Everybody slept.

Less than twenty-four hours after we tied up at the pier we
backed out again, and slipped down to anchorage to wait for the
other ships and for the convoying naval force. As we moved down
the North River the salutes from ships in the river and ships at
their piers, from tug-boats and ferries and Sunday-morning excursion steamers, made us realize the errand we were bound on more
than all the routine of embarkation. We spent that night within a
ring of cruisers and destroyers.

We stayed several days with that ring of destroyers and cruisers around us, close to the submarine net. Our ship was the
first of the transports to make the anchorage. The others joined
us at long intervals. No one was allowed to go ashore, and no
one was allowed to come aboard. Everybody longed to be at sea,
the ship's crew because "a week in any port is long enough,"
and the soldiers and nurses because of the confinement. Fog set
in, and held even the gaze restricted most of the time. Nobody
slept well or settled well to any interest or occupation. We all felt
relieved when two privates of the regulars quarreled in mess-line
the fourth morning of our "hold-up," and after breakfast were
allowed to fight it out with bare fists, ringed round by the men of

their company and many others. It cleared the air for them and for all of us. The supply of text-books in elementary French was appalling; only less appalling than the oral tutoring of those who were held to have made some progress.

At last we went out, just after noon, in weather that contained every portent. The brilliant sun smoked on the water from a vivid blue sky piled with clean, white clouds. A lively breeze played on us from the southwest. In Ambrose Channel, and before we had dropped the pilot, black, streaked clouds climbed quickly from the southwestern horizon, overshadowed us, and swept the decks with a vicious summer shower that lasted ten minutes. Incoming coastal steamers from Newport News and Savannah, British cargo-boats bound in and out, had their rails lined as we passed. It was a brisk breeze, with a slight sea; but slight as it was, it killed much of the interest in elementary French along the promenade-deck, and subdued the horseplay fore and aft, where the soldiers were stowed. Most of them were on salt water for the first time. Fortunately, the sea was not bad enough to overpower any but the most susceptible; it simply subdued the others. The three groups of watches, military, naval, and merchant marine, were posted. The soldiers assigned to the upper crow's-nests faced the horrors of a first climb up the side of a ship's mast along with the misery of sea-sickness. One unfortunate had just strength left to yell "Look out below!" to the crowded forecastle-head a hundred feet below him. Another climbed successfully to the crow's-nest, but went in head first instead of feet first, and it took three minutes by the watch for his mates in the nest to get him right side up in that narrow space.

While at anchor bridge watches had been deluxe. Moving-pictures by the foremast, band concerts on the promenade deck forward, boxing-bouts in the well of the ship between, made bridge life seem like an over-idealized La Follette shipping bill.[16] Now that we were at sea, only the boxing-bouts were held. They came on regularly and with gusto about six-thirty every evening.

We went out in three groups, all headed, we surmised, for the same port in France. This surmise was largely confirmed when we found systematic rendezvous of the groups established from time to

16. The La Follette Seamen's Act in 1915 improved labor conditions for American seamen.

time on the voyage. We put to sea on a Thursday, a group of seven ships in all. So far as that night and Friday went, we were alone on the journey. But occasionally a wisp of smoke was reported to starboard, sometimes forward, sometimes abaft the beam. A wisp of smoke or wisps of smoke might be anything, cargo- or passenger-boats headed east or west, even a German raider[17]—anything but a German squadron, thanks to an overwhelming fleet of an ally in the North Sea. But the wisp of smoke grew to two, to three, to more, and kept pace with us. Late that first Saturday afternoon one of our other two groups was in good view to starboard and astern—ten ships in all, an imposing cruiser, transports, and other escort. That midnight the group sailed past us. At four in the morning they were well ahead of us, getting low down on our horizon. Two days later we had not seen them again.

The whole ship's company soon fell into its routine and its settled mood. There was setting-up drill for the soldiers morning, afternoon, and evening; there was frequent gun practice for the naval crews. Fire and boat drill came for all hands. Maneuvers of the transports and escort kept everybody either busy or interested. The tension of organization was down to a working basis.

I was in and out among the soldiers more or less. I had a curiosity to know the individual attitude among them toward this expedition to France. Here were regulars who were in the service before 1914 sprang its cataclysmic surprise on the world, recruits who enlisted six months before our own declaration of war last April, recruits who signed up after the declaration. All the teens and the twenties and early thirties were represented, and all grades from men of the college and other well-bred types to men representing our least excellent American citizenship. I ran on people from every part of the country except New England and the Pacific Northeast. All offered themselves to the army. Why did they? And of those who did it after our declaration of war, what was their idea of our reason for being in the war and their reason for wishing to take part in it at the outset?

The main answer to all these questions—and many more that might come up regarding the origins and progress and outcomes of the war—was astoundingly simple. They understood their country had to go to war, was forced into it because there was no other

---

17. German raiders were surface warships that preyed on commercial vessels.

resource that had not been exhausted, and so they signed up. That seemed an all-sufficient reason, and once offered naively as all-sufficient, it did seem so. I had been associating for a year and a half with a young man who thought perhaps he ought to go into the war. There was no real reason under the sun why he should not go if he felt that way; but he had weighed it and discussed it and decided for it and decided against it. Finally he committed himself to the auxiliary cruiser service, and two days before he was to start backed out. He then started off to enlist in the National Guard of his State for more preliminary training just before the Conscription Bill would have ended all his agonizings and hesitations. In some way these fellows of the regiments aboard made him seem unbelievably grotesque. One private, nineteen years old, from the open-pit iron-ore mines of northern Michigan, stated the stark proposition:

"I figured I was born an American, I'd had my schooling and got my first job in Michigan, and that it was up to me to quit and fight. If I was good enough for all I had had from the country, the country was good enough for me to fight for. I have a brother who was earning seven dollars a day running a winch at one of the mines. He quit, too, feeling the same way. He's in the navy. I've got another brother in the cavalry. My first brother would have gone, too, first crack off the bat, only he's married; and so he'll wait awhile. My mother's German, and my father's French. No wonder I got a boil on my neck. They're both dead. I don't know either language."

So far as the justification of the war is concerned, these soldiers seemed to accept President Wilson's phrase "making the world safe for democracy"[18] at its full face-value. There is a general acceptance of the fact that Germany has "gone the limit," and, if not defeated, would push that same limit a little further, in war or peace.

The simple truth is interesting and not discreditable. There were young recruits in the bunks down in the hatchways weeping as we sailed out of New York harbor. Homesickness and sheer horror of brutal warfare in a strange land hurt to tears. The same condition prevailed with a few of them after we sighted the French coast and neared the port. And I, at least, was not ashamed of them. They will be none the worse fighters and none the less willing fighters for it.

---

18. In his April 2, 1917, address to Congress, requesting war with Germany, President Wilson used as part of his justification a line that would become famous—"The world must be made safe for democracy."

On the twelfth day we entered the danger zone[19] or thereabouts. Shortly after four that Monday morning the cruiser wigwagged[20] that we would make rendezvous with two United States destroyers sometime around six o'clock. The sea was dull; the sky was overcast; mist hung on the horizon. At five-twenty, a couple of points off our bow to port, a low, swift shape came through the mist, telegraphing her identification across the transient half dark of belated dawn. Her yellow eye blinked her name and number, — No. —, the S—[21], —and as she drew nearer her name was given us again in the signal-flags of the international code. Off to starboard, heading in toward us at about the same angle as the S— had come in off to port, another destroyer was reported from the forward crow's-nest, and was immediately visible from the bridge. A little forward of the beam another one was seen farther out. That seemed like good measure for the two we expected. Five minutes later the J—, No. —, tore through the mist to port, and before long the M— showed up abaft the beam, also to port. Five of Uncle Sam's finest destroyers from somewhere off the coast of England and France had showed up to us somewhere else off the coast of England and France, and with our steady escorts, the A— and the P—, made seven destroyers for our little column of the cruiser, three transports, and the collier. We swung into the actual, official danger zone amply protected.

Boat drill came at nine-thirty. We swung the boats to the level of the promenade-deck rail, and lashed them there. Portable steps were placed along the deck at each of the boats. It seemed almost a pity that so much preparation might, probably would, be wasted. But the destroyers had come through the mist to a dot for a rendezvous appointed a month ago for this place and hour. They were cutting in and out among us. A submarine's chances were pretty slim.

It was all very impressive. We took it a little sardonically, necessary and admirable as it was. You see, we were simply a merchant ship's company who had been used to carrying the ship and its crew and its passengers and its cargo "through the zone" for two years and a half, with an occasional zigzag, in about ten days' time

19. German submarines operated in the coastal waters of Britain and France, the "danger zone."

20. Sending messages by the use of signal flags.

21. Under wartime censorship, the names of individuals, military units, and ships were often camouflaged in this way.

between New York and Liverpool. For eleven days now we had been in the midst of changing speeds, maneuvers, flag-signaling, until we had wondered vaguely how we ever got across before. The expedition was too important to omit any precaution; but we were a little sated, if the truth must be told. We had had a paraphernalia of military lookouts aboard in extra crow's-nests, strung along the promenade-deck, on each end of the bridge, who certainly were zealous, whatever else they were. We half suspected inadequacy in our own extra man out on the forecastle-head, our regular man in the regular crow's-nest, and our usual close watch on the bridge in other voyaging, though we longed for it. When we were not stepping on military lookouts in the wings of the bridge we were tripping over signal halyards lying all over the place. It was all very colorful and comprehensive, but distracting. The bridge will never seem the same again on routine merchant marine watches. I wonder if it will be any the less effective.

The signal-men were our chief delight. "Jig, X-Ray, Tare," they would sing out, which meant simply that the flag-ship had hoisted a three-flag signal in the international code for the three letters, J, X, and T, meaning whatever the code-book or the secret instructions said they meant in that combination. "Love, Mike, Quack," they would call out, and hoist L, M, and Q to our yard-arm in confirmation of the flag-ship's signal. Words for the letters is a device that helps distinctness, but has its humor. Military lookouts on a ship are equally delightful, even though, if the truth be told, not so useful. I can imagine, just imagine, that in peace times, or even in other war times, where everything to be sighted loomed well above the water, they would be useful additions to the regular ship's lookout. But lookout in waters infested with submarines is specialized lookout. It is minute, but not too minute; inferential, but not wildly imaginative; cool and collected. Anything that clutters it impairs it. Well, the services of soldiers on their one voyage across certainly clutters and distracts the regular ship's lookout. Reports to the bridge became fantastic, with no principle of selection employed. An aeroplane astern in mid-ocean that disappeared the instant it was observed; a "log" three hundred yards off the starboard beam that was finally reduced, under questioning of the lookout, to a length of two inches; a dead fish eight hundred yards away; and of course periscopes innumerable were incidents of two days. The sailor out of the ship's crew, stationed in the forward lower crow's-nest, was seldom heard from.

We steered by "pegs" instead of degrees or points; that is, black-and-white staffs placed on the bridge-rail for the quartermaster at the wheel to keep his line with the cruiser ahead, an excellent device and new to us. We received reports of ships or logs or submarines at two o'clock, at three o'clock instead of abeam to starboard, at six o'clock instead of astern, at nine o'clock instead of abeam to port, at half-past ten instead of four points off the port bow. All these are novelties that we can assimilate; but the reports of our soldier lookouts! It were a strange sea that actually held all their marvels.

The ship was bound to be a house of rumors, and many more floated up to the bridge than drifted down from it. Nobody aboard the ship knew where we were going, but almost every place along the Atlantic coast of France had been the choice of various groups. Rumors that one or the other two groups that made up our total convoy had been attacked by submarines were followed by rumors that both of them were safely in port well ahead of us. The soldier lookouts had heard that they were to go back with the ship, because they could see so many things, presumably. Chaucer's "House of Rumor," with its thousand openings and shifting, whispering little airs, was no more crowded with items than our ship with the airs of mid-ocean playing upon it.

We drew near the shore of sunny France in dull weather with an overcast sky, squalls of driving rain, and a troubled sea. At night the waxing moon had a thin light, and got few chances between clouds. We had notification on Tuesday evening of a French escort, and late Wednesday morning—late, that is, as watches go; it was near nine o'clock—they showed up, two specks off our port bow, mosquito destroyers of the French navy, tiny craft, midgets alongside even our own escorting destroyers, but speedy. They swung to off the cruiser, and one remained to port, while the other cut across our line and took its position to starboard. They scouted ahead for the thirty hours that remained of the journey.

Land does not "loom" on this low-lying' Biscayan shore. It showed faintly, heralded by a lighthouse or two, toward six o'clock. We had already known from six o'clock the night before that our port was S—, at the mouth of a small river, the interesting city of N— lying two hours' or more travel inland. The rain pelted, half a mist persisted, and the whole experience was oddly without inspiration or excitement—about as thrilling as a Hoboken ferry docking at Twenty-third Street. S— lies in a bay of its own off the Bay of Biscay. Two great points reach out into the open, with some indications of bluff cut into by sandy beaches. Clumps of pine stood here and there along these bluffs, and the cultivated fields ran to their very edges. This has been a cool summer, a backward season, but the green and yellow fields and the foliage of the trees showed from the ship as we drew into the harbor channel in all the lushness of the end of June. We passed slowly between the buoys, with an occasional dipping of the ensign from a harbor ferryboat or a coastwise freighter. A British tramp slid past us, bound out, and a Norwegian tramp as well. The shore boulevard, with its stone facing, lay alongside our course, and the beaches were bare with half a tide. We took the turn and swung into the harbor proper, and then we saw the American base. Cruisers at anchor, transports in the bay. United States naval launches plying between, the collier N—, a five-masted sailing schooner—everything afloat in that harbor was American except the French tugboats and the ferry-boats that run up the river. Meantime the rain pelted steadily, an increasing blow came in from the old Bay of Biscay, and, to our disappointment, we dropped anchor off the docks. and lay there all that day and until ten o'clock at night. The S—, lucky ship, drawing only sixteen feet, went into dock at once. She had been tail-end ship all the way over, and the officers on her bridge grinned as she passed us on her way to dock. It cleared in the late afternoon to a sky of curious steely gray for a summer sky, too thin and too cold, suggestive of November or February. Great ovals of dirty gray and nearly black clouds stood up in this thin light ahead, and the moon in her first quarter rose astern of us and to port as we weighed anchor to pass in. The N— had weighed her anchor just ahead of us, and swept past us with bugle-calls going, bound out. All our company aboard cheered as we passed on our opposite errands.

The French pilot, a short, heavily whiskered man, had been aboard all day. He and I had "hit it off together," and he had talked of the war naturally, of the sea even more naturally, of Catholics and Protestants in France, of the vineyards and orchards and grain-fields and cattle pastures in sight from the bridge, even of poetry, particularly of Breteil,[22] the people's poet living at St. Malot.

It was weather of all the portents, just as it had been the early afternoon we passed out from Sandy Hook. The pilot handled the ship, new to him, with greater dash and accuracy than any other pilot I ever have watched. He swung her around in narrow quarters off the first dock gate, and drove her with beautiful directness and exactness into the first basin. Then he passed into a lock that seemed hardly wide enough to accommodate her huge girth, though as a matter of fact a thousand-ton local freighter was able to lie alongside her there.

Here it was, in this lock, waiting for twenty minutes to pass into the second dock, which was the one where our own berth was assigned, that we met the French people. There is a street on both sides of this lock, and the rue du Port, which was on our port side, as it happened, though that is a poor pun, was crowded. Since Tuesday ships of the convoy had been arriving and passing in, and this was Thursday night. But the spontaneous heartiness of the French welcome had not worn down. The rue du Port was jammed with French men, French women, French girls (it is worth while making the division), French children, and American sailors and soldiers.

This was at ten forty-five, and the moon had worked around toward the ship's head a bit. Just as the people cheered, she came out from behind a berg of cloud and filled in between the sparse electric lights along the quay. The houses were within a girl's stone-throw of the ship's side, and the long French windows of their second stories, the living-quarters above a line of shops, were wide open, the lighted interiors giving us ship-folk a frank glimpse of their domesticity over the shoulders of the residents in their little iron balconies. The quay is lined with an iron railing, and the crowd hung over it, or were pressed over its spikes almost perilously.

The first attempt after the general cheer was typically French in its attempt at adaptability. A group of young Frenchmen yelled, "Heep—heep—boo—rah!" and the familiar words in the unfamiliar inflections set the American into a good natured roar. Some American sailor already ashore from the earlier ships saved the situation by yelling to us aboard:

"Sing a song! Say, the French girls want you to sing a song."

---

22. An unclear reference, perhaps to the writer, politician, diplomat François-René de Chateaubriand (1768–1848), born in St. Malo. Chateaubriand is considered the founder of French Romanticism for his descriptions of nature and analysis of emotion.

They started to sing themselves, and the first song that rose from ship and shore was "Columbia, the Gem of the Ocean." The next one was "John Brown's Body." In among the singing came the routine calls from bridge and quay for locking through the ship, "Heave away that port bow line!" and calls from the pilot in French. Our regimental band played the "Marseillaise" first, and the crowd greeted it with a great roar. Then it played "God Save the King," then "The Star-Spangled Banner," and the roar from the crowd almost outdid the first response to the "Marseillaise."

The girls on the quay astonished everybody then by singing the chorus to "Tipperary," the substitute in this war for "The Girl I Left behind me." The next songs came from the ship, "Suwanee River" and "Old Black Joe." The Johns Hopkins crowd of medical students were forward on the promenade-deck, out of the lights. They put pep into the proceedings by singing "Hail, Hail, the Gang's all here," and an American voice from the quay called, "Give us another; give us a rag." The university men tried to resurrect "There'll be a Hot Time in the Old Town to-night," but it languished and faded away. They sang "America" finally, with, it must be admitted, the usual groping for words after the first stanza.

At eleven-twenty we left the lock and passed into our dock. We warped into our particular quay there very slowly, leaving the crowd behind at the lock. Only a group of American soldiers watched for us there on the quay. "Taps" was heard somewhere. "Well, good night," they called to the privates of the regiment forward. "Pleasant dreams. See you in the morning," and one man added, "How do you like France so far?" "Avast heaving," sounded the order from the bridge, the signal, "Finished with the engines," was flashed below, and the transport with its first American contingent had arrived.

Women Respond to the Call for Nurses

"A Nurse is a Soldier."

"Fighting Sisters of Fighting Men"
The Bourbon News (Paris, KY), May 21, 1918

Of the eighty odd thousand registered trained nurses in the United States about 20,000 have enrolled as Red Cross nurses, volunteering their services at the front, in cantonments and hospitals or in any other needed capacities. This enrollment is the nursing reserve of the United States Army Nurse Corps and the United States Navy Nurse Corps, and from it will also be drawn contingents for service under other allied flags than our own. The enrollment goes on at the rate of 1,000 volunteers a month. On a basis of an army of a million men over 30,000 nurses will be required for active duty in the present year.

Up to the last of February over 7,000 nurses had been actually detailed; to duty or were ready for immediate mobilization.[23] So it is seen that there are none too many, in view of the requirements of the service, since between time of enrollment and actual assignment to duty the nurse must undergo a period of special study and training for war service, and the work of organizing and mobilizing this "army of mercy" is no small thing.

A Nurse is a Soldier

Surgeon General Gorgas[24] has called upon the Red Cross to supply 5,000 nurses for the Army Nurse Corps by June 1, and if this quota is forthcoming the total number detailed will have reached 12,000. So the mobilization of another 18,000 to 25,000 by Jan. 1, 1919, will be a big problem to solve.

Now, a nurse is a soldier. She is recognized officially by the government and included in those eligible for soldiers' and sailors' war insurance. A nurse goes into actual danger of wounds and death by shell fire and bomb explosion. Her work is arduous, exacting, calling for the finest qualities of mind and heart. She is the right hand of the surgeon.

So, because nursing is primarily a woman's job, the war nurse is properly the peculiar responsibility of the women of America. While the trained nurse is urged to volunteer the risk of her life at the front, the American woman at home is commanded by every dictate of patriotism and humanity to support her "fighting sister."

The nurse fights pain, disease and death, making her sacrifice with amazing, cheerfulness and enthusiasm.[25]

----

23. The first U.S. Army nurses sailed for Europe in April 1917, before the American troops, to work with the British. They began to serve with the AEF in October 1917.
24. Surgeon General William C. Gorgas.
25. Army nurses held no rank and received only half the pay of an Army private.

Women Recruited as Bi-Lingual Telephone Operators

"In perhaps no other women's corps is there such strict military discipline."

Hazel V. Carter
"Army 'Hello Girls,' Trained in New York, Will be a Picturesque Unit in France"
The Evening World (NY), June 24, 1918

At 7 o'clock every morning reveille sounds through the upper corridor of the National Board of the Young Women's Christian Association Building, No. 600 Lexington Avenue, and sixty young women rise, don uniforms of blue, with U.S.A. buttons, and march to the roof, where a drill opens the routine of the military day, which closes with "taps" at 10 o'clock and retirement to the barracks.

They are Gen. Pershing's "hello" girls the 4th Unit of Signal Corps Operators billeted at the Y.W.C.A ready for orders at any minute to sail.

In perhaps no other women's corps is there such strict military discipline and such a recognition of the responsibility of being members of the only woman's organization that is a part of the United States Army.[26]

"You will notice that we wear the official buttons with the raised eagle," points out Miss Geneva Marsh, formerly a lawyer from Omaha and now chief operator of the corps—which office bears the same relation to the operators as the Captain to the privates. And there is something beautiful about the pride with which Miss Marsh points to the buttons.

"We never put aside our uniforms, except for the night—while we sleep," she said. "We are pledged for the duration of the war to wear the blue serge in winter and the alpaca in summer. Not the most fashionable party nor the most formal ball would be an excuse for a girl of the Signal Corps to change from her official uniform. We are enlisted women. Just as every man in Pershing's Army is an enlisted man."

---

26. Although the "Hello Girls" were members of the Signal Corps Female Telephone Operators Unit, wore army uniforms, and were subject to military regulations, they were considered civilian employees. Not until 1978, did Congress officially grant veteran status to the remaining Hello Girls.

As Miss Marsh explained the insignia of the uniform, a young operator, also in uniform, passed and saluted. Miss Marsh returned the salute with the dignity and the snap of the army Captain.

The suits have the high military collar on the coat, with a U.S. insignia on one side and the Signal Corps insignia on the other. The aviator's cap fits snugly to the head and is more than becoming. On the left arm the Signal Corps girl wears a white brassard representing her rank.

The operator's brassard has a telephone receiver embroidered on it. She receives a salary of $60 a month. The supervisor wears a telephone receiver and a wreath and her salary is $72.

Miss Marsh, the chief operator, wears a telephone receiver with a wreath and lightning flashes embroidered from it. Her salary is $125. The living expenses are paid by the Government.

The sixty girls come from every part of the country, from Washington to Maine and from Michigan to Texas. Most of the girls are of French descent and the corps includes a Belgian and a French girl.

A fluent speaking knowledge of French is a requisite of the Signal Corps girl, and many of those in the 4th unit are talented linguists— some of them speaking Spanish, Italian and German. Out of 5,000 applicants from all over the United States, 150 were chosen. From 70 to 80 per cent of the girls of the 4th unit are college girls, representing almost every college in the United States. Twenty-eight of the members are from California.

Eleanor Hoppack, one of members of the 4th unit, is a graduate of the Sorbonne in Paris. Many of her relatives have been killed in service and she is eager to get across and do her part.

Miss Melanie van Gastel is the Belgian member of the unit. She is from Antwerp and lost her entire family in the devastation of Belgium. Since then she has attended California University and was graduated there this month.

"I shall be willing to brave any dangers," Miss van Gastel said, "and I believe that we will have an opportunity to do some big service as soon as we can get over."

Mrs. Pauline McDonnell and Miss Louise Ruffee are two sisters who heard the news of the death of their father in France just as they were being outfitted for Signal Corps service.

"It will be a pleasure to think that we were billeted for our last few days in this country with the Y.W.C.A. and that we shall be again billeting with the Y.W.C.A. when we reach Paris," Miss Marsh said. "We will go across on an American transport. Many of us will go first to Hotel Petrograd, the Y.W.C.A. Hostess House there, and await distribution to our various posts. Some of us will go to important communication centres where Hostess Houses have been set up for us by the Y.W.C.A."

Chapter 2

✦

✦

✦

✦

✦

First American Troops
Arrive in Europe

Introduction

The month the United States entered the war, mutinies erupted in the French army, in the wake of the failed Second Battle of the Aisne. The new commander of the French army, General Robert Nivelle, had promised a quick, war-ending victory to a dispirited army and nation that had suffered nearly one million deaths since the start of the war. French troops enthusiastically threw themselves into the "Nivelle Offensive."[1] But when it failed, the mood of the French army soured overnight.

This offensive seemed like a repeat of the same futile strategies that had bled France dry at the mammoth battles of Verdun and the Somme. Army morale collapsed. Many French units now refused to follow their officers' orders to return to the trenches. The replacement of Nivelle with General Phillipe Pétain on May 15 largely diffused the situation.

However, in light of continuing morale problems, the French now assumed a defensive posture and initiated no new major offensives. *"J'attends les chars et les américains"* Pétain pronounced.

---

1. The Second Battle of the Aisne, which took on the name of the French commander, was a combined French-British offensive, designed to be an overwhelming assault on the German lines. It failed miserably, resulting in a combined 317,000 casualties in five weeks of fighting.

"I am waiting for the tanks and the Americans." The "tanks" were the Renault FT light tanks. The "Americans" were the American Expeditionary Forces (AEF), one division of which was being hurried to France.

Commander of the AEF, General John J. Pershing, arrived in Paris on June 15 to a tumultuous welcome. "Crowds shouted themselves hoarse with cheers for America," the Associated Press reported. Pershing was followed over the next few weeks by 14,000 American troops. By any measure, it was a meager force, in number and capability. Its most recent experience had been chasing bandits in Mexico.

But no one missed the huge symbolic value of the accomplishment, not least the crowds that welcomed the Americans at their ports of arrival and in the Allied capitals. With the Stars and Stripes flying and regimental bands playing, U.S. troops marched in England and France to show that the Allied cause was getting an injection of fresh American spirit. From three thousand miles away, running the gauntlet of Germany's formidable U-boats, America had come to join the fight.

The articles in this chapter reveal the various levels of euphoric welcome and invigorated hope that greeted the arrival of U.S. troops in England and France. However, in "France in Dire Need of U.S. Aid," reporter Henri Bazin tempers the joyous tone by acknowledging that "the United States is but a lusty infant in the military sense, that much patient, hard disciplining preparation is necessary ere America can go up against the Boche[2] in a fight."

Although there was little reason to be optimistic about the chance of an Allied victory at this point in the war, the arrival of the first American troops in Europe—and all it portended—gave heart to the Allied cause.

Paris Celebrates General Pershing's Arrival

"The first shout of welcome became a continuous roar."

Associated Press
"Paris Wildly Enthusiastic Over Pershing"
Harrisburg Telegraph, June 14, 1917

2. A contemptuous term for German soldiers.

Paris, Wednesday, June 13—Paris welcomed General Pershing and his staff with an outburst of spontaneous enthusiasm such as only Paris is capable of. No conquering hero returning home could have hoped for or received such a tremendous reception as greeted the American commander as his automobile sped through hundreds of thousands of cheering people. Paris, particularly the French authorities, had planned and hoped for a great reception, but it is doubtful whether even the most optimistic pictured the almost frantic crowds that all but blocked the progress of the automobiles. Men and women cheered themselves hoarse and flung masses of flowers into the cars. Parisians themselves declare that the only event in their lifetime that approximated the reception in enthusiasm was that accorded to King George of England in 1914.

Cheering Shakes Station

When the special train reached the station Gen. Pershing and Field Marshal Joffre[3] were the first to appear. Behind them came a stream of American officers, each with a French officer as his host. The first shout of welcome became a continuous roar that seemed to shake the station to its foundations. The police hurriedly began to clear a lane down which a half dozen automobiles moved at a snail's pace between stirring throngs.

From hundreds of windows American flags were waved by men, women and children. French girls, with flags pinned to their breasts, and their arms filled with flowers, bought from their scanty savings, fairly fought for a chance to get near enough to the machines to hurl their offerings into the laps and shoulders of the astonished American officers.

Struggle to Shake Hands

The Americans apparently had not imagined the heights to which Parisian enthusiasm could rise. Boys, men and girls and even some old women struggled to jump on the running board of Gen. Pershing's car to shake hands with him.

---

3. General Joseph Joffre, the former Commander-in-Chief of French forces, had visited the United States in April to urge that a small American force be rushed to France. Pershing's arrival marked the success of Joffre's mission.

The demonstration was the more significant because it came from a great outpouring of people who, for the time being, seemed almost to forget that war was in progress. It was not Gen. Pershing alone who came in for unprecedented ovations, for every American caught sight of by the people was almost burdened with flowers. Crowds shouted themselves hoarse with cheers for America. From every house top all along the route, from every window, from every elevation and from thousands upon thousands who choked every thoroughfare in the vicinity of the line of march, there was hurled a welcome that no American in Paris will ever forget.

Transportation Tied Up

Gen. Pershing was expected to arrive from Boulogne at 3 o'clock but his special train did not reach Paris until 6:30. This gave opportunity for thousands who work until 6 o'clock to mass themselves along the route, until the congestion became so great that transportation was tied up. Gen Pershing's features were not familiar to the people but "Papa" Joffre's cap caught the eye of the people and revealed the identity of the soldier in khaki at his side.

At the station Gen. Pershing was met by a group of French officials, including Minister Viviani, Marshal Joffre and Generals Foch, Painleve and Peltier and by a group of Americans headed by Ambassador Sharp.[4] At one end of the station was an improvised throne with red tapestries such as is erected when royalty is visiting the city, which had been put up for the occasion. Before leaving the station the party assembled at this point. Speeches of welcome were delivered by prominent Frenchmen.

Given Informal Dinner

An informal dinner was given to Gen. Pershing at the American embassy. Premier Ribot, Marshal Joffre, Ministers Viviani and Painleve and other leading military and naval officers and public men were present. Toward the close Ambassador Sharp proposed the health of the presidents of France and the United States and the success of the expedition. The premier responded by greeting the American commander as representing the American army and people in the

---

4. William Graves Sharp, U.S Ambassador to France throughout the war.

undertaking on which they are now embarking. He wished them all success and proposed the health of President Wilson.

The first day spent in Paris by Major Gen. Pershing was a continuous succession of enthusiastic popular demonstrations, given wherever the American commander made an appearance. Great throngs filled the Place de La Concorde early in the day, hoping to catch a glimpse of the American. Hundreds of French soldiers on leave from the front mingled in the throngs and gave hearty greetings to the troops of the Second cavalry who accompanied Gen. Pershing. A large American flag waved over the general's hotel and everywhere the French and American colors were flying. One of the first events on today's crowded program was a visit this morning to the Hotel Des Invalides,[5] wherein is the historical monument containing Napoleon's body.

Makes Formal Call

After a brief ceremony at the Invalides, Gen. Pershing made a formal call on Ambassador Sharp and was then escorted with military honors to the Palace of the Elysees[6] to be presented to President Poincare.[7] At 12:30 o'clock the president and Madame Poincare gave a state breakfast in honor of the American commander. Other guests were Premier Ribot, Gen. Painleve, Marshal Joffre, Minister Viviani, Ambassador Sharp and other prominent figures in official and civilian life.

First U.S. Troops Land in France

"Tears of gratitude welled up in the eyes of French wives,
mothers and sweethearts"

Lincoln Eyre
"U.S. Troops Quickly Landed on Arriving at French Port"
The Sunday Star (Washington, DC), July 1, 1917

At a French port, June 30—All of the first expeditionary corps of Gen. Pershing's army are safely on French soil. Convoyed by naval

5. The *Hôtel national des Invalides* is a complex of museums and monuments relating to the military history of France. It includes a church, *Dôme des Invalides*, that is the burial site of Napoleon Bonaparte.
6. The Élysée Palace is the official residence of the President of France.
7. Raymond Poincaré was President of France from 1913–1920.

vessels they passed through the German U-boat zone without a mishap and the soldiers landed in fit condition to take up their intensive training.

The feat of the warships and destroyers in escorting them through the cordon of watchful submarines without the loss of a life rivals, perhaps surpasses, the marvelous success of the British in bringing their expeditionary force across the channel in August, 1914.

What risks they ran, what perils the American navy's efficiency and vigilance faced and vanquished, may not be told now. Suffice to say that the dangers were very real and very close, and that they were overcome reflects the greatest credit upon the commander of the convoying war vessels and all his officers and crews.

The transports once moored to the quays which had been prepared to receive them, the troops speedily disembarked and regiment by regiment, without the slightest confusion and with a total absence of fuss and within a few hours marched away to the camp outside of the city.

Mistaken at First for Canadians

Men, women and children lined the sidewalks as the Americans passed and wonderingly eyed the fighting men of their ally overseas. There was no boisterous manifestation of welcome, because the secrecy surrounding the newcomers' arrival precluded all accurate advance knowledge of the historic event among the townspeople themselves. There were, of course, numberless rumors afloat, but so vague was the public's appreciation of what they were witnessing that even after more than half of the contingent had passed through the town, I overheard bystanders discussing the reason for the "Canadians" coming to this port of France.

But if the cheers of greeting to the boys in olive drab lacked the volume of those that fell upon the ears of their commander-in-chief when he first drove through the streets of Paris, it was not because such French folk as realized what was going on were not deeply stirred by the spectacle. Tears of gratitude welled up in the eyes of French wives, mothers and sweethearts as they gazed upon the living symbols of their sister republic's resolve to fight at the side of their own Poilus'[8] fight for all humanity.

---

8. The name Poilu was an informal term of endearment for French soldiers in World War I. The literal translation is "hairy one," a reference of the bushy mustaches and beards often worn by these soldiers.

In a little shop here I heard a trench stained veteran in horizon blue[9] grumbling like "Grognards" or Napoleon's old guard[10] about the frightful pressure of the three years of war. "How long must we continue this slaughter?" he demanded bitterly. At that moment the strains of a military band playing the glorious marching song "Le Regiment de Gambre et Meuse," burst in upon the poilu's words, it was an American band, and behind it at the end of a long column of American soldiers was borne an American flag.

An old woman in the shop laid a hand on the war-weary soldier's arm and said gently: "Not so long, perhaps. See, my son. Americans already are here." The man in the uniform of France silently raised his hand in salute as the Stars and Stripes swept by.

Disembarked Without a Hitch

To say that the disembarkation of the men composing the initial contingent of Gen. Pershing's command was carried out with clock-like precision would be understating the facts. No clock was ever so smoothly efficient in its time-keeping as was the landing of the first expeditionary force ever sent from the United States to battle on European soil. There never was a hitch in the machinery from the time the advance guard of destroyers brought the first transports into the safety of the roads outside the port proper until the rear guard of the last battalion had marched in camp.

Edging gingerly alongside the quay the first vessel was tied to the soil of France shortly after 8 o'clock in the morning. Within half an hour the gangplank was creaking beneath the steady tramp of United States infantry and marines. As the men reached the wharf they were formed in line by their officers. As soon as the entire regiment was ashore it was marched off headed by its band to camp.

The second transport reached its berth and the operation was repeated at about the same interval with the first arrivals. Then

---

9. French soldiers began the war wearing their traditional uniforms of blue coats and red pants. The highly visible uniforms contributed to higher casualty rates. A change was made to a blue-grey uniform, known as "horizon blue," because it did not stand out against the skyline.

10. Grognards and Old Guard are references to elite soldiers who served in Napoleon's personal guard. One of the privileges granted them was the freedom to freely express their discontent. *Les Grognards* translates as "the Grumblers."

there was an hour's lull, after which the rest of the fleet began coming in at regular intervals. After awhile the novelty wore off even for the German prisoners at work on the piers, who, with their French guards, sent from Paris to supervise the landing, and a little group of correspondents, were the only witnesses to the actual disembarkation.

American Meat in Evidence

Following the troops on the road to camp came interminable files of motor trucks driven by French soldiers and bearing the heavier supplies, equipment and ammunition. American frozen meat, a noticeable feature of the load carted from the ships in earnest of Uncle Sam's desire to feed his men himself.

I joined the major general commanding Gen. Pershing's forces, who spared a few minutes of what time he had to say it was sure the busiest day of his life and to tell how glad he was to be in France. "It feels mighty good to get here," he said. "There is not one of us who is not bubbling over with the desire to get at the enemy. Of course, it will be a good while yet before our chance comes, and meantime we have got a healthy spell of hard work ahead of us. There's plenty to be done before we will be fit to enter the trenches alongside the French. We had a fine trip and owe a great deal to the navy for the way it got us through safely."

The Yankee twang, the southern drawl and the western burr are being wafted up into the bedroom of the hotel where I am writing this dispatch. Already "American" is being heard more frequently than French on the main street. At least, so it seems to me.

Tonight there are throngs of soldiers and sailors in every restaurant and cafe, and every now and then the provost marshal's guard marches past corralling men who have strayed too far from camp and is restraining the exuberance of those to whom the ability to buy drinks—forbidden them in their own countries, has proved a bit too strong.

French Delighted with Americans

The French so far are delighted with Uncle Sam's fighting "envoys." The American's boyishness and high spirits are pleasing even to these folk whom the great struggle has weighed so crushingly.

"It is their youth that is so wonderful to see," the proprietress of my hotel informed me. "They seem so much younger than our poilus. Why, I have not seen a single mustache among them all. God grant that they do not lose their youthfulness as I have lost it."

Whenever the American companies march by, and that's all day long, one finds the French officers gravely regarding them, estimating their worth as warriors.

"There are many who require the most intensive training before they are fit for the front, I think," the gray-haired commandant replied to my question as to what he thought of our men. "But the material is there in plenty. "We shall be glad to place them on the same high level as our own poilus before long."

He did not know what percentage of the Americans are recruits.

Think All Americans Millionaires

Other things about new allies, somewhat surprising to the French, are their prodigality and their bands. From every transport, as it passed through a certain narrow passage within arm's length of the quay, showers of pennies and nickels descended upon the crowds of children, who were cheering "Les Americans." The French soldiers, drawing 5 cents a day,[11] cannot afford to dispense largess to youngsters, however much they may desire to do so. Americans are more than ever regarded as a nation of millionaires as a result of this coin scattering from the transports.

As far as the bands are concerned they have exerted the most stirring influence upon the townsfolk who seldom hear music of any kind and never military bands. French bandsmen have all become stretcher-bearers nowadays.

Although very few of the enlisted men have any knowledge whatever of French one discovers them chatting amicably with the natives on every street corner. Already a large proportion of the town's fair sex has been enrolled as voluntary instructors to the would-be linguists in olive drab. The soldiers engaged in learning French in this pleasant manner are generally adorned with boutonnieres, for the French damsels invariably register their admiration by putting flowers in the heroic ones' buttonholes.

---

11. The lowest private in the American army earned ten times this amount, or around $0.50 a day.

Interested in German Prisoners

The Americans are taking an almost morbid interest in the German prisoners of war, of whom there are considerable numbers employed in and about this port. They have captured the enemy with their frank, impersonal kind of curiosity, to which the Boche replies with sullen, sidelong glances. I stood alongside a group of prisoners who ceased work to watch the American regiments go by. None of them said a word except one non-commissioned officer, who, eyeing the column with professional interest, suddenly muttered: "They look like recruits."

On my way out to visit the American camp I passed a field where a ball team from one of the naval vessels was practicing for the game it was going to have with another navy nine. A little crowd of French spectators was watching with mouth agape at the activities, which they doubtless considered a bit light hearted. I venture the prophecy that baseball will become as familiar as tennis to the inhabitants of this section of this country before long, for the army intends to organize a league of its own as soon as it finds the time. The navy's league already is in process of organization and games already are scheduled.

The camp is situated on particularly well chosen grounds. The troops are lodged in wooden huts which stretch forth endlessly in even rows. In each there are electric lights and running water. There is already splendid accommodation for a great many men—just how many it is not permissible to say. American sentries are posted at every entrance to the camp and French territorials guard the roads leading to it.

America's "Solemn-Looking Blokes" March in London

"It was as though upon the anvil of the New World all the troubles of the Old, after being passed through a white-hot furnace, had been forged into something clear and splendid."

Stacy Aumonier
"Solemn-Looking Blokes"
The Century Magazine, December 1917

At midday on August 15 I stood on the pavement on Cockspur Street and watched the first contingent of American troops pass through London.

I had been attracted thither by the lure of a public "show," by the blare of a band, and by a subconscious desire to pay tribute in my small way to a great people. It was a good day for London, intermittently bright, with great scurrying masses of cumuli overhead, and a characteristic threat of rain, which fortunately held off. Cockspur Street, as you know, is a turning off Trafalgar Street, and I chose it because the crowd was less dense there than in the square itself. By getting behind a group of shortish people and by standing on tiptoe I caught a fleeting view of the faces of nearly every one of the passing soldiers.

London is schooled to shows of this kind. The people gather and wait patiently on the line of route. And then some genial policemen appear and mother people back into some sort of line, an action performed with little fuss or trouble. Then mounted police appear headed by some fat official in a cockade hat and with many ribbons on his chest. And someone in the crowd calls out:

"Hullo, Percy! Mind you don't fall off yer 'orse!"

Then the hearers laugh and begin to be on good terms with themselves, for they know the "show" is coming. Then follows the inevitable band, and we begin to cheer.

It is easy and natural for a London crowd to cheer. I have heard Kaiser William II[12] cheered in the streets of London! We always cheer our guests, and we love a band and a "show" almost as much as our republican friends across the channel. I have seen royal funerals and weddings, processions in honor of visiting presidents and kings, the return of victorious generals, processions of Canadian, Australian, Indian, French, and Italian troops and bands. I wouldn't miss these things for worlds. They give color to our social life and accent to our every-day emotions. It is, moreover, peculiarly interesting to observe national traits on march: the French, with their exuberant élan, throwing kisses to the women as they pass;

---

12. As a grandson of British Queen Victoria, German Emperor Kaiser Wilhelm II was the first cousin of the reigning British monarch George V. Although he didn't get along well with his English relatives, he made numerous visits to England and was at Victoria's bedside when she died in January 1901.

our Tommies,[13] who have surprised the world with their gaiety, and keep up a constant ragging intercourse with the crowd and cannot cease from singing; the Indians, who pass like splendidly carved frieze; the Canadians, who move with a free and independent swing and grin in a friendly manner; the Scotch, who carry it off better than any one. But I had never seen American troops, and I was anxious to see how they behaved. I said to myself, "The American is volatile and impressionable, like a child." I had met Americans who within an hour's acquaintance had told me their life-story, given me their views on religion, politics, and art, and invited me to go out to Iowa or Wisconsin or California and spend the summer with them. More-over, the American above all things is emotional and—may I say it?—sentimental. It would therefore be extremely interesting to see how he came through the ordeal.

The first band passed, and the people were waving flags and handkerchiefs from the windows. We could hear the cheers go up from the great throng in the square. And there at last, sure enough, was Old Glory, with its silken tassels floating in the London breeze, carried by a solemn giant, with another on each side.

And then they came, marching in fours, with their rifles at the slope, the vanguard of Uncle Sam's army. And we in Cockspur Street raised a mighty cheer. They were solemn, bronzed men, loose of limb, hard, and strong, with a curious set expression of purpose about them.

Tramp, tramp, tramp, tramp.

And they looked neither to the right nor the left; nor did they look up or smile or apparently take any notice of the cheers we raised. We strained forward to see their faces, and we cried out to them our welcome.

Tramp, tramp, tramp, tramp.

They were not all tall; some were short and wiry. Some of the officers were rather elderly and wore horn spectacles. But they did not look at us or raise a smile or response. They held themselves very erect, but their eyes were cast down or fixed upon the back of the man in front of them. There came an interval, and another band, and then Old Glory once more, and we cheered the flag even more than the men. Fully a thousand men passed in this solemn

13. A slang term for the common British soldier was "Tommy Atkins," usually shortened to "Tommy."

American troops on the way to the front march through London amid cheering crowds, on September 5, 1917. *Source:* National Archives and Records Administration, 530734.

procession, not one of them smiling or looking up. It became almost disconcerting. It was a thing we were not used to. A fellow-cockney near me murmured:

"They're solemn-looking blokes, ain't they?"

Tramp, tramp, tramp, tramp.

The band blared forth once more, a drum-and-fife corps with a vibrant thrill behind it. We strained forward more eagerly to see the faces of our friends from the New World. We loved it best when the sound of the band had died away and the only music was the steady throb of those friendly boots upon our London streets. And still they did not smile. I had a brief moment of some vague apprehension, as though something could not be quite right. Some such wave, I think, was passing through the crowd. What did it mean?

Tramp, tramp, tramp, tramp.

The cheers died away for a few moments in an exhausted diminuendo. Among those people, racked by three years of strain and suffering, there probably was not one who had not lost some one dear to them. Even the best nerves have their limitation of endurance. Suddenly the ready voice of a woman from the pavement called out:

"God bless you, Sammy!"[14]

And then we cheered again in a different key, and I noticed a boy in the ranks throw back his head and look up. On his face was that expression we see only on the faces of those who know the finer sensibilities—a fierce, exultant joy that is very akin to tears. And gradually I became aware that on the faces of these grim men was written an emotion almost too deep for expression.

As they passed it was easy to detect their ethnological heritage. There was the Anglo-Saxon type, perhaps predominant; the Celt; the Slav; the Latin; and in many cases definitely the Teuton: and yet there was not one of them that had not something else, who was not pre-eminently a good "United States-man." It was as though upon the anvil of the New World all the troubles of the Old, after being passed through a white-hot furnace, had been forged into something clear and splendid. And they were hurrying on to get this accomplished. For once and all the matter must be settled.

Tramp, tramp, tramp, tramp.

There was a slight congestion, and the body of men near me halted and marked time. A diminutive officer with a pointed beard was walking alone. He saluted, made some kindly remark, and then passed on.

Tramp, tramp, tramp, tramp.

The world must be made safe for democracy.

And I thought inevitably of the story of the Titan myth, of Prometheus, the first real democrat, who held out against the gods because they despised humanity. And they nailed him to a rock, and cut off his eyelids, and a vulture fed upon his entrails.

But Prometheus held on, his line of reasoning being:

"After Uranus came Cronus. After Cronus came Zeus. After Zeus will come other gods."

14. At one time or another the following names had been suggested for the American soldier: Yank, Yankee, Johnnie, Johnny Yank, Broncho, Gringo, Liberty Boy, and Doughboy. Sammie got some usage early on, but Yank and Doughboy won out.

It is the finest epic in human life, and all the great teachers and reformers who came after told the same story—Christ, Vishnu, Confucius, Mohammed, Luther, Shakspere. The fundamental basis of their teaching was love and faith in humanity. And whenever humanity is threatened, the fires which Prometheus stole from the gods will burn more brightly in the heart of man, and they will come from all quarters of the world.

> He is trampling out the vintage where the
> grapes of wrath are stored;
> He hath loosed the fateful lightning of his
> Terrible swift sword.[15]

There is no quarter, no mercy, to the enemies of humanity. This is no longer a war; it is a crusade. And as I stood on the flags of Cockspur Street I think I understood the silence of those grim men. They seemed to epitomize not merely a nation, not merely a flag, but the unbreakable sanctity of human rights and human life. And I knew that whatever might happen, whatever the powers of darkness might devise, whatever cunning schemes or diabolical plans, or whatever temporary successes they might attain, they would ultimately go down into the dust before "the fateful lightning." "After Zeus will come other gods."

Tramp, tramp, tramp, tramp.

Nothing could live and endure against that steady and irresistible progression. And we know how you can do things, America. We have seen your workshops, your factories, and your engines of peace. And we have seen those young men of yours at the Olympic Games, with their loose, supple limbs, their square, strong faces. When the Spartans, lightly clad, but girt for war, ran across the hills of Athens and, finding the Persian hosts defeated, laughed, congratulated the Athenians, and ran back again—since those days there never were such runners, such athletes, as those boys of yours from Yale and Harvard, Princeton and Cornell.

And so on that day, if we cheered the flag more than the men, it was because the flag was the symbol of the men's hearts, which were too charged with the fires of Prometheus to trust themselves expression.

---

15. Lines from the Civil War song "The Battle Hymn of the Republic."

At least that is how it appeared to me on that forenoon in Cock-spur Street, and I know that later in the day, when I met a casual friend, and he addressed me with the usual formula of the day:

"Any news?"

I was able to say:

"Yes, the best news in the world."

And then he replied:

"What news?"

I could say with all sincerity:

"I have seen a portent. The world is safe for democracy."

Long, Disappointing Delay before U.S. Joins the Fight

"The United States is but a lusty infant in the military sense."

Henri Bazin
"France in Dire Need of U.S. Aid"
Evening Ledger (Philadelphia), July 6, 1917

The arrival of the first American division will he history by the time this story is in print. No single event in the annals of the war was ever awaited with more intensity and ardor, with more earnest well-wishing, with so much desire, with so much pent-up enthusiasm that is straining at the leash, eager to make dents of joy in the atmosphere of Paris.

All over Paris there is talk and rumor and hearsay and exaggeration about the army of the United States. The trim cavalrymen who stand at attention about the door of General Pershing's headquarters are surrounded by admiring throngs from dawn to darkness. The members of the staff, as they ride about Paris or walk upon its streets, are pointed out and followed. They are looked upon as the vanguard of civilization's final crusade against evil. They are referred to as "straight, tall men" and the trim cut of their uniforms is favorably commented upon. As for General Pershing himself, he is looked upon as a savior. His approximate hours of work are known, and always about the Crillon,[16] where he resides, a crowd collects at 8:15 a.m. to see him enter his car for the Rue Constantine.

16. The Hotel Crillon in Paris, where General Pershing made his headquarters.

The same story can be told as to his return in the evening. And all this, in large measure, is because General Pershing and his staff and the cavalrymen are something seen, something tangible that could be touched with the hand.

Hope and Expectancy

With this seeing and sensing, there is a great hope and expectancy. In a certain measure unreasonable to be sure, and also in a certain sense lamentable because of illogical ideas prevailing among the masses, that, for instance the territorials at the front will very presently be relieved by American troops.

No one has circulated the story. It has just come from nowhere. It is, of course, known in French official circles, as it is generally known in America, that the United States is but a lusty infant in the military sense, that much patient, hard disciplining preparation is necessary ere America can go up against the Boche in a fight. But the people here cannot see it, or, if they do, refuse to believe it possible.

There is therefore something to be feared in a certain disillusionment among the millions who, in personal losses, know how much of France's army is under the sod, and who have not or will not learn to reason that before a child or a nation learns to run, it must learn to walk.

Much has been written in French newspapers on this subject, and much has been said, too, upon the transportation problem.

But the masses read and forget figures and, in any event, do not take into calculation their meaning nor the problems involved, nor the ships essential; nor do they reason out the why. They only know of their own desolated hearthstones, of their wounded and mutilated, of the death of their youth, of the fact that in the man sense, France is bled almost to the bone; and they have staked their all on the United States as the one land in the world whence men and guns and equipment can come soon "bientot," in untold quantity.

They want these living and inanimate things now; and, more's the pity, they need them now. They need them to an extent beyond compare, save Germany's needs toward her vicious ends. And as human nature is but human nature, and, after all, men and women are but children who want a thing when they want it, the masses in

France are going to become, in some sense, disappointed through relative future face-to-face realization of the fact that all America's good will and resources, all America's intense earnestness cannot be manufactured in a few months into disciplined fighting men who will fight to the last under orders. For there you are.

That's the real reason the United States cannot place a big army in the field quickly. You can teach a man to salute and how to handle a gun and all the rest of it in a few weeks, but you cannot take a bunch of men fresh from desks, and factories, and farms, and even Plattsburg training camps[17] and have them stand all unflinchingly the test of fire even to the death. It is not a question of their courage or their willingness. They require a year's disciplining as to what soldiers really are, as what war really means.

There is the reason England's splendid army took eighteen months or more in the making. And in the reverse sense there is the reason through service in compulsion the armies of Germany and France stood and died for their cause. It's the reason, too, why the poilu is so wonderful. His fellow countrymen with him are the most democratic in the world, and yet his submission to military service was an institution with him and his fathers before him. Hence he took to its discipline as a duck to water, the very moment he was mobilized, thirty-four months ago.

Doomed to Disappointment

Summed up, all this means to one who has lived long close to the French people, who knows them so well as to be able almost to say what they will think, eat and say at a given moment, that there is an additional understanding as to how eagerly they are waiting for something immediate, that perforce cannot be else but relatively distant, and that they are going to be disappointed ere American hosts, fresh, strong, youthful, disciplined, carry the bulk of the burden, carry the war into Belgium, and if God is good, into Germany.

And it is because of this knowledge of French people and temperament that I deplore most earnestly the decision of mainly training at home, where, despite installations based upon modem

17. Plattsburg camps were volunteer, civilian, training programs, run over the summers of 1915 and 1916. They were designed to prepare college graduates to be available as potential army officers, when the U.S. entered the war.

warfare, psychologically it will not only be impossible to bring about as rapid a transformation of civilians into soldiers as were the men in France, but prevent also the great moral salutary effect of their presence as a thing the blood-weary French people could sense and see and touch; produce a great moral effect upon the nation while more quickly fitting the men, under a French sky, amid the atmosphere of France, within the smell of war itself.

We should have 100,000 of them here as quickly as it is possible to have ships carry them over. They would mean more toward quick action and the upholding of French morale than five times the quantity six months hence.

France is like a man battling with a still strong devil. The devil is tired, but France is tired too even if, thanks to England, less so. And because willing, sympathetic hands are not ready to gird themselves in war gauntlets, France must wearily hang on. She will of course, because France is wonderful. And she has the wonderful youth of England beside her. But she is nevertheless in sore need of help now. That's the situation in a word.

Nothing will be gained of course, in this writing. Far be it from the writer's mind to presume better or even equal judgment with those trained in the American sense military. There is seen only the immediate need and also the deplorable short-sighted political policies that through congressional lassitude permitted the greatest nation in the world to live over a volcano all the years it was smoldering, all the years, too, after it had broken out into evil and engulfing flame had crossed the Atlantic Ocean and struck us in the face ere we unsheathed swords and began training men to stand behind them.

It's a far cry from a widowed French or English or American woman whose widowhood might have been prevented and the aims, of politicians of all parties in America during the last twenty years. But there is a connecting link nevertheless in this story.

Chapter 3

❖

❖

❖

❖

❖

Learning to Fight

Introduction

After the United States entered the war, there was a general perception among the American public that the army it was hurrying to France would quickly get into the fighting and, more than likely, put an end to this nasty war. Something in the American character, the country's vast resources, and its know-how would bring the victory that had eluded the allied armies for three years.

Long-time American expatriate, Mary King Waddington, commented on the American soldiers she saw in France in the summer of 1917: "Their attitude was a little puzzling when they first came over; they were half shy, half arrogant. The American eagle spread his wings extensively, they were going to finish the War, and show the Old World what the young Republic across the sea could do."

Unfortunately, the "regular army" and National Guard divisions that landed in France were seriously unprepared to wage war, lacking experience with modern warfare and the weapons and equipment needed to fight. The U.S. Army had not kept pace with the development of modern artillery, machine guns, and warplanes. It had no experience with the type of trench fighting it would soon face or the weapons there employed: the hand grenade, flamethrower, and poison gas. Plus, since regular army units had been rushed to full strength with new recruits, many soldiers had not even received basic military training.

In July 1917, correspondent Wythe Williams began to correct American thinking by filling his article, "Stars and Stripes with Tri-Color Fly at Verdun Citadel," with the reality for which AEF troops must prepare. He painted the "ghastly picture" of trench fighting, the barbed wire, artillery barrages, machine guns, the killed and wounded, the merciless enemy. Then he struck the proper nationalistic tone by noting that the American soldier would soon be the best fighter, "privileged to spend his blood" for the principles of his country.

For most of 1917, news stories about America in the war focused on training and the buildup of the infrastructure necessary to support an American army that would eventually be several million strong. It was during this period that U.S. soldiers acquired the nickname Sammies, for Uncle Sam's boys. The Sammies began training with war-hardened French soldiers, affectionately known as Poilu (hairy one), and with British soldiers, referred to as Tommies.

News stories told how quickly and how well the Sammies learned to throw grenades or fire artillery, how they had won the respect of their French trainers, how eagerly they awaited their chance at the enemy, and how they would employ the more aggressive "open warfare" favored by General Pershing, rather than stay on the defensive in the trenches. In short, the press delivered a catalog of the American soldier's attitudes and capabilities that would lead to his success. However, correspondents such as Wythe Williams cautioned their readers that long before U.S. troops saw any fighting, America first faced the "biggest, hardest, and greatest" task of building an army in France.

U.S. Army Must Become Greatest Force in the World

"The time of fiery trial and sacrifice for the American army
is still in the future."

Wythe Williams
"Stars and Stripes with Tri-Color[1] Fly at Verdun Citadel"
The Sunday Star (Washington, DC), July 29, 1917

1. The French flag, known as the tri-color for its three vertical stripes of blue, white, and red.

Field headquarters of the American Army in France, July 26 (via Paris, July 27)—The biggest, hardest and greatest work ever attempted by a people since mankind flocked into nations at Babel has been well begun.

The Stars and Stripes are flying above the citadel of Verdun.[2] Our army is not there or anywhere near, but Old Glory floats beside the tri-color, a fitting recognition from the greatest army that ever existed to the new champion now at hand, preparing to take up the struggle for civilization and peace. It seemed to me when I visited the citadel a few days ago, it was more significant that the flag should fly above that battered gray and grim old shrine of war than even its hoisting over Westminster tower by order of the king. It means the tribute of an army to an army as well as the salute of a nation. It means the hand grip of brothers. It means the French army knows the American army will carry on to the end. It means that the poilu has seen the Sammy and pronounced him all to the good.

Many Weeks Before Fiery Trial

When I left French headquarters to come to the American army it was with a feeling it would be difficult to send news dispatches from what is now only a training camp. The time of fiery trial and sacrifice for the American army is still in the future. It will be many weeks before the recording of our casualty lists, not just a list of killed, wounded, prisoners and missing. It will be long before the cables carry the news that the Germans attacked our lines with gas and liquid flames, gained a footing in certain salients by pulverizing our barbed wire barricades and trenches with military barrage, after which the infantry charged with hand grenades and bayonets. That will all come. Just as bad and worse.

The Germans hate us more than they fear their future. They will give us no quarter. Many of our boys, drilling this morning in

2. Fought from February to December 1916, the Battle of Verdun was one of the longest and deadliest in history, with over 700,000 casualties. No other battle of WWI carries the symbolic resonance in France as Verdun. For ten months, the Germans threw overwhelming numbers of troops at the Verdun forts and pulverized them with siege guns. The French defenders suffered staggering losses but held out. The immortal order by French General Robert Nivelle—"They shall not pass."—is firmly enshrined in the mythology of the war.

the fields surrounding this quiet village, are going to a last bivouac
in No Man's Land,[3] where even the buzzard dare not interfere with
the tortures of shrapnel and gelignite. This is a ghastly picture.
We will cable it. It is already written that we shall cable it before we
can record the glory of our triumphs. But that is the end for which
the American army has its being. The beginning, the cause for
which it was created, in the parlance of journalism already carries
a date line that is old.

Hard Job Back Home

We are now in the middle of the story—training camps. And training
camps, it seemed to me, were apt to be dull. I have commenced this
dispatch by saying that the biggest, hardest and greatest work ever
attempted by a people has been well begun. This work to which
I refer is the American army in France. This summing up is the only
message that can be sent to the folks at home from this training
camp at this stage of our war against Germany. The American army
must become the biggest force the world has ever produced to crush
a foe.[4] To make it such will be a harder job back home than anything
our government has ever tackled in its existence. Its accomplishment will be so great a thing that this planet hardly seems big enough
in which to give its record proper place.

And today the work has only just begun. The censor forbids
details. This sudden reference to my old acquaintance from every
battle front does not mean that I would like to become critical. Far
from that. Since joining this camp, two days ago, I became more
proud that I was an American than ever in my life, and criticism
this morning is not in my nature. Only the scribes and the censors
can never see quite alike on all questions of details.

I would like to take one phase of this summing up that I have
given—the hardness of the job that the American army has on
hand—and simply burn it into the understanding of every man
and woman back home who has a single ounce of force that might
be used in bringing this war to victory and an end. We are a proud
and a great people. Our eagle has soared high and far. We have the

3. The disputed space between opposing trenches, no man's land was a blasted terrain
of barbed wire defenses, shell craters, and dead bodies.
4. By July 1918, the U.S. Army had over one million men in France. The number would
eventually grow to over two million, but many arrived too late to participate in the fighting.

right to be proud because we are great. But now we must become greater. We must equip ourselves now—today, not tomorrow—to perform, our greatest act, the establishment and maintenance of an American army on the European battle front.

Must Fill in the Gaps

Our army in France is small—all the world knows that, including Germany. Compared with the armies of our allies, it is about as big as a fife and drum corps in a monster parade before a presidential election. And if we had a million men in France today it would not mean we could put a million men in the battle line. I may not become specific on percentages or numbers, but I may say this:

"The first question after our men take their section of line is that known here as 'refits.' We must have enough men behind—not reserves, but just in training in France, as all our army is today—to fill every gap in every company, battalion and regiment. Every division must be kept to its strength. A regiment of 2,000 men may have 20,000 names on its roster before the war is over. That means ten complete refits—that it has been wiped out and made over ten times—always keeping the same number and name and thus adding to its regimental history. Long before the time comes when for every man in line ten men have gone before at one battle or another, that regiment whatever it is called, will do as that Coldstream Guards have done since Waterloo, like the French Chasseurs and even the Guards of Prussia[5]—it will go out and fight for the honor and glory of its name. Refits, then, are the first consideration for the final end after the first line of khaki are big and strong enough to be given a sector of the actual front."

Supplies Necessary for Success

Then there are all the services of the rear—not only food and munition, but literally a hundred different kinds of army material and supplies that are absolutely necessary for success. We must have motor lorries, not by dozens, but by thousands: tools of every description, materiel to construct new trenches and emplacements for big guns, materials to make bombproof shelters, clothing, boots

---

5. Long-standing units in the various national armies that had venerable histories.

and arms, guns themselves, thousands of them, too, of all sizes, so that when we let loose the hell of our artillery upon the Germans we can cable that we, instead of anybody else, had the greatest concentration of cannon fire that has ever been known. If any other army concentrates guns so that if stretched in line they would be only a few yards apart—as already has been the case—our guns, in a similar line, must stand wheel to wheel. For that is the only way we are going to beat the Germans.

When our work here is finished it must be recorded that the activities lumped together are greater than those of a world metropolis. We are not part of the British army, we are not part of the French army or any army. We are just the American army, fighting under the Stars and Stripes in France. We must build railroads, main lines and narrow-gauge spurs, literally by the thousands of miles to keep our troops moving and our supplies right behind them.

I say nothing of our activities in the air, which may take so great a part in winning the war. The airplanes are only an arm of the service. I proceed from the front to the rear, to the base of our organization in France, on sea.

What America Must Do

Now comes the portion of my message the most important of all. From the time an American Sammy steps off a transport that lands in France to the time he kills or gets killed in the trenches of the enemy everything that happens to him must be made possible by America. Aside from the very intensive training that France is giving the first detachment of our forces already here, we must depend upon nobody; we must do everything for ourselves. Our next detachments must be trained by the detachment already here, so that the French troops now having them in hand can go back to the line. America must bring them here and keep them here; she must feed them and transport them; she must supply every single item that is necessary.

There is no use to say the sea is too wide, the ships too few and the task too difficult. True, it is far greater than the formation of business trusts. It makes San Juan[6] seem like a baseball game and

---

6. The Battle of San Juan Hill (1898), the largest land battle of the Spanish-American War, involved some 8,500 troops, scarcely more than a skirmish by World War I standards.

building of the Panama Canal[7] like the afternoon of the child at play. In connection with the allied plans, the generals of our army must make their own plans. Our intelligence department must depend first on itself. We must plan and map our own ground; we must conduct our own fight. We are to have an army all our own in the allied line; it must be all ours to the last button on its boots.[8] We are committed to this task; we must see it through, and the quicker every American realizes how hard and big it is the better. There is no use sending over hundreds of pairs of mules with only dozens of sets of harness. It is useless to send officers and horses and forget to send bridles and saddles. America has had three years to watch the mistakes by the allies, so if we go ahead making the same mistakes, to which our distance from the conflict lends even greater importance, we will have no one to blame but our precious selves.

Message of Officers and Men

To this task every officer and every man now in this training camp has dedicated his life. The day is not far distant when it will be his privilege to spend his blood for the principles upon which his country is founded and for the freedom and peace she has prized so highly. It is the message of our officers and men that I am sending, and nothing more. I have tried for three years to give an understanding by cable of the magnitude of this task, if ever it would be necessary that we take it up. Our army is here now, and true to American standards only a very few weeks have been necessary for it to gather to itself a complete understanding of its size today compared with its job in hand.

I was on the quay when Gen. Pershing set foot on French soil, and when the same troops with whom I am living today marched off their transports. Even in the short time I have known them I can see a great campaign, not so much in the way they look, although they seem much harder now than then, but in the way they think.

7. The Panama Canal officially opened to traffic on August 15, 1914, only weeks after the start of the war, capping a decade-long, monumental construction project.
8. The AEF would not conduct the first American-planned and commanded offensive, in which it operated as an independent army, until the Battle of St. Mihiel, September 12–15, 1918.

An officer at whose mess I lunched summed up the situation. He said:

"This army has had to forget practically everything it ever knew and start all over again."

Figures Outcurve on Grenade

How that start has been made I am able to judge for myself. America may not be considered a military nation, but the Americans are certainly a fighting race. Sammy has taken hold of this new way to fight better and more quickly than any other soldiers on the allied line. Show him a new fangled machine gun and he takes it apart and finds out all about it for himself. Give him a hand grenade and he has already figured out an outcurve on the way to throw it that bids fair to beat the distance record of the entire allied line.

French soldiers responsible for our training are frankly delightedly amazed. A French liaison captain of an American machine gun squad told me yesterday that his gang knew more in twenty-four hours than even his own chasseurs could learn in two weeks. Not a man in that squad had ever handled a machine gun before, yet I saw them go through a drill that for snap, quickness and "chic," as the Frenchman called it, was so near perfection that several British callers who knew the particular gun in hand very well were goggle-eyed with wonder.

Although there are plenty of interpreters, Sammy does not need interpreters, he gets on by himself, and as one of our colonels said yesterday:

"These interpreters all learned English instead of American, anyhow."

But one French officer best dismissed the subject of interpreters. He said:

"Your men do not pay any attention to interpreters. They watch what our men do, then they do the same thing themselves."

Finest Brand of Fighter

So, you see, taking everything into consideration. there is nothing the matter with Sammy today, and he will be a great deal better tomorrow, and in a very short time he will be the finest brand of fighting man that the war has produced. The countryside in which he lives already loves him. He is a lovable chap; that is why. He is a gentleman, this Sammy of ours, despite his cuss words and his noise. He is often noisy, there is no gainsaying that, but he has an inherent gallantry that appeals especially to the French. In dozens of French villages where he is billeted—tiny hamlets where all the men have long ago gone to war—the coming of Sammy has brought the greatest joy. When he is off duty, he usually has all the children of the place in tow and seems to enjoy it as much as they. Sammy's fondness for children is also aiding him to learn the language, for the children speak far more slowly and distinctly than their elders, and inasmuch as Sammy's blunders are so amusing, they have far more time and patience in making him understand.

On an old stone wall I found a Sammy sitting beside a little girl of six, solemnly teaching him how to count. He held up his fingers and the child told him the number in French, while he repeated it over and over until he got the pronunciation. It was funny. It was pathetic. Sammy seemed so far away from home, and a look into his future probably would not indicate anything very gay or enduring. Later in the day I ran across the same lad at a peddler's cart telling his pals he could speak French and he would interpret for any who wished to buy. He did not do so badly, either. The teacher had taught the numbers well.

Fields their Workground

With the poilus assisting him in training, Sammy is equally popular. For every battalion of Americans there is a corresponding battalion of French billeted in the next village along the road. The fields, valleys and hills between are their workground from morning until night, and they share a common midday meal, hot from the camp kitchen on the field. Each battalion of every regiment has already laid out its French systems of defense and begun minor operations which will gradually develop until the full scale of mimic front is established which will be held against a mimic assault and modern war action.

Custom has established that on alternate Sundays the poilus and Sammies entertain each other in their home village to the music of the regimental band, so already the fraternity of the two armies is a matter of firm fact.

Of course, there have been minor difficulties on minor subjects. Sammy does not like French tobacco, and shouts his dislike at the top of his lungs. He has to learn that common French table wine, which has no kick whatever if consumed the way the French consume it, cannot be imbibed by the barrel without trouble. There have been other little annoyances on which he vented verbal displeasure, but, as one of our old sergeants remarked on one of these occasions to the French interpreter, who since expressed hopes that Sammy was not insulted: "Don't you worry, old man, there never was an American who didn't have to raise a holler about somethin'."

A Credit to his Country

So, as I said before, there is nothing the matter with Sammy as he stands today in France. He is a credit to his country, and the country should be proud of him. But Sammy who is here cannot do the job alone. There is not enough of him to do that, and I have already tried to explain his message to the folks back home. The French army has placed the seal of approval upon us.

With them we register 100 per cent, so far as we go. Winter is coming. We have got to the limit. Something more than a flag has got to represent us in that holy of holies of war—the citadel of Verdun.

Learning to Fight a Modern War

"Should the grenade thrower hold the bomb longer than the time
allotted for its flight and explosion he will be blown to bits."

"Teaching Our Soldiers the New Warfare"
The South Bend News-Times, August 19, 1917

From the Atlantic to the Pacific and behind the farflung battle line of the allies on the western front, the soldiers of the United States, the "Sammies," as the French have dubbed them, are learning the new method of waging war.

First of all, the men who will carry the Stars and Stripes forward in France and in Flanders are learning the rudiments of trench warfare,[9] a form of conflict practically unknown until German hosts dug themselves into underground fortifications after their defeat on the Marne.

The National Guardsmen of the various States, who are now enlisted under the Federal banner, have drilled and maneuvered for years in accordance with regular army tactics, founded on the lessons learned in the Civil, Indian and Spanish-American wars. Most of these tactics, so far as they apply to fighting in France and Belgium, are now practically obsolete. The National Guardsmen, like the regulars, must forget a large part of what they have been taught for years and take up an entirely new course in warfare. The volunteer recruits and the men drawn by draft have nothing to unlearn, but a whole lot to learn. The regulars and the National Guardsmen have a slight advantage—they are already instructed in discipline; they know how to handle a rifle and shoot; they know the military formations of squad, platoon, company, regiment and battalion. With these differences the regular, the National Guardsman, the volunteer and the conscript who go into training in a camp behind the Western front will face the same problem. All will have the same tactics to learn. The major portion of the lessons will be new to all.

In accordance with these changed conditions the efforts of the instructors, many of them English and French officers who wear valor decorations won in the first two years of the war, who are teaching American soldiers the first rudiments of the new warfare, are concentrated on the use of the bayonet, hand grenade throwing, machine gun operation, trench construction and the erection and destruction of barbed wire defenses. The primary evolutions of the various military units and arms are not forgotten—enough attention is paid to them to insure efficiency in them, but the main effort is expended on the various forms of offense and defense in relation to the trenches.

The trench being the soldiers' base, either for offense or defense, he is first shown how to construct it in its various forms, he learns how to build the first line defense trench and its communicating, supporting and reserve trenches, with their mazes of

---

9. Following a brief period of mobile warfare in August-September 1914, the fighting settled into the static trench warfare associated with World War I. That type of fighting would predominate on the Western Front until the final months of the war.

first aid, supply and rest stations. He learns how either to string a barbed wire barricade in front of his own advanced trenches or to cut a similar barrier so as to allow his passage in front of an enemy trench which he is attacking in case his artillery fire has failed to destroy it. Next he is taught the art of what is referred to in the war dispatches as "consolidating our gains." This means the reconstruction and fortification in sufficient strength to withstand a counter attack of captured enemy trenches; trenches which have previously practically been destroyed by the artillery fire which precedes every attack in force. Third he is shown how to use to the best advantage either for offense or defense, the shell holes or craters of the No Man's Land which always lies between the advanced trenches of opposing forces.

The bayonet and the hand grenade are as important in trench defense as they are in offense. Time and time again, as at Verdun, German infantry waves have swept into French trenches through seemingly impassable artillery and machine gun fire, only to be stopped and driven back by the bayonet and hand grenade. Compared with the bayonet practice of the United States Manual of Arms,[10] the bayonet drill of the allies now being taught to the United States soldiers is as a bolt of lightning to a Summer zephyr. One of the student officers at Plattsburg died from the effects of a nervous shock sustained in bayonet practice, although his opponent was only a stuffed bag.

The soldiers are being taught to kill with the bayonet. Practice is not merely a pretty exhibition of thrust and parry. If wooden bayonets were not used in man-to-man practice the ranks of the recruits would already have been appreciably thinned. It is absolutely cold-blooded practice in cold steel killing. To quote from the instructor:

"You must learn to drive your bayonet into your opponent only so far as it will enable you to withdraw it without unlocking it from your rifle or wrenching it free by putting your foot on your opponent's body. In the meantime you might be bayoneted; moreover, you would be wasting valuable time."

Hand grenades weigh from a pound to a pound and five ounces each. They are the same shape as a turkey egg and a little larger.

10. A Manual of Arms provides precise instructions about how weapons are meant to be used. The suggestion here is that how the bayonet was being used by the Allies in trench fighting differed considerably from Manual of Arms instructions.

British instructors training American soldiers in bayonet fighting in the trenches. Near Moulle, France, May 22, 1918. *Source:* Ministry of Information First World War Official Collection, Imperial War Museum, Q9079. Wikimedia Commons.

The man who can hurl a hand grenade ninety feet is worth half a dozen crack rifle shots, and that is why dependence on the rifle bullet is growing less and less. One hand grenade will kill or put out of action every man in a ten-foot trench section. These grenades are so arranged that the withdrawal of a firing pin releases a lever and lights a fuse timed to fire the explosive within a given number of seconds. Should the grenade thrower hold the bomb longer than the time allotted for its flight and explosion he will be blown to bits.

The American soldiers are being taught hand grenade and bomb defense and attack. It already has been officially announced that the organization of the United States army units has been changed to conform to the French organization. Under this arrangement each trench section in practice work contains riflemen, hand grenade throwers and trench mortar operators for defense. Each man is instructed in the use of his specific weapon. Since they are not supposed to show their heads above the trench, the soldiers must learn to throw the grenades and launch the trench mortars at a mark the distance and location of which are given by an

American soldiers in training with the French. *Source:* Author's collection.

observer using a trench periscope. In an offensive or on a raid the grenadiers carry four-second grenades, smoke bombs of petrol and phosphorus weighing three pounds each and six-second fuse bombs weighing nine pounds for wrecking dugouts and machine gun emplacements.

The officers and rank and file of the engineering, pioneering and sapping units at the various instruction camps and in the American camp in France are learning how to tunnel through the earth, and construct and explode the underground mines which have been used to such great advantage by both sides in the terrific European struggle.

Troops Eager to Get in the Fight

"Our men have learned nearly all that their excellent French teachers can show them."

Junius Wood
"American Troops in France Want to Get to Firing Line"
Evening Star (Washington, DC), August 17, 1917

American field headquarters in France. August 16 (delayed).[11]

"Let us get into the trenches. We want to fight." These expressions are frequently heard among the soldiers and marines in France. Eagerness to show their mettle is a striking characteristic of the troops. They seem undaunted by any anticipation of heavy casualties or by the stories of hardships, the merciless rain of fire, deadly gases and other dangers of trench life. Officers and men are confident that our forces will make a wonderfully creditable showing once the opportunity comes for real action.[12]

Though just as keen as the men, the officers realize that despite great progress made in a month of intensive training much remains to be done before all the intricacies of the life and death struggle in the trenches are mastered. If it were left to the men probably half of them would vote to start tomorrow, so great is their enthusiasm.

"Because of the present rapid rate of progress our men have learned nearly all that their excellent French teachers can show them," said an officer of the marines. "We will soon have an excellent teaching force which can take the later arrivals in hand. They will be able to teach four times their own number and they should do it in half the time it has required the French to teach us. It will not be necessary to use interpreters, which always takes time, or to explain fundamentals which the later arrivals will already know. If the later contingents are fairly well drilled it will not take more than a month to teach them the intricacies and new angles of trench warfare. It will be rapid work and I have no hesitation in saying that the world will be astounded at the speed with which America builds an immense army with tremendous striking power."

When the long list of Army promotions was received by cable the officers were stirred to great enthusiasm. Congratulations were extended on all sides. The men also had cause for rejoicing when they saw the first "movie" show arrive in the shape of a Red Cross[13] motor truck from Paris, equipped with a projecting machine,

---

11. Dispatches from war correspondents occasionally carried such designations in their dateline as "delayed," "delayed by Censor," "by mail," or "via cable," to explain when and how they had arrived on the page of the newspaper.

12. The armies of all the belligerents entered the war with a naïve confidence and high spirits.

13. The American Red Cross provided many services to the AEF. In addition to its better-known medical support of doctors and nurses, it ran a Camp Services unit that provided everything from movies and refreshments to communications with home and financial aid.

which throws the antics of favorite comedians, languishing vampires and other scenes on an open-air screen. The truck makes a one-night stand in each camp.

American Artillery to Beat Infantry to the Front

"Modern artillery training is a maze of technical details,
a labyrinth of mathematical problems, a never-ending
series of intricate puzzles."

Associated Press, September 14, 1917
"American Guns on French Front"

American training camp in France, Sept 12—American guns are booming in France, booming under the eyes of observation balloons and airplanes[14] to trace each singing shrapnel shell, each missile of high explosive destructiveness. Thus far the guns have not been turned against the enemy, but there is every likelihood that the artillery will beat the infantry to the front, for it is now planned to complete the intensive training of the gunners under actual battle conditions, under the fire of German guns and with their own weapons directed against occupied German trenches in various positions behind enemy lines.

While the plans of the American commanders are unknown, it would seem logical from a military standpoint that after the American artillery has completed several weeks of training at the front in liaison with the French infantry and supporting guns, the greater part of it would be withdrawn for maneuvers with the gradually multiplying American infantry.

The co-operation of artillery and infantry is so close under modern battle tactics that it is essential they be trained to act together almost as one unit. And just as the first contingent of American infantry will devote itself largely through the fall and winter to training other units as they arrive, so the first contingent of artillery will train the batteries, regiments and brigades which will be thrown into France before the spring campaign of 1918 is likely to begin.

14. Both balloons and airplanes were used by artillery observers to direct fire onto enemy targets.

Carefully Guarded Secret

While it is not known here what announcements may have been
made from Washington, the arrival of a large section of American
field artillery in France has been kept a carefully guarded secret, so
far as Europe is concerned. The announcement is permitted now,
only after the officers and men have progressed far in their intensive training under general supervision of France's most expert
artillerists. There are no longer any French officers or Poilus
actually serving at the guns, the crews having been Americanized
throughout. At the observation posts and in the schools of instruction French officers sit now only in an advisory capacity.

Through various reports received from trained observers, atta-
chés and other confidential sources during the last three years, the
American artillery officers of the regular army have been enabled
to keep in fairly close touch with all the gunnery development
in the world war—sufficiently close, in any event, to change many
of their older practices within the last twelve months, while at the
same time keeping them abreast of the more modern theories of
the various artillery schools. What the American artillery has now
and never had before is plenty of shells. It is easily conceived what
this means to enthusiastic officers and men, whose batteries are
expending in two or three weeks ten times the number of shells
formerly allotted to them for an entire year.

Modern artillery training is a maze of technical details, a labyrinth of mathematical problems, a never-ending series of intricate
puzzles, in which such elusive and subtle subjects as orientation,
triangulation, deflection, drift, elevation, calibration, meteorology,
range finding and a dozen other branches of optics and geometry
and the general application of the concentrated powers of destruction are involved.

Famous Seventy-fives[15]

In meeting its fulfillment of its contract with Washington, the
French government has supplied the American artillery units with
the latest output of the famous seventy-fives, which it is generally
conceded is the finest light field piece the world has ever known.

15. The French 75 mm artillery piece was a highly effective, rapid-fire weapon that was
also used by U.S. troops.

It corresponds with and takes the place of the old three-inch gun in the American army. The French have also supplied the Americans with six inch howitzers—a gun of great power and accuracy which corresponds to the noted German 9.9, probably the most effective weapon in the entire German gun list.

Examine the Guns

The Americans have been quick to master the details of the French weapons and are handling them now as if they had been friends of many years standing. Under the watchful supervision of a splendid old French major, who speaks English as it if were his own tongue, they have taken down and reassembled the two types of guns with which they have been training, so that the most minute detail of construction and the particular use of each part, no matter how small, has become thoroughly known. The mastery of artillery, as a whole, however, is a matter of months rather than weeks, and there still remains much for even the first American artillery contingent to learn.

The work of cooperation with balloons and airplanes has only recently been started. The airplane service has attracted many of the brightest young officers in the artillery, who are practicing now to qualify as observers. The American chief of artillery in France recently gave each officer of the lower grades an opportunity to indicate his preference in any special branch of artillery work. It is striking evidence of the spirit of the expeditionary force that an overwhelming majority expressed the desire to become airplane observers, which is the branch of the service holding undoubtedly the greatest hazard.

Americans Trained to Attack Rather than Defend

"The American army is one wherein officers are trained to lead men into action in the most energetic fashion."

Newton C. Parke
"Aggressive Spirit Instilled in Sammees"
International News Service, October 17, 1917

Field headquarters of the American army in France, Oct 17.

The instilling of a vigorous offensive spirit[16] in every American soldier in France will be the keynote of the instruction and training in every army and corps school this winter. Every phase of training will accentuate this until, when the time comes to enter the trenches, the men will be fired with the aggressive zeal summed up in the phrase, "Kan the Kaiser."

The British instruction in bayoneting in the divisional school already fits in well with this program. British tactics are based upon the principle of "Forward! Forward."

The officers are confident that continued emphasis upon aggressiveness in training will develop the men into a magnificent army possessed of the same supreme confidence that made the Roman legions invincible in battle.

It is pointed out in the schools that, despite the important changes in modern warfare, the rifle and bayonet are still the principal weapons of the infantrymen. Training in marksmanship and bayoneting consequently are highly important.

The American army is one wherein officers are trained to lead men into action in the most energetic fashion, this giving the rank and file examples of aggressiveness. One of the objects of the schools is to develop sound and vigorous leadership. Maintaining discipline of the highest order and a West Point standard is required, but at the same time officers are obliged to assist in keeping the morale at a high standard by doing everything possible that means comfort for their men.

All problems of tactical maneuvers will be worked out with a view to developing the officer's initiative to the greatest possible extent. The use of normal methods of attack with fixed formations are forbidden. On the contrary, subordinate officers will be required to assume various formations that are likely to develop on the battlefield. The best students emerging from the army schools will become instructors of the corps schools and staff officers of divisions and higher units.

---

16. Although the Allies wanted to train AEF troops to fight beside them in the trenches, General Pershing thought the long stalemate on the Western Front could only be broken with "open warfare" that emphasized a more aggressive spirit of the offensive.

Chapter 4

✦

✦

✦

✦

✦

American Firsts

Introduction

On October 27, 1917, the artillery batteries of America's First Division moved into the French trenches on a quiet sector of the line. Following months of behind-the-lines training, the unit was getting its first exposure to front line combat conditions. A hard driving rain had created mud so deep that the horses could not even haul the artillery pieces—the famous French 75's—into position. But one battery of artillerymen, obsessed with the single idea to be the first to fire their gun, manhandled their piece through thigh-deep ooze to position it for firing. They did not stop to sight it in, just pointed it in the general direction of the German trenches and fired off a round. These First Division gunners had just fired the first American shot of the war. The brass shell casing was hustled off to Division headquarters and from there shipped to President Wilson.[1]

This event and the other American "Firsts," carried enormous symbolic value and were played up mightily in the press. The string of Firsts spanned nearly the entire course of American involvement, from the arrival of U.S. troops in France to the routing of the Germans

---

1. Actually, the first American shot of the war had been fired at sea six months earlier, but no one was splitting hairs.

in the Argonne. "Firsts" chronicled the incremental introduction of U.S. troops into the fighting—first time in the trenches, first attack repelled, first prisoners taken, first deaths suffered. Symbolically they served to demonstrate that the Yanks were evolving from green soldiers to capable veterans, as they acquired the technical skills necessary to join their allies in the trenches and the experience to take the fight to the enemy.

First U.S. Attack on a U-Boat

"There's a submarine off the port bow."

Associated Press
"German Sub Is Sent to the Bottom by First Shot of Yankee Gunners"
The Rock Island Argus, April 25, 1917

London, April 25, (4:45 p.m.) Captain Rice of the American steamship *Mongolia,*[2] which has arrived at a British port, told the Associated Press today that the *Mongolia* had fired the first gun of the war for the United States and sunk a German submarine.

The submarine, Captain Rice said, was about to attack the great liner in British waters on April 19. He declared there was absolutely no doubt that the U boat was hit and that there was every reason to believe it was destroyed.

The naval gunners on board made a clean hit at 1,000 yards. The periscope was seen to be shattered. Even more pertinent a fact, as regards the ultimate fate of the submarine, was that the shell disappeared immediately after the hit was made. The captain stated that a shell always ricochets in the water and can be seen again unless it finds its mark. Oil also was seen in the water after the submarine disappeared.

Sure Sub Sunk

The *Mongolia* was going at full speed and was a long distance away when the spray and foam subsided, but from the bridge the officers

---

2. The USS *Mongolia* was an armed freighter (later troopship) that carried three 6-inch deck guns manned by U.S. Navy crews. Contrary to the claims of its captain, it was never confirmed that it sank the U-boat during the encounter mentioned in this article.

observed the spot through their glasses and they are confident the submarine was sunk.

The periscope was sighted dead ahead on the last afternoon of the voyage. The captain gave the order for full speed ahead with the intention of ramming the submarine.

The periscope disappeared and a few minutes later reappeared on the ship's broadside. The gunners fired, hitting the periscope squarely and throwing up a mountain of water.

Captain Tells Story

Captain Rice outlined the incident with modesty, but could not quite conceal the pride he felt in the achievement of his ship. He paid a high tribute to the gunners and especially to the manner in which they were handled by the officer who directed the firing of the telling shot.

"For five days and nights," said Captain Rice, "I hadn't had my clothes off and we kept a big force of lookouts on duty all the time. It was 5:20 o'clock in the afternoon of the 19th, that we sighted the submarine. The officer commanding the gunners was with me on the bridge where in fact we had been most of the time of the voyage.

U-Boat Sighted

"There was a haze over the sea at the time. We had just taken a sounding for we were getting near shallow water and we were looking at the lead when the first mate cried: 'There's a submarine off the port bow.'

"The submarine was close to us, too close in fact for her purposes, and she was submerging again in order to maneuver in a better position for torpedoing us."

On Second Trip

The American steamship *Mongolia*, a vessel of 16,638 tons, owned by the International Mercantile Marine company, left an American port for London April 7 on her second trip since Germany's submarine declaration of Feb. 1.

April 19, the day on which the *Mongolia* fired the first shot of the war, is the anniversary, it was recalled here today, of the battle of Lexington, when the first shot was fired in the American Revolution.

America's First Shot of the War

"Defending American honor against barbarism"

Henri Bazin
"Fired the First Shot for America in War"
Evening Ledger (Philadelphia), November 26, 1917

American field headquarters in France, Oct. 28—The gun was so well camouflaged that six feet away no living soul could tell it was there. It was a French seventy-five, pointed towards invaded country, as are and have been many thousands of its fellows these last few years. The interest in it, and the reasons for this writing, were in the facts that its crew were khaki clad Sammees,[3] and that at exactly 6:27 o'clock upon a recent October morning, its lanyard was pulled by an American gunner, launching the first hostile shot in the war defending American honor against barbarism, and the Kaiser's rule.

We stood, seven accredited correspondents in company with the American Major, who is our chief press officer, ankle deep in rich red mud amid a driving rain. It was Sunday afternoon. Above us upon a rise in the ground between the gun and the telephone station, stood the lieutenant commanding, a youngster of perhaps twenty-two, slight, smooth-faced, brown-haired, hazel-eyed. His voice was low and musical with something of a Southern drawl, although he told us afterward he came from Indiana. I wish I could tell his name and the name of the gunner. But there is the censor, forbidding![4]

As the rain pattered upon the officer's helmet and upon ours for all the world as upon so many tin roofs and trickled in streams from the sleeves of our raincoats he told us this story, interrupting himself to give orders as the piece was intermittently discharged.

---

3. Bazin uses the French spelling of "Sammies," one of the nicknames for U.S. soldiers.
4. Army censors restricted the mention of the names of individual soldiers, except in certain circumstances, such as the recipients of medals.

"The first American gun fired in France for cause of humanity." *Source:* U.S. Army Signal Corps, Prints and Photographs Division, Library of Congress, LC-USZ62-67000.

Gun Placed by Manpower

"It was raining like this, only harder. We were told we could fire as soon as the gun was in position; but the mud was so thick it was impossible to pull it to this place with our horses. So in eagerness to get on the job, the crew unanimously agreed to drag it by hand if I gave permission. It was some job. It was the hardest job perhaps we ever tackled together. The morass was as deep as the hubs and over our knees. But in the dark and the rain we turned the trick.

"Three five hundred," interrupted a voice at the phone, a phone camouflaged as was the gun.

"Three five hundred," repeated the lieutenant, "watch the bubble."

"Ready to fire," continued the voice.

"Ready to fire," again repeated the lieutenant.

"Fire!" came the voice from the phone. And as we opened our mouths and placed dripping gloved fingers to ears the lieutenant repeated, "Fire!"

"We had eighteen shells, including five shrapnel. We did not wait for any range. We just shoved her nose where you see it, jammed a shrapnel home and let her fly beyond no man's land over there. We wanted to beat any other battery to it, and we did! The whole crew took part, of course, even if that lanyard was pulled by Sergeant -----, for afterward each man took the trick. We used all our shells with a given range after the first one, and then we had to phone quit for lack of ammunition. You see, we could not bring up more and the gun besides."

They Don't Mind the Rain

"We are sure glad to be here, every man. The weather is nothing. It rains everywhere, here or at home. We wish it was ours to stay instead of going back after a while to give way to others."

"Did you give any special order for that first shell?" I asked.

"No, sir; nothing but like that you have just heard. It was just as any other discharge and did not count for more beyond the honor of being the first."

"Cease firing," came the voice from the phone.

"Cease firing," commanded the lieutenant.

"Right, sir," came from the unseen crew under the camouflage.

As we shook hands before going on, we asked the lieutenant if we could see the gunner. At a request, he came forth, a simple, clear cut, red headed Sammee of Irish extraction, who blushed in modest pleasure. With that of his officer, I repeat I wish I could tell his name. But it is not for this time—for a later date when it is destined to be associated, not with the mere pulling of a 75's lanyard, but the thing significant and exemplified in the pulling.

We walked on a mile and a half through mud and water to Major -----'s quarters, camouflaged again. Here, in the only dry spot in the afternoon, we welcomed and were welcomed by recent friends of the training camps back of the lines as well as older French interpreters. After greetings, we went on, now with a French lieutenant added to our little company. In conversation with him, I found again how very small the world is; for he knew my father's country, and some of his friends in the army of France were mine.

The rain had increased. It was coming down literally in torrents, the wind had slightly risen, and the gray day was dying. We made the additional mile in silence save for heavy breathing, for the ground was full rolling and here, there and everywhere were little lakes and pools of muddy water, at times due to natural grades, at others to shell craters.

And then we reached the first communicator. It was ankle deep in water, with here and there a stepping stone, here and there a glimpse of flooded slatted walls.

Standing in it, crowded against the interlaced barked twig linings, were soldiers of the United States army, the Sammee from home, in his khaki and his helmet and his slicker; and with his rifle. He and his fellows were the very first I had ever seen on active service for the United States, and I looked in new perspective, recognizing in a sort of astonishment the same faces I had seen all these past weeks throwing grenades at imaginary enemies, stabbing sand-stuffed bags depicting imaginary Boche. It came as a shock, although I had been expecting it, picturing it. It struck home nevertheless, and despite mental forecalculation that here, before me, in the pelting, driving rain, amid the gray dying daylight, were boys from over the sea, near the front line, and that each and all were there with their breasts and faces confronting these hated enemies of my father's France.

At last I saw and sensed that for which I had dreamed and hoped during all these dreary, weary past months and months when I had been sustained but by my faith, comforted but by the oft-viewed valor of the poilu. At last!

We went on through the mud and water and mist and rain— onto the front line. There we found the trenches newer, unlined with interlaced twigs, and further out in No Man's Land than they had been, I was told, a few months before.

Finally a sharp turn brought us to an observation post, set low in the trench, and roofed over with sheeted corrugated iron. Peering out from it toward the barbarian beyond was a mitrailleuse [machine gun], and beside it a tall well-built young American figure, his khaki as wet as his helmet, vigilant, waiting, ready for his bit, Sammees on active service, barring his little piece of the way with those of France and England and Belgium on this front, where in the end war is to be won.

First Prisoner Taken

"The [German] soldiers do not know you Americans are here."

Associated Press
"Pershing's Troops Capture First Prisoner, Mortally Wounded by Patrol; Another Escapes"
New York Times, October 30, 1917

With the American army in France, Oct. 29, (By the Associated Press)—The first German prisoner of war taken by the American expeditionary forces died today in an American field hospital, having been shot when he encountered an American patrol in No Man's land in front of the American trenches.

The man, with another German, was discovered Saturday night by the patrol and was called on to halt. The Germans ran, the patrol fired, and one of the enemy was hit. The prisoner was treated at a dressing station and removed to a field hospital, where the combined efforts of several surgeons failed to save his life.

The prisoner was a mail carrier, and letters of some value were found on him. He explained his presence near the American trenches, saying he had lost his way in the dark. The prisoner talked freely after reaching the hospital. He was a slight blond youth. From his cot he said in German:

"I was going from our trenches with the mail, following another man in the dark. We kept turning to the left when we should have kept turning to the right, and as a result encountered the patrol. The soldiers do not know you Americans are here, but the officers probably do. They tell us nothing.

"The German soldiers in the ranks are tired of the war and want it to end, but the officers want it to continue, as they are well paid. Our food is good, but we know nothing of conditions in the interior of Germany. Sometimes no mail is permitted to reach us for eight weeks at a time."

The American doctor who operated said that the prisoner was very game, despite his painful wound. American batteries are continuing to shell the German lines at regular intervals, the enemy following similar tactics.

First Americans to Die in the Fighting

"Eleven fresh sod-topped mounds marked the resting places of American dead."

W. S. Forrest
"Visit to Trenches of First Sammies Who Gave Up Lives"
The Daily Capital Journal (Salem, OR), December 13, 1917

With the French armies in the field, Dec. 13—I have walked over hallowed ground today—over ground dyed by the blood of the first Americans of the army to die in action fighting the fight of right against might.

Through courtesy of the French army headquarters the United Press correspondent was permitted to spend a day and night in the very trenches where Privates Gresham, Hay and Enright perished in the German raid November 2.[5]

The night was spent in a dugout a few feet distant from the spot where the first American was taken prisoner by the Germans. Before dawn the United Press correspondent accompanied a French patrol party over the exact spot on No Man's Land where the Americans made their first reconnaissance. Later our party talked to a French surgeon who prized as his most precious possession a piece of the historic German shell which wounded the first American.

Then, later with an American colleague, Paul Scott Mowrer of Chicago we were guided by a French chaplain to a tiny village two miles to the rear of the fighting lines.

We found the town simply a hamlet typical of this part of France.

We were guided to a ten-acre field surrounded by a high stone wall. The field's sloping surface was marred by rusted wire entanglements.

At the bottom angle of the wall, eleven fresh sod-topped mounds marked the resting places of American dead. Wilted flowers covered them. At the head of each was a five foot roughly hewn wooden cross.

Of the eleven mounds, the first three at one end were enclosed in tiny, unpainted pine fences. Farther away the crosses told us there lay the body of Private Thomas Enright. Next was the grave

---

5. They actually died on November 3.

of Private Merle D. Hay and nearest of the three was the mound covering the resting place of Private James B. Gresham.

The markers for these three heroic Americans were octagonal wooden nameplates. Their full names, with the regimental numbers of each man and the date of their death, was inscribed on each and an inter-twined background of the Stars and Stripes and the French tri-color made them stand out prominently.[6]

On the fence inclosing these graves of the first three Americans to fall is a wooden sign with black painted on a white background.

The inscription, translated, is:

"Here lie the first soldiers of the noble republic of the United States to fall on French soil for justice and liberty."

We paused at the graves of this heroic trio and then passed to the other eight graves—not so well garnished with flowers.

The first three in this group were the graves of Abraham Meadows, Stanley Janovicy and Harry Meyers—according to the roughly printed name boards.

Here, while the scream of shells came unceasingly through the air, with occasional explosions vibrating the very earth in which these Americans rest, our chaplain said a brief prayer. My colleague and myself placed sprigs of evergreen foliage on each grave—and then went back under drenching skies toward the trenches.

First-Time Experience in the Trenches

"This ain't no way to die, Billy, to be blowed all to pieces
by a shell."

C.C. Lyon
"Sammies Demand Chance at Boche as Guns Roar"
The Washington Herald, December 28, 1917

With the American army in France, Dec. 27—A soldier boy from a Middle Western State, after having taken his turn in the first

6. The three were buried where they fell, and the French Government erected a monument to their memory, but it was destroyed by the Germans in 1940. A new monument was built near Bathelémont, France after World War II.

line trenches, tried to describe his feelings to me one afternoon recently, between drills.

This is his story, just as he told it:

"Well, sir, friend, I'm a-tellin' ye, I was scared plumb stiff the first time them Boches opened up on us with their big guns.

"They's a lot of the fellas, now that it's all over, who'll tell ye they wasn't scared, but I know they was. I could see their legs a-shakin' and I s'pose they could see mine if they'd taken the time to look.

"You see, it was a new game for all of us."

Huns[7] Open Fire

"In this whole company here they's only four men besides our captain who was ever in a real battle before. They'd done their fightin' in the Philippines where about the only things the natives had to fight with was a lot of old corn cutters. So, they wasn't much better off'n the rest of us.

"The Germans musta known it was Americans opposite them, because they began pouring about five times as many shells into our trenches as they had been doin' before we went into the line.

"When the shellin' began, our officers cam runnin' through the trenches.

"'Get into the dugouts, all of you, quick,' they yelled, and you bet we got. The little one I and some other of the boys crawled into looked mighty safe and invitin', I'm tellin' ye.

"Inside the dugout there wasn't nothin' for us to do but wait for the Germans to quit shellin' us. The captain said they was at it only a little more'n an hour but it seemed like ten hours to me."

I urged him to tell me what he thought about that first night under fire in the dugout. He hesitated rather shamefacedly but finally went on:

"Mostly about myself, friend. You see, I thought that every minute was a goin' to be my last and all the mean, ornery things I'd ever done kept coming up in my mind."

Only Two Men Hit

"Huddln' right next to me was my pal Billy. Billy and I are from the same town, and we joined the army together.

7. Because their invasion brought wide-spread death and destruction, Germans were often referred to as Huns, the nomadic warriors who terrorized Europe in the fifth century.

"'This ain't no way to die, Billy,' I said to him, 'to be blowed all to pieces by a shell when you hain't got no chance to help yourself. Why don't they let us go over the tops after them sons-a-guns?'

"'That's what I say, too,' Billy said. 'I certainly could take one or two of them Boches over the river with me.'

"But after the Germans had wasted a lot of shells on us we discovered that only two men in our outfit had been hit, and neither one was wounded badly.

"We began to feel that maybe there was a good deal of bluff about this bombarding stuff. Nobody was gettin' killed; just a lot of noise.

"After that first shellin' we all settled down and got over our nervous spells and began feelin' like old-timers.

"After a couple days in the first line we began to like it. None of this seven or eight hours a day drillin' out there! They bring your meals to you steamin' hot and the hash boys treat you like you was some kind of King. Honest, it was soft compared to this trainin' game back of the lines.

"There's been a lot of hot air spilled about the hard life in the trenches and about the dangers, too.

"I'm tellin' the truth when I say it woulda took them German guns a week of solid shellin' to shot away all the barbed wire in front of our trench. Why, we couldn't a got through it in a day ourselves with wire cutters."

Wanted Shot at Boche

This boy was not in the American trench which was the object of the first German raid and in which several American soldiers were killed and wounded and about a dozen captured.

"That's the only thing I'm sorry about—that I didn't get a chance at one of them Boches at short range," he said.

"The whole game in the trenches," he said as a parting shot before falling in for drill again. "Is to keep cool. I saw three of our guys killed by a shell one day. After a shell had taken off a corner of their dugout they busted out and started to run and they run right into another shell. Two shells never hit in the same place and they'd be alive today if they'd stuck in their own dugout."

"Fall in," called out a sergeant.

"Lord, how I hate to drill!" protested the narrator to me. "I wish I was back in the trenches right now."

And he hurried off with a wave of the hand.

Americans Suffer First Gas Attack

"The men's hands were outstretched as though they were drowning."

Fred S. Ferguson
"German Gas Attack Kills Five Americans, Poisoning Sixty-one"
The Daily Capital Journal (Salem, OR), February 27, 1918

With the American Army in France, Feb. 27—Sixty-one American soldiers, gas victims, lay in the hospitals today, following a night of horror. The doctors worked all night on the cases.

Five others were killed in the gas attack. Many of the hospital cases included artillerymen, who were overcome by fumes from gas shells. The first victims included boys from Massachusetts, Pennsylvania, North Carolina, Indiana, Kentucky, New Jersey, Tennessee, Rhode Island, Ohio, New York, Washington and Arkansas.

The attack came suddenly this morning after an all day rain. The clouds had parted and the moon was shining brightly in the trenches. Stillness prevailed.

Suddenly there was a huge flare from the German trenches as the minewerfers[8] were discharged. Then came the detonations of high explosives with the quick spread of deadly gases.

Three officers ran into a dugout and closed the curtain so tight they narrowly escaped death through asphyxiation from the charcoal fire. They were taken to a hospital but their condition is not serious.

Three men were killed and nine were overcome in the first attack.

When the attack came over the men endeavored to adjust their gas masks. Those who weren't quick enough were soon gasping for breath. These were carried to a hospital. A child could not look more helpless than those Americans. Their huge chests raised and

8. A short-range trench mortar used by the German army.

Americans in a trench, wearing gas masks. *Source: U.S. Official Pictures of the World War: Showing America's Participation*, Washington, DC: Pictorial Bureau, 1920. Wikimedia Commons.

lowered the covers as they fought for breath. As their breathing grew louder and more difficult and choking started, the doctors hurried an oxygen tank to the side of one of the victim's cot. He drank in the oxygen from the rubber cup and with a sigh of satisfaction at the temporary relief.

The American army has gas equipment and will use it as the occasion demands, but it is a matter of self-defense. The Boche introduced the gas terror to the world. Its first use against the Americans has aroused the entire army to the stage of "seeing red."

It would stir the fighting blood of every American to view the hospital where lay the victims of the first German gas attack.

At the hour of cabling five were dead and twenty were in hospitals struggling like drowning men for breath. Word came that thirty additional were enroute to the hospitals.

At the field hospital where the first twenty victims of German gas frightfulness were taken, the doctors were stirred to the deepest hatred toward the Boches after having seen the suffering. The struggles of the victims for life could be heard a hundred feet away.

With closed eyes and blue faces, these American boys gasped and struggled for every breath, while the attendants, in charge of a captain, worked tirelessly. Among the doctors was one from Waco, Texas, and one from Milford, Pa. Every effort to relieve the sufferers was resorted to. Blood-letting and the giving of oxygen were tried. Every breath was a groan. The Americans' eager drawing in of the God-given air sounded like bellows, so nearly were the lungs closed. As the sufferings became worse, the men's hands were outstretched as though they were drowning. Their fingers distended, they stiffened; there was a sudden foaming at the mouth, then—the end.

The doctors cursed the Boches for every minute the men suffered. They treat wounded men with no special feeling of hatred for the enemy. But watching gas victims is like watching twenty men slowly drowning or dangling from a rope, gradually suffocating.

The gas victims were in a hospital which was recently repeatedly bombed. Doctors declared that the final act they might expect from the Huns would be an air raid on the hospital while the gassed men were slowly passing out.

Between one and two o'clock Tuesday morning, gas projectiles were hurled from minewerfers. There were two attacks, in which about 73 chlorine and phosgene[9] gas shells, accompanied by high explosives, were thrown. Small balls of fire were first visible, then the entire battery of minewerfers let go, hurling gas and explosives simultaneously. The Sammies tried to reach their dugouts and also to signal their artillery for a barrage. The wire from this sector was

---

9. Both chlorine and phosgene gas irritated the eyes and lungs. As a reaction to the gas, the body produced secretions that blocked breathing and could cause suffocation.

found to have been severed and the barrage was delayed more than forty minutes while rockets were sent up.

The barrage started at 2:20 and continued for forty minutes.

Minewerfers are fired electrically, the entire battery being set off simultaneously, the second attack coming before an attack of gas projectiles. The projectiles were equipped with time fuses. They did not explode until they had landed in the American trenches. This is the first time the boche have used time fuses.

In addition to this attack, an important village was gas shelled three times during the night. The gas attacks continued during the day.

Americans Get their Own Section of the Front Line

"As the Americans were swallowed into the mouth of their trench every poilu in the line stood at rigid salute."

Wythe Williams
"We're in the Line!"
Collier's Weekly, March 23, 1918

We are in. A small portion of the American army has taken over its line on the front in France—the tenth month of our war against Germany. Last June I stood on the quai at Boulogne when General Pershing and his staff first set foot on French soil. A few weeks later I saw the first detachment of our army land at a French port. It was this same detachment that, a few days ago, I saw disappear into the night as they turned in toward the trenches of their front line. I shall never see them again—that is, not all of them; for even now, as I write, it is more than probable that some have already paid the price of war.

In Paris one day, among the other boulevard rumors and gossip, I heard a whisper: "Some Americans are about to take over their line." I at once hurried over to the office of officialdom and inquired if this were true.

I was asked to divulge where I had secured my information. My questioner was somewhat taken aback when I told him my informant was not an American officer nor an American anybody, nor even a Frenchman, but an Englishman whose whisper had really been quite a vocal effort in a public place. Officialdom then remarked that, inasmuch as I seemed to know about it, I would be told later the exact time to leave Paris for the front—that my name was "on the list."

Getting to the Front

I was never notified, because this Paris office of officialdom never found out any more about it. After several days of vain inquiry, in company with fellow correspondents, I went by train and automobile to the town that shelters the Press Headquarters of our army, situated some thirty-odd miles from another town, the headquarters of General Pershing and our General Staff.[10]

The chief press officer revealed the date when our men would take over their line. He told us where we might go to witness the undertaking, and told us what we could and could not write, according to his definite instructions from General Pershing. And there was more, far more, that we could not write than that we could. In view of the restrictions, which seemed to include everything except what I have said in the first paragraph of this article, the arrangements for the cable correspondents seemed amusing.[11] After long and heavy conference, it was decided that as soon as the official communique arrived from the Staff Headquarters town, thirty-odd miles away, the three press agencies were to be given a one-hundred-word "flash" on the wire. After this overture all of the eight special cable correspondents were to have another "flash" of one hundred words each. Then these same eight, filing their dispatches in the order drawn by ballot, were to be allowed one thousand words of descriptive cable. This would close the performance.[12]

It was carefully explained that these almost ten thousand words would completely choke the telegraph wires from that town for

10. Headquarters for the credentialed correspondents was located a Neufchâteau, purposefully separated from General Pershing's headquarters at Chaumont.

11. In addition to strict censorship, the AEF and other armies, managed the news by credentialing reporters, strictly controlling what they saw, and issuing official communiqués that gave the authorized version of events. During the war, several reporters lost their AEF credentials for bucking this system, including *New York Times* and *Collier's Weekly* correspondent Wythe Williams.

12. This "performance" was typical of the protocol required to satisfy the highly competitive war correspondents, who always attempted to scoop their rivals with breaking news.

thirty-six hours. In as much as the stories of at least half of the eight Correspondents would reach America after the first half had already been printed, it would be scarcely worthwhile for the latter to write any "descriptive stuff" at all. Again I point out that the press telegraphic arrangements for the benefit of the American public, have been existent in this town for six months. To-day the number of French operators who cannot understand English is the same as on the first day that a cable was ever sent from that part of France on the subject of the American troops.

I will give no further chronology of what we correspondents did in order to get the facts and to understand this taking over of our line. Once it was decided that we could not go near the troops at all. We pointed out that the occasion was a part of the vital history of the war, if not indeed of the world; in as much as the performers were all Americans, we argued that the American people had a right to have some of that history written from the ground. Finally the order was changed, after twenty-four hours of backing and filling, and we were permitted to go into the zone to see the men, but were absolutely forbidden to enter or go near the trenches. This last order was quite understandable, because the relief of a section of trenches is a difficult and ticklish performance at any time, and was especially so in this case because of possible confusion resulting from the difference of languages. I wish again to assert that at this writing not a single correspondent has ever gone into a trench at its taking over by American troops.

From Horizon Blue to Khaki

Several years ago I visited these present American trenches when they were held by the French. I went over every yard of that front when it was one of the important sectors of the line. Looking back to my nights and days passed there, it was quite easy to shift the color scheme from horizon blue to khaki; it was a simple matter to change the bearded poilus and grinning Africans[13] into slim, clear-skinned young Americans, and to look forward to the American "zero hour" when our soldiers would make their first attack. "Contempt-ible little armies" can grow fast once they are planted. Our force

13. Many soldiers recruited from French colonies in Africa fought with the French army during the war.

now in the line could not numerically be called an army (unless it were acting as a punitive expedition in Mexico[14]); but the mere fact that the first section of American troops is now guarding its own trenches, sending its own patrols and its own raiding parties through the barbed wire and across No Man's Land, should force our army chiefs to speed up and finish the training of new divisions landed and landing. We shall need them all too quickly to make good the losses of the First Army and to form new armies to expand the American military zone.

Our regiments left the tiny villages where they were billeted, some miles behind the trenches, just at sundown. The day had been somber and the air dank, like almost every day in France at this time of year. The roads were unending streams of mud and water. Machine-gun companies went first, sloshing and slipping along under a fine drizzle that would at least prevent any German reception in the form of a gas attack. The air was too dense and still for gas. The men were calm and quiet, and those who said anything at all simply expressed the general opinion that they were glad they were moving—moving to the real front, to fight; they were completely fed up with training and waiting.

An imperative whispered command soon silenced all conversation, and there was only the gentle padding of feet in the mud as the infantry then took up the march, platoon after platoon. Cigarettes were prohibited in the general order that no lights were permitted so close to the lines. At a certain point French liaison officers met each platoon and silently signaled the American officers to follow them into the dark, along a narrow, slippery path that wound slightly uphill through a black forest. One of these Frenchmen explained that there had been some slight artillery activity along about dusk, but that the French batteries had quickly silenced it. There might be a return barrage fire, he explained, so every precaution was necessary. The Germans had the range of the mud path, so that even a "slow barrage"—that is, one shell every few minutes—might seriously impede "la releve."

After a few moments of climbing, the last file of our infantry could feel—for they could not see—passing bodies of men headed

---

14. In March 1916, General Pershing led the Punitive Expedition into Mexico in pursuit of Mexican bandit/revolutionary Francisco "Pancho" Villa, in response to his cross-border attack on the town of Columbus, New Mexico.

toward the rear. Occasionally our men would brush against them
on the narrow road and slip aside into the ditches knee deep with
water. By a muttered imprecation in French after one of these
collisions the Americans realized that these soldiers were the
French troops they were relieving, probably the first platoons to go
out as our first platoons marched in. But the Frenchmen did not
know that the long-awaited "American relief" was passing them.
The effort of the High Command to keep the matter secret had
prevented even a whisper reaching the front. Another case where
news concerning troops reached them after open discussion in the
cafes of Paris!

No indication was given by any of the Americans of their identity. Both files plodded silently along, a weariness in the march
rhythm of the one, an alertness in the other that was significant.
There were no salutes from the almost invisible officers who
marched at the heads of their columns. The last American platoon
left the narrow path, turning toward the position on the right it was
to occupy. It passed through a mass of broken stones that had once
formed a village. Our men had never seen a demolished village, so
they peered eagerly about. Again they sensed soldiers filing toward
them. The Frenchmen had seen so many ruins that those through
which they were soon stumbling registered no new impression.
A few of them sank down among the stones to rest just as several
flares from distant hills rocketed up and for a moment illuminated
the scene.

The American Relief Has Come!

The poilus sitting at rest were scarcely recognizable, they toned
in so exactly in color with the ruin all about. Their figures looked
more like the high reliefs carved on the walls of ancient churches
than like human beings. They were as motionless as the debris.
They were covered with dirt and mud. Their packs and helmets
were crusted with clay, and their faces gray with fatigue and
streaked with grimy sweat. All they wanted was rest; they looked
with unseeing eye at the staring Americans. The fact that "la
releve americaine" was at hand was not yet known in the zone of
the armies.

The Americans marched out into an open field. Their trenches
were just on the other side. It was downhill now, into a little valley.

On hills opposite were the German lines; these hills toned into the blackness of the starless, moonless sky.

There came a suspicion of swagger into the walk of the Americans, swinging down the hill. None of them were tired. The climb had been nothing They were fresh and clean and recently fed. Their packs were in good condition. True, some of them had wet feet, because their new boots had not been sufficiently oiled before starting out, but, all in all, there was nothing the matter with them. The hour was still early, so there would be plenty of time for the field kitchens to follow to their positions and send morning coffee up through the communication *boyaux*.

Another file of French soldiers was climbing up the field from the communication trench that led to the front line. There were only a few of them, and they marched slowly. A few stumbled. As the Americans came abreast there was a succession of flares on the hills, so that for a few seconds the field was bathed in flickering blue light. At the head of the French column was a bedraggled, bearded sergeant. He stared straight ahead, his eyes so fixed and lifeless they might have been blind. Then he saw the column of Americans. He did not recognize them, but his hand came up in a mechanical salute. A young American lieutenant returned it; and then the man's eyes and mind awoke. The flares flickered out and the American officer disappeared in the dark.

In the light of another rocket the French sergeant could have been seen still standing at salute. He smiled now, and as the light again died he gave the first signal to French troops that Americans had taken over their line. It was the phrase which every soldier in the French army had been repeating as a question for months: "La releve americaine est venue?" ("The American relief has come.") The sergeant reiterated the miracle in a whisper: "La releve americaine est venue." And as the Americans were swallowed into the mouth of their trench every poilu in the line stood at rigid salute: inky, vague forms in the occasional glare from the rockets.

As I came away I saw the moon had risen and was sending a pale gleam through the heavy dark. The relief of the trenches was successfully carried out without incident, says the War Office dispatch.

First U.S. Division to Engage in a Fight

"When they eventually launched two attacks we dropt them
in their trenches."

Hamilton Holt
"The Shot Heard 'Round the World'"
The Independent, August 3, 1918

The one American division above all others I wanted to visit was the Twenty-sixth. It ranked as the first National Guard division in France. It was the first American division to engage in a battle in this war.[15] It was made up entirely of New England troops. And the 102d Connecticut boys of that division, upon whom devolved the honor of holding the line against the German shock troops at Seicheprey on April 20 and 21st, were the boys who came from the hills and valleys in the neighborhood of my summer home, from the region where for over 200 years all my ancestors have lived and died.

Accordingly, it was with the anticipatory delight of returning for an "Old Home Week" festival that I started out from American headquarters on May 12, exactly three weeks after the battle of Seicheprey, to see my home boys in the trenches and to hear from their own lips some account of how, as Irvin Cobb would say, they took the mania out of Germania. Our party consisted of Judge Wadhams, an adopted son of Connecticut on account of his four years at Yale, two escorting American lieutenants, and myself.

Our objectives were, first, an American aviation field, and then General Edwards's headquarters, where we were to receive final instructions before proceeding to the front lines. I shall reserve comment on the various aerodromes I visited till another paper— suffice it to say that after mess with the American aviators we motored to Toul and thence on to a little village where we found General Edwards at his headquarters, in a beautiful old twelfth century chateau that I was informed belonged to the French general who commanded Verdun during the great German drive in 1916. Major General Clarence Edwards, commanding the Twenty-sixth

---

15. The battle referred to here occurred at the village of Seicheprey, on April 20, 1918, when German storm troopers launched a surprise attack against green American troops. The Germans captured the village but then lost it in an American counter attack. Although it suffered 650 casualties, the U.S. Army could claim its first victory for holding its ground.

Division, received us in a noble room furnished with rich draperies, gilt and pink antique furniture, and old French portraits on
the walls of periwigged gentlemen and lace-collared ladies. General
Edwards is evidently a "character." I have come within the spell of
very few soldier personalities that impressed me more. He seemed
to be a man of great personal dash and decision, and yet withal full
of humanity and even tenderness. In one breath he would damn the
Germans and in the next exhibit the most fatherly solicitation for
his troops. "Heart and guts," he said, were the prime ingredients of
a true soldier, and he looked as tho he had both. He was especially
concerned for the morale of his boys, which he said depended as
much on proper food, sleep and clothes as dry powder. He even
insisted on my reading aloud to Judge Wadhams his recent orders
for the "delousing" of the troops, and his eyes twinkled with merri-
ment as I proceeded.

Then the general asked his aide to bring us a map of the
sector he was holding and proceeded to explain to us the battle of
Seicheprey.

From the general's account and also from the stories, more or less
conflicting, of a dozen other participants, I take it the Americans' first
real battle went about as follows:

Altho there had been two or three skirmishes between our troops
and the Germans immediately after we took over the sector, it was
several weeks before the enemy finally planned to go over the top
and attack us. When they eventually launched two attacks we dropt
them in their trenches. The Germans then summoned 600 shock
troops and sent them over to teach us a lesson. But only three
got to our front trenches, and of these two were killed and one was
captured. The next morning the barb wires in front of our lines were
full of German dead. On the 20th, 3500 Germans started for us and
the French on our left. They came over in close formation and drove
us out of the front trenches. We fell back and reformed. The boys
could hardly wait to get the orders to counterattack, but finally
permission was given and in two tries we regained all our lines.
The 102d Connecticut boys got badly cut up, losing 123 men, about
the same number gassed, the same number captured and some 500
wounded. They fired during that fight between 5000 and 10,000
rounds of ammunition. Three of our batteries[16] were rolled out into

16. Artillery units.

the open and fired at the enemy for over five hours, tho under a severe bombardment. Major Rau met a counterattack with cooks, signal men and every one available. Our machine gun squad was nearly annihilated. When we regained our line our doctors found the Germans had left there poisoned coffee for our troops.

General Edwards then said, "The best thing for you to do is to have a talk with the boys themselves. Come with me and you shall hear them tell their story in their own words. I'll tell the officers to keep away, so they will talk to you freely."

So he ordered his car and we jumped into ours. He led us a pretty chase up and down the hills at a clip of forty miles an hour till we came to a two mile stretch alongside of a ridge of hills in full view of the German trenches not two miles away. We now hit up the pace to at least fifty miles an hour, but the day was misty and either the Germans did not see us or they decided not to take a pot shot, for we received no reminder of their presence. I was not in the least unhappy when we shortly turned behind a hill out of sight of the German observation balloons and quickly drew up at a little crossroads village. The boys who were lounging about came swarming out of the yards and billets to meet us, for the General and two civilians, the first they had seen since the fight, were as much objects of curiosity to them as would be General Pershing walking down the streets of any inland American town. The boys collected about the car in a circle twenty deep, and I instantly established friendly relations by calling out, "I'm from Connecticut, too. I have a home in Woodstock. Is there any fellow here from there?" One private had an uncle who lived in town, and wished to send his regards. Then I asked if there were any who came from Pomfret, Thompson, Eastford, Danielson, Willimantic, etc., and as boys replied, "That's my home," "I come from there," I said, "If you will give me your name I will be glad to write to your family, saying that I've seen you and that you're still determined to get the Kaiser." And before I knew it I had 242 soldiers hand me names of parents, sweethearts and friends at home, for me to send letters to. One of the boys gave me a German bayonet that he had taken off the body of a dead German. Another gave me a German water bottle which had been jabbed thru with an American bayonet, and another a belt of cartridges which he wished me to give to his parents in Torrington. The boys were in superb spirits and yelled frantically and affirmatively when I asked them if they wanted to get back at the Germans. "Only let us get another crack at them," they shouted. Without any request on my part they told me that they had the best officers in the American Army and that they would do anything that their officers asked.

I have only space to tell one story of the many the boys gave us from their personal experience. Private Clyde Thompson, of New Haven, said: "The battle started at 3 a.m. I was in my dugout at headquarters 350 yards behind the lines. The Boche came over from the flank and not directly behind their barrage—a very pretty trick. When I came out of my dugout there were five Boches yelling 'heraus mit.' I shoved the door back. They threw grenades at the door and blew it in. I came out the other door, drew my revolver and opened fire. One threw up his hands and fell backward. Two carried him away. The other two fell back. I threw two grenades at them and killed one. The other ran away. I then went to headquarters, picking up the major's orderly on the way; we joined Lieutenant Ingersoll and we held the reserve trench with one squad of eight men until 5 or 6, when the Boche left town. While carrying in wounded men I saw three Boches coming up the side of a fence. I opened fire and killed one of them; the other two disappeared. I am recommended for a cross."

After listening to the various experiences, I walked across the street to where the officers were waiting in a group and talked with them. They told me they had the best boys in the United States Army. Lieutenant-Colonel Dowell said, "The boys will do more than you ask them to. They never have to be driven." I then said to the Colonel, "When I get back to my summer home in Connecticut the people will probably ask me to stand up in the village church and tell them something of how their boys are getting along. Can you give me some message that will interest them?" The Colonel thought a moment and then said, "Tell them this." And then he related the following story, which I wish every American could have heard him tell: "When the Germans made their great attack on that fateful night, one of our boys, First Lieutenant Lockhart, a Yale graduate and a school teacher in New Haven, was isolated with a band of thirty-seven men when the command to retreat was given. The report got thru that they had been badly cut up, but we heard no more from them and we thought the entire lot was killed or captured. On the evening of the 21ˢᵗ, after two days of fighting, when we regained our trenches, I went to Colonel Parker, in command of the 102d, and suggested that he and I go out and look for Lockhart and his command. Just as we left the trenches we met Lockhart coming back. The first thing he did was to draw himself up and salute, apologizing for his two days' growth of beard and his disheveled appearance. In response to our requests as to how he had fared, he replied, 'I am glad to report, sir, that we are all here. We have eight men alive, the others are dead in the trench with us.'"

Just think what this story of Colonel Dowell means. Here was the first fight in the Great War in which America took part on the soil of France. The honor of representing America fell to a band of Connecticut boys. When the order was given to retreat, this little group being isolated did not receive it. They therefore stayed in their trenches for two days, altho completely surrounded by the Germans. And when they were finally relieved, there they were, every single man, dead or alive, at his post. There was not a man who had run away. Our histories tell us that America probably never produced a braver soldier than old Israel Putnam.[17] I cannot help feeling that were that old gentleman alive today he would not be ashamed of these boys from his native state.

That evening we were invited to dine at the field hospital run by the Yale unit, which is the closest to the front line of any American hospital in France. There were fifteen physicians and over eighty Yale boys under them, and fifteen trained nurses, all from Connecticut. After supper we adjourned to one of the hospital huts for vesper services. Judge Waldhams and I, both Yale men, made addresses. The meeting ended with the famous Brek-ek-ek-ex Yale cheer, which must have astonished the Germans if they heard it in their trenches over the hills not far away.

---

17. A U.S. general during the American Revolution who fought with distinction at the Battle of Bunker Hill and gained fame for his bravery and fighting spirit.

Chapter 5

✦

✦

✦

✦

✦

At Sea

Introduction

The American passenger/cargo ship *Antilles* had just unloaded troops and cargo at Saint-Nazaire, France and begun its homeward voyage, when it fell victim to a German submarine on October 17, 1917, taking sixty-seven seamen to their deaths. It was the largest single loss of American lives to that point in the war. *The Literary Digest* editorial included here summarized America's shocked reaction, as reported in newspapers across the country.

The Atlantic Ocean was America's first battlefield. Not only did the United States need to put several million men into the European war zone, along with the weapons, equipment, and supplies to sustain them, but it had to transport everything across 3,000 miles of U-boat-infested ocean.

U-boats had been highly effective at disrupting shipping to England and France in the early years of the war. When the United States entered the conflict, it began to convoy ships, sending a group of transports along with armed escort vessels. Although the convoy system proved a dramatic success, it did not remove the danger. *Antilles* had been in a convoy.

From late 1917 through 1918, a ceaseless flow of shipping crossed the Atlantic. Although various strategies were employed to defend against lurking submarines, U-boats still took their toll. The two magazine articles in this chapter strike contrasting attitudes towards the danger. The writer of "When the Sea-Asp Stings," is forced to watch helplessly as a torpedoed troop ship sinks, while convoy rules prevent his ship from rescuing survivors. Later in the war, the article "Chasing the Periscope," about the Navy's destroyer fleet, made the case that the U-boat had been vanquished.[1] That was somewhat wishful thinking, but the tide had certainly turned in the battle with Germany's submarines, and American destroyers had played an important role.

U-Boat Sinks First U.S. Ship

"We all felt at once a new sense of the actuality of being at war."

Editorial
"The Foe's First Blow"
The Literary Digest, November 3, 1917

In Germany's first successful attack upon us since we entered the war, our press sees the true beginning of the conflict for the United States. There have been deaths from accident and disease, gunners on armed merchant men have been lost, and on October 16 the destroyer *Cassin* was slightly damaged by a U-boat, one of its men being killed and five injured. But on the 17th there befell, as the *Boston Transcript* notes, the first considerable disaster directly consequent upon our military and naval operations, when an unseen torpedo sent the homeward-bound troop-ship *Antilles* to the bottom with sixty-seven soldiers and seamen. "It has come," was the *Chicago Herald*'s first word, and the *Springfield Republican* noted how we all felt at once a new sense of the actuality of being at war. Practically all the newspapers found the event a stimulant for the Liberty Loan campaign. In Washington, as Mr. David Lawrence, of the *New York Evening Post*, reported, it was predicted that among the certain nation-wide effects of the tragedy would be

1. In April 1917, the month America entered the war, U-boats sank 516 ships. By February 1918, the month in which *Tuscania* was lost, the monthly tally was down to 166. In October 1918, the month when the article "Chasing the Periscope" appeared, U-boats claimed 94 ships.

"keener realization by the people of the great sacrifices that must be made in the future," and better "appreciation of the ruthlessness of German warfare."

The Government's prompt publication of the news of the loss of the *Antilles* should end once and for all, the *New York World* thinks, "the malicious and traitorous business which has been filling the land with horrifying lies of ships sunk and soldiers by thousands sent to the bottom. The people will now know that when any disaster of the kind does happen they will be informed officially." And there is another mischievous impression which this New York newspaper is glad to see dispelled by the disaster:

"The pacifying notion that Germany regards the United States as a negligible quantity in the war and views with indifference our efforts to get troops to Europe is now effectually exploded. Germany has been after these American troop transports with all of its available submarine power ever since they began to move. It has been waging war against the United States in the deadliest manner it has been able to."

The death of three score and seven seamen and soldiers in the sinking of the *Antilles* suggests still another thought to several editors. As the *Syracuse Herald* puts it:

"We already see our sons dying by the score for our protection, and in vindication of a just and noble cause; yet we are still permitting recreant Americans to raise their vicious clamor and engineer their dastardly conspiracies against the national interests for which the victims of the *Antilles* forfeited their lives. We shall but imperfectly comprehend the meaning of the *Antilles* catastrophe, and, worse yet, we shall be shamefully false to the memories of the seventy men swallowed up by the Atlantic, without a warning or a chance for their lives, if we do not resolve to take a firmer and sterner attitude toward the miscreants at home who are plotting to destroy or shackle the very Government to which the victims of the *Antilles* have paid the greatest possible tribute of devotion."

Now that our men have died in the nation's cause, declares the *New York Sun*, "we must stamp out sternly, emphatically, and decisively all caviling and discussion as to the justice of this war, or the righteousness of the participation of the United States in it." And a writer on the *Chicago Tribune's* editorial staff thus briefly and pungently puts a question which has been troubling the minds of many Americans:

"The first American casualty-list has come in. Shall we continue to find excuses for the pro-Germans? Or nooses?"

In a leading editorial the same Chicago daily calls attention to the consolation to be found in the prompt and full report of the *Antilles* disaster, in the knowledge "that an army larger than most Americans have supposed is already in France," that the loss of the *Antilles* is less calamitous than what might have occurred had the Germans managed to sink an outward bound troop-laden transport, "and that it emphasizes thus early the fundamental necessity of keeping open our lines of communication." In a succeeding paragraph comes a sharp call for vengeance upon the nation responsible for the death of these Americans. And coming vengeance at the hands of American soldiers and sailors is confidently predicted on many an editorial page.

The fact that no submarine or torpedo was sighted has led some to wonder whether the explosion which tore the *Antilles* apart on the morning of October 17 may not have been due to a mine or a treacherously placed bomb. But officers aboard, according to the dispatches, are certain that it was the work of the Schwarzkopf torpedo used by the Germans. Survivors from the *Antilles*, in safety in a French port, told press correspondents of the excellent discipline which prevailed after the men rushed to the deck in the early morning, and of the bravery of the gun-crews who stuck to their posts to the last, watching for a telltale periscope.

Watching a Troop Ship Sink

"Near at hand a ship was in distress, a ship laden with a precious freightage of American soldier boys, and here were we legging it like a frightened rabbit."

Irvin Cobb
"When the Sea-Asp Stings"
Saturday Evening Post, March 9, 1918

Because the *Tuscania* rode high out of the water, and wallowed as she rode, because during all those days of our crossing she hugged up close to our ship, splashing through the foam of our wake as though craving the comfort of our company, we called her things no self-respecting ship should have to bear. But when that night, we stood on the afterdeck of our ship, we running away as fast as our kicking screw would take us, and saw her going down, taking American soldier boys to death with her in alien waters, we drank toasts standing up to the poor old *Tuscania*.

I was one of those who were in at the death of the *Tuscania*. Her sinking was the climax of the most memorable voyage I ever expect to take. Five days have elapsed since she was torpedoed, and even though these words are being cabled across from London to the home side of the ocean, at least three weeks more must elapse before they can see printer's ink. So to some this will seem an old story; but the memory of what happened that night off the Irish coast is going to abide with me while I live. It was one of those big moments in a man's life that stick in a man's brain as long as he has a brain to think with.

The Sober Departure

Transatlantic journeys these days aren't what they used to be before America went into the war. Ours began to be different even before our ship pulled out from port. It is forbidden me now to tell her name, and anyhow her name doesn't in the least matter, but she was a big ship with a famous skipper, and in peacetimes her sailing would have made some small stir. There would have been crowds of relations and friends at the pier bidding farewell to departing travellers; and steamer baskets and steamer boxes would have been coming aboard in streams. Beforehand there would have been a pleasant and mildly exciting bustle, and as we drew away from the dock and headed out into midstream and down the river for our long hike overseas, the pierhead would have been alive with waving handkerchiefs, and all our decks would have been fringed with voyagers shouting back farewells to those they had left behind them. Instead we slipped away almost as if we had done something wrong. There was no waving of hands and handkerchiefs, no good-byes on the gang-planks, no rush to get back on land when the shore bell sounded. To reach the dock we passed through trochas of barbed-wire entanglements, past sentries standing with fixed bayonets at entryways. When we got inside the pier our people

bade us farewell at a guarded gate. None but travellers whose pass-
ports read straight were allowed beyond that point. So alone and
unescorted each one of us went soberly up the side of the ship,
and then sundry hours later our journey began, as the ship, like
a big grey ghost, slid away from land, as quietly as might be, into
the congenial grey fog which instantly swallowed her up and left
her in a little grey world of sea mist that was all her own. After this
fashion, then, we started.

As for the first legs of the trip they were much like the first
legs of almost any sea trip except that we travelled in a convoy
with sundry other ships, with warcraft to guard us on our way.
Our ship was quite full of soldiers—officers in the first cabin,
and the steerage packed with khakied troopers—ninety per cent
of whom had never smelled bilge water before they embarked
upon their great adventure overseas. There were fewer civilians
than one formerly might have found on a ship bound for Europe.
In these times only those civilians who have urgent business in
foreign climes venture to go abroad.

I sat at the purser's table. His table was fairly typical of the
ship's personnel. With me there sat, of course, the purser, likewise
two Canadian officers, two members of a British Commission
returning from America, and an Irish brewer. There were not very
many women on our passenger list. Of these women half a dozen
or so were professional nurses, and two were pretty Canadian
girls bound for England to be married on arrival there to young
Canadian officers. There were only three children on board, and
they were travelling with their parents in the second class.

Except for a touch of seriousness about the daily lifeboat drill,
and except that regimental discipline went forward, with the troops
drilling on the open deck spaces when the weather and the sea
permitted, there was at first nothing about this voyage to distinguish it from any other midwinter voyage. Strangers got acquainted
one with another and swapped views on politics, religion, symptoms
and Germans; flirtations started and ripened furiously; concerts
were organized and took place, proving to be what concerts at sea
usually are. Twice a day the regimental band played, and once a day,
up on the bridge, the second officer took the sun, squinting into his
sextant[2] with the deep absorption with which in happier times a

2. A navigational instrument used for measuring the angle between the sun or a star
and the horizon, to determine a ship's longitude and latitude.

certain type of tourist was wont to stare through an enlarging device at a certain type of Parisian photograph.[3] At night, though, we were in a darkened ship, a gliding black shape upon black waters, with heavy shades over all the portholes and thick draperies over all the doors, and only dim lights burning in the passageways and cross halls, so that every odd corner on deck or within was as dark as a coal pocket.[4] It took some time to get used to being in the state in which Moses was when the light went out; but then, we had time to get used to it, believe me! Ocean travel is slower these days, for obvious reasons. Personally, I retired from the ship's society during three days of the first week of the trip. I missed only two meals, missing them, I may add, shortly after having eaten them; but at the same time I felt safer in my berth than up on deck—not happier, particularly, but safer. The man who first said that you can't eat your cake and have it too had such cases as mine in mind, I am sure of that. I can't and I don't—at least not when I am taking an ocean voyage. I have been seasick on many waters, and I have never learned to care for the sensation yet.

Crossing the Danger Zone

When I emerged from semiretirement it was to learn that we had reached the so-called danger zone. The escort of warcraft for our transport had been augmented. Under orders the military men wore their life jackets, and during all their waking hours they went about with cork flaps hugging them about their necks fore and aft, so that they rather suggested Chinese malefactors with their heads incased in punishment casques. By request the civilian passengers were expected to carry their life preservers with them wherever they went; but some of them forgot the injunction. I know I did frequently. Also, a good many of them turned in at night with most of their outer clothing on their bodies; but I followed the old Southern custom and took most of mine off before going to bed.

Our captain no longer came to the saloon for his meals. He lived upon the bridge—ate there and, I think, slept there too—what sleeping he did. Standing there all muffled in his oilskins he looked

3. A reference to viewing a risqué photograph through some sort of viewing device. Paris was famous for its racy cabarets and lewd postcards.
4. Such measures to mask all lights were a necessary precaution to prevent the ship from being observed at nighttime by a lurking enemy submarine.

even more of a squatty and unheroic figure than he had in his naval blue presiding at the head of the table; but by repute we knew him for a man who had gone through one torpedoing with great credit to himself and through numbers of narrow escapes, and we valued him accordingly and put our faith in him. It was faith well placed, as shall presently transpire.

I should not say that there was much fear aboard; at least if there was it did not manifest itself in the manner or the voice or the behaviour of a single passenger seen by me; but there was a sort of nagging, persistent sense of uneasiness betraying itself in various small ways. For one thing, all of us made more jokes about submarines, mines and other perils of the deep than was natural. There was something a little forced, artificial, about this gaiety—the laughs came from the lips, but not from points farther south.

We knew by hearsay that the *Tuscania* was a troopship bearing some of our soldiers over to do their share of the job of again making this world a fit place for human beings to live in. There was something pathetic in the fashion after which she so persistently and constantly strove to stick as closely under our stern as safety and the big waves would permit. It was as though her skipper placed all reliance in our skipper, looking to him to lead his ship out of peril should peril befall. Therefore, we of our little group watched her from our afterdecks, with her sharp nose forever half or wholly buried in the creaming white smother we kicked up behind us.

It was a crisp bright February day when we neared the coasts of the British Empire. At two o'clock in the afternoon we passed, some hundreds of yards to starboard, a round, dark, bobbing object which some observers thought was a floating mine. Others thought it might be the head and shoulders of a human body held upright in a life ring. Whatever it was, our ship gave it a wide berth, sheering off from the object in a sharp swing. Almost at the same moment upon our other bow, at a distance of not more than one hundred yards from the crooked course we were then pursuing, there appeared out through one of the swells a lifeboat, oarless, abandoned, empty, except for what looked like a woman's cloak lying across the thwarts. Rising and falling to the swing of the sea it drifted down alongside of us so that we could look almost straight down into it. We did not stop to investigate but kept going, zigzagging[5] as we went, and that old painted-up copy cat of a *Tuscania* came zigzagging behind us. A good many persons decided to tie on their life preservers.

Winter twilight was drawing on when we sighted land—Northern Ireland it was. The wind was going down with the sun and the sharp crests of the waves were dulling off, and blunt oily rollers began to splash with greasy sounds against our plates. Far away somewhere we saw the revolving light of a lighthouse winking across the face of the waters like a drunken eye. That little beam coming and going gave me a feeling of security. I was one of a party of six who went below to the stateroom of a member of the group for a farewell card game.

Perhaps an hour later, as we sat there each intently engaged upon the favoured indoor American sport of trying to better two pairs, we heard against our side of the ship a queer knocking sound rapidly repeated—a sound that somehow suggested a boy dragging a stick along a picket fence.

"I suppose that's a torpedo rapping for admission," said one of us, looking up from his cards and listening with a cheerful grin on his face.

I think it was not more than five minutes after that when an American officer opened the stateroom door and poked his head in.

"Better come along, you fellows," he said; "but come quietly so as not to give alarm or frighten any of the women. Something has happened. It's the *Tuscania* —she's in trouble!"

Up we got and hurried aft down the decks, each one taking with him his cork jacket and adjusting it over his shoulders as he went. We came to the edge of the promenade deck aft. There were not many persons there, as well as we could tell in the thick darkness through which we felt our way, and not many more came afterward—in all I should say not more than seventy-five.

All the rest were in ignorance of what had occurred—a good many were at dinner. Accounts of the disaster which I have read since my arrival in London said that the torpedo from the U-boat thudded into the vitals of the *Tuscania*, disarranged her engines, and left her in utter darkness for a while until her crew could switch on the auxiliary dynamo. I think this must have been a mistake, for at the moment of our reaching the deck of our ship the *Tuscania*

5. Sailing the ship in a zigzag course made it harder for a submarine to aim its torpedo.

was lighted up all over. Her illumination seemed especially brilliant, but that, I suppose, was largely because we had become accustomed to seeing our fellow transports as dark hulks at night. I should say she was not more than a mile from us, almost due aft and a trifle to the left. But the distance between us visibly increased each passing moment, for we were running away from her as fast as our engines could drive us. We could feel our ship throb under our feet as she picked up speed. It made us feel like cowards. Near at hand a ship was in distress, a ship laden with a precious freightage of American soldier boys, and here were we legging it like a frightened rabbit, weaving in and out on sharp tacks.

We knew, of course, that we were under orders to get safely away if we could in case one of those sea adders, the submarines, should attack our convoy. We knew that guardian destroyers would even now be hurrying to the rescue, and we knew land was not many miles, away; but all the same, I think I never felt such an object of shame as I felt that first moment when the realisation dawned on me that we were fleeing from a stricken vessel instead of hastening back to give what succour we could.

As I stood there in the darkness, with silent, indistinct shapes all about me, it came upon me with almost the shock of a physical blow that the rows of lights I saw yonder through the murk were all slanting slightly downward toward what would be the bow of the disabled steamer. These oblique lines of light told the story. The *Tuscania* had been struck forward and was settling by the head.

Suddenly a little subdued "Ah! Ah!" burst like a chorus from us all. A red rocket—a rocket as red as blood—sprang up high into the air above those rows of lights. It hung aloft for a moment, then burst into a score of red balls, which fell, dimming out as they descended. After a bit two more rockets followed in rapid succession. I always thought a rocket to be a beautiful thing. Probably this belief is a heritage from that time in my boyhood when first I saw Fourth-of-July fireworks. But never again will a red rocket fired at night be to me anything except a reminder of the most pitiable, the most heart-racking thing I have ever seen—that poor appeal for help from the sinking *Tuscania* flaming against that foreign sky.

There was silence among us as we watched. None of us, I take it, had words within him to express what he felt; so we said nothing at all, but just stared out across the waters until our eyeballs ached in their sockets. So quiet were we that I jumped when right at my elbow a low, steady voice spoke. Turning my head I could make out that the speaker was one of the younger American officers.

"If what I heard before we sailed is true," he said, "my brother is in the outfit on that boat yonder. Well, if they get him it will only add a little more interest to the debt I already owe those damned Germans."

That was all he said, and to it I made no answer, for there was no answer to be made.

Fifteen minutes passed, then twenty, then twenty-five. Now instead of many small lights we could make out only a few faint pin pricks of light against the blackness to mark the spot where the foundering vessel must be. Presently we could distinguish but one speck of light. Alongside this one special gleam a red glow suddenly appeared—not a rocket this time, but a flare, undoubtedly. Together the two lights—the steady white one and the spreading red one—descended and together were extinguished. Without being told we knew, all of us—landsmen and seamen alike—what we had seen. We had seen the last of that poor ship, stung to death by a Hunnish sea-asp.

Still silent, we went below. Those of us who had not yet dined went and dined. Very solemnly, like men performing a rite, we ordered wine and we drank to the *Tuscania* and her British crew and her living cargo of American soldiers.

Banner headlines reflect American shock at the sinking of the troop ship *Tuscania*, torpedoed on February 5, 1918. Two hundred and ten soldiers and crew lost their lives. *Source:* Chronicling America, Historic American Newspapers Collection, Library of Congress.

Next morning, after a night during which perilous things happened about us that may not be described here and now, we came out of our perils and into safety at an English port, and there it was that we heard what made us ask God to bless that valorous, vigilant little pot-bellied skipper of ours, may he live forever! We were told that the torpedo which pierced the *Tuscania* was meant for us, that the U-boat rising unseen in the twilight fired it at us, and that our captain up on the bridge saw it coming when it was yet some way off, and swinging the ship hard over to one side, dodged the flittering devil-thing by a margin that can be measured literally in inches. The call was a close one. The torpedo, it was said, actually grazed the plates of our vessel—it was that we heard as we sat at cards—and passing aft struck the bow of the *Tuscania* as she swung along not two hundred yards behind us. We heard, too, that twice within the next hour torpedoes were fired at us, and again a fourth one early in the hours of the morning. Each time chance or poor aim or sharp seamanship or a combination of all three saved us. We were lucky.

Next day, here in London, I read that not a man aboard the *Tuscania*, whether sailor or soldier, showed weakness or fright. I read how those Yankee boys, many of them at sea for the first time in their lives, stood in ranks waiting for rescue or for death while the ship listed and yawed and settled under them; how the British sang "God Save the King," and the Americans sang to the same good Allied air, "My Country, 'Tis of Thee;" and how at last, descending over the side, some of them to be drowned but more of them to be saved, those American lads of ours sang what before then had been a meaningless, trivial jingle, but which is destined forevermore, I think, to mean a great deal to Americans. Perry said: "We have met the enemy, and they are ours."[6] Lawrence said: "Don't give up the ship!"[7] Farragut said: "Damn the torpedoes, go ahead."[8] Dewey said: "You may fire, Gridley, when you are ready."[9] Our history is full of splendid sea slogans, but I think there can never be a more splendid one that we

6. Oliver Hazard Perry, an American naval commander in the War of 1812. This quote is from his battle report following his victory over a British Navy squadron in the Battle of Lake Erie, September 10, 1813.

7. The dying words of U.S. naval officer James Lawrence to his officers, when he fell mortally wounded during an engagement with a British ship in the War of 1812.

8. The words of Civil War admiral David Farragut during the Battle of Mobile Bay, urging his ships to pass through a mine field. Mines were known as torpedoes.

9. The words of Commodore George Dewey to Captain Charles Gridley during the Spanish-American War Battle of Manila Bay. The order was to begin firing on the Spanish fleet in the Manila harbor.

Americans will cherish than the first line, which is also the title of the song now suddenly freighted with a meaning and a message to American hearts, which our boys sang that black February night in the Irish Sea when two hundred of them, first fruits of our national sacrifice in this war, went over the sides of the *Tuscania* to death: "Where do we go from here, boys; where do we go from here?"[10]

Convoy System Reducing Losses to U-Boats

"On one day in July there were 100,000 soldiers at sea at once."

Howard Edwin Bechtol
"Convoys Make Trip to Front Safe as a Church"
Bismarck Daily Tribune, August 17, 1918

London, England.

This news story is for American mothers.

The facts which follow are now permitted to be assembled and presented in this form by Admiral Sims'[11] U.S. Navy Staff in London.

When your soldier son starts across the Atlantic he has better than a 4600 to 1 chance-of arriving at his destination safe and well.

Since the United States declared War, about 1,400,000 American fighters have come across. The total casualties at sea have been 291.[12] That's only one man lost in 4600.

There's another point: That proportion, as small as it is, covers all the men sent across since early 1917. And every month methods and appliances safeguarding the transports have improved and broadened.

As Safe as a Church

So the 4600 to 1 chance which the long-period figures prove, does not actually show the percentage today. It's better than that.

"As safe as a church," one Sammy who landed recently put it.

---

10. "Where Do We Go from Here?" was a popular song in 1917, after the United States entered the war.

11. Vice Admiral William Sims commanded all U.S. naval forces operating in European waters.

12. The final figure for the number of U.S. troops lost to U-boats was 637.

Practically every American soldier now comes to Europe in a convoy—a group of ships. Which means, in case of the improbable torpedo, that there are other ships very near for rescue work.

Practically every one of these transports is armed—that is, there are big guns on the actual vessels carrying the soldiers.

Additional protection to the form of escorting war vessels is provided for every convoy in so-called danger zones, and many have escorting war vessels all the way across.

More war craft, especially designed for beating down the U-boats, are constantly getting on the job, as the shipbuilding plants turn them out in constantly increasing numbers. More carrying ships are being put into service too. On one day in July there were 100,000 soldiers at sea at once.

More U-Boats Being Sunk

The percentage of U-boats sunk by the allied navies is climbing. A recent British official statement shows that, for the first time in the war the number of U-boats sunk in the past six months exceeds the number Germany has been able to build. In short, they are being sunk faster than they're being built.

The German government, through inspired articles in the German press, has begun a campaign to "explain" to the people at home why they haven't been able to stop or even interfere with the flow of American troops to France.

In these inspired articles it is now admitted as a final fact that it is impossible under the convoy system that the Allies have perfected, to attack the transports with hope of success.

In other words, the German government realizes that the danger to a U-boat which attacks a convoy is far greater than the danger to the convoy. So they're not showing their heads.

Vanquishing the U-Boat

"Of all the hunting in the world, it is difficult to imagine anything more thrilling than the hunt for submarines."

William G. Shepherd
"Chasing the Periscope"
Everybody's Magazine, October 1918

Youth has whipped the submarine. Waning muscles and aging nerves of mature man could not have done it. It was more than a man-sized job; it was a youth-sized job.

Maturity has the credit for devising the weapons and the plans, but youth took these to sea and used them with success.

American boys have had their part in this mighty task, and it has made them the most upstanding, the happiest, proudest, bravest boys that have ever appeared, as a mass, on the pages of American naval history.

Navy officials, early in the war, selected groups of young men, with officers trained to a dot, and gave to each group that wonderful tool known as a destroyer. The civilian thinks a destroyer is "just a sort of some kind of a little boat that runs around looking for things." He's wrong. A destroyer is almost the last word in ships. It costs two million dollars. It is really two exquisitely mounted turbine engines with a thin skin of steel put around them to keep them afloat. These engines have the power of twenty-seven thousand horses, enough to drive a great liner. The destroyer is so loaded with bombs and torpedoes and explosive deviltries that it is, potentially, a huge bomb in itself. It slices the ocean at forty miles an hour. It is all power and danger. It can not upset. While an ordinary ship is doomed if she rolls much lower than forty-five degrees, or half-way down to the surface of the sea, the destroyer on the side of a wave can roll over to one hundred and seven degrees, which is seventeen degrees below level, and still right herself.

When an ordinary ship rolls beyond forty-five degrees you can see part of the bulge of her bottom as you stand on her deck, but I have met young destroyer sailors from Iowa, Nevada and elsewhere who have told me that they have stood on their decks and seen clear underneath their own boats. Such is an effect of destroyer service upon happy, care free youth. Destroyers are not easy to build; not every shipyard can turn them out. They are the jewel-mounted watch of ships, and you might as well expect an ordinary shipyard to turn them out as to expect a dollar-watch factory to make you a platinum chronometer.

Such is the tool that Young America, in the European anti-submarine patrol, has used. And he has used it exultingly, with the blood of excitement and adventure surging through his young body. Master of the power of twenty-seven thousand horses, riding its thin shell like an aviator on silk wings, conqueror of the ten-month storm that sweeps yearly across the ocean and about the shores of England, Ireland and France, he is a component part of a piece of hurtling death. What American boy who isn't subject to seasickness wouldn't like a job like that?

It is a twentieth-century job; something new on the sea. Pirates, Spanish explorers, Norse sailors never knew such moments as come to these fellows. Just as Hannibal or Napoleon might gaze with astonishment on the great land battle of this year, so John Paul Jones might listen with astonishment and unbelief to the yarns which might be spun by any of the American boys in the antisubmarine patrol.

There's something pathetic in the efforts of these boys to find words to tell their stories.

"Talk about reading thrilling stories in the magazines about rafts and wrecks and things!! We are living them," wrote Stanton F. Kalk, who went from the war-time whirl of Washington, D.C., to the submarine haunt in the Irish Sea on the destroyer *Jacob Jones*.[13] True, he went to his death, a few days later, from swimming about in icy-cold water to herd his men onto the life-rafts, but he had gone through such an experience as no sea-fighters of old could ever have imagined.

The game of these ocean hunters is a certain steel fish, which they hate. It isn't in cold blood they hunt. To explain:

One day, not long ago, bright American eyes from the deck of a destroyer saw, out on the lonely water, a tiny rowboat. In it sat a drooping figure. The whole twenty-seven thousand horse-power of the destroyer was immediately turned on and the young American hearts aboard pounded with excitement as their ship rushed to save the castaway. The glasses of the commander were turned to the little boat. But his ship didn't slow down as it approached the rowboat. No signal went down to the engine-room to take off way. He dashed past the little boat at express-time speed. He ordered the rudder thrown over. His ship whirled broadside onto the tiny derelict. As he went away from there at full speed the commander gave an order:

"Fire at it until it sinks," he ordered. And one small shell that hit the drooping figure broke into a shower of tattered canvas

13. The *Jacob Jones* was sunk by the German submarine U-53 on December 6, 1917, becoming the first U.S. destroyer sunk by enemy action. Sixty-six officers and men lost their lives.

and splintered wood. The figure had been a dummy, a trap set by the submarine men to lure some destroyer to its death. The eye of some periscope had been fixed on the trap, waiting for the prey it expected.

A German navy man might smile at a trick like that; might say: "That's nothing to hate us for."

But what about this:

Our American boys on the destroyers dare not stop to pick up life boats containing shipwrecked men; they must do the job at top speed. Or, if there be two destroyers on the scene, one may slow down for the rescue while the other circles about it to protect it.

Life-boats full of thirsty, starving, freezing, dying men, women and children are German submarine bait. Our destroyer men, and the English and French destroyer men in these waters, know it to be a fact. There's nothing more priceless to a German submarine than to come across a life boat, full of signaling human beings, far from shore. The German submarine men don't rescue the survivors; they just let them wave. Those human beings out there in the little boat are live bait; with their trousers and coats and other desperately improvised flags they are drawing prey to the submarine's zone. That cold, glassy eye of the periscope, that comes up out of the water, circles and circles and circles with pitiless diligence that boatload of human suffering. If no rescuer comes before the bait has died and ceased its attractive wavings, the submarine goes its way. Dead bait is almost worthless.

It is a horrible story, indeed, but so many American and other destroyers have had torpedoes fired at them while they were engaged in rescuing the occupants of life-boats on the high seas, and so many German submarines are always so handily near to a life-boat, that every pitiful little cluster of shipwrecked human beings, on rafts or in boats, is looked upon as a bit of submarine lure.

There is an ardent hate, therefore, in the hearts of the American destroyer men for most of the German submarine sailors.

I used "most" advisedly. These very human young Americans, who range the storms for submarines, have found one submarine commander for whom they have a weakness. That's "Kelly." In spite of all they know of the perfidy and cruelty of the submarine men, they hesitate to believe any great ill of "Kelly." "Kelly" has hit them square in their sense of humor, a fair shot. They've never seen "Kelly," but they all say they'd like to. And, indeed, "Kelly" is a mystery. Not long ago, so the destroyer tales go—and I tell them as they were told to me—a German submarine came up alongside a British lightship.[14] Lightships, it is understood, are not sunk by either side. A head popped out of the submarine turret.

"Here," said the head, to a wondering lightship man. "Here's a bunch of papers you might like to read. I had a good time the other evening and I want you fellows to know about it. But if you fellows tell on me, I'll come and sink you."

The bundle contained, so the story goes, several English newspapers, a receipted bill from a certain hotel in the British Isles made out to "Kelly," and two seat-checks for a certain theatre in the same well-known islands, all of recent date.

"Did they tell on 'Kelly'?" I asked one of the submarine hunters who told me the story.

"They did. And 'Kelly' did, too. They had to get a new lightship."

"How did 'Kelly' find out they'd told on him?" I asked.

"That's the big puzzle. That's what makes 'Kelly' interesting."

"Kelly," the Good German

Another time, as the story goes, "Kelly" came up alongside a fishing fleet, popped his head out and said: "I haven't any money with me because I've been away from home for a long while, but if you'll sell me some fish and trust me for a couple of weeks, I'll be much obliged." The fisherman gave him the fish and he submerged. About two months later a submarine came up near the same fishing-boat. The turret was opened and a package was thrown onto the deck of a trawler. It contained the money for the fish and a note which said: "Kelly always pays his bills."

The destroyer patrols have a whole batch of "Kelly" stories.

"He can't be a German," is the opinion of the destroyer fleet. "He must be some rebel Irishman, because he's got a sense of humor."

---

14. Lightships are vessels that provide a navigational beacon, just like a lighthouse. They are positioned in waters that are too deep or otherwise unsuited for the construction of a lighthouse.

The first task of these American boys on the destroyers was to fit in with the English. Their elders, sitting back at their desks in the Navy Department in Washington, wondered, as the first American destroyers approached the other side, whether everything would be smooth sailing between the British navy men and the American navy men. Would the Britishers have a chip on their shoulders because of their ancient sea traditions? Or would the American boys be reluctant to blindly follow British orders?

It's interesting to know just exactly what happened when the American destroyers, after having crossed the Atlantic, reported for patrol duty. The young officers of the destroyers were called together and shown maps of the infested waters. They were told just what areas were to be patrolled. And then their orders came to them. The whole issue of how well they could work with the British navy men hung on those first orders. They came from a man's man, those orders, from a man who knew men. In effect those orders said:

"Go out to your stations and use your own judgment. Don't ask me by wireless what to do or whether to do it. Do it! And then send in your wireless, telling me you've done it. That's all I want to hear."

It was signed by Admiral Bayley[15] of the British navy. What could have been more American than that? No American admiral ever gave a more pleasing order. Under such instructions the destroyers fairly leaped to their tasks. All the self-reliance that is taught American youth was challenged by that first order. At the very first jump-off the American navy men decided that "that British admiral was a regular fellow" and it is a decision that has not been changed after more than a year of war. They call him "the best American admiral in the British navy."

Of all the hunting in the world, it is difficult to imagine anything more thrilling than the hunt for submarines in these wild waters. It is the biggest, meanest, snakiest game that was ever sought in the justest cause ever known to hunters. There is little wonder that the American boys on the destroyers like it.

There are two aspects of patrol work—the offensive and the defensive. Each has its peculiar problems.

15. Royal Navy admiral Lewis Bayly commanded the mixed British-American naval forces protecting the busy shipping lanes that approached Britain from America.

Let us take, first, the offensive. Just as soon as the Germans had sketched that huge geometrical figure on the face of the waters which they called the submarine zone, the Allied naval men took their maps and pencils and superimposed on the German drawing a geometrical design of their own. This design was made up of squares which were designated by letters. With the quick imagination of seamen, where the sea is concerned, these letters formed an acrostic made out of a phrase which meant, in effect: "This is not a German ocean." These lettered areas were detailed off to various destroyers. I find that it appealed tremendously to the imagination of the American destroyer men to play their life-and-death game on the face of this hugest acrostic ever devised. To be out in the zone marked by the first letter of the acrostic meant to be tossing far out at sea.

When the submarine war was at its height, the departure of a destroyer for its distant area in the huge acrostic marked the beginning of the unending excitement. Just as soon as the wireless was rigged and the destroyer left port, the cries of the sea began coming through the wireless room. There were times when these cries were almost incessant. "We are being fired on by a submarine at such and such a place." "We have been torpedoed and are sinking." "Submarine sighted at such and such a place." "Men on our decks are being killed by submarine shell-fire." "S.O.S.!" "S.O.S.!" "S.O.S.!"—the air was filled with calls of distress. In his room, at his maps, it was the task of the destroyer commander to discover the location of each one of these disasters and decide whether or not it might be his particular duty to answer any one of them. He might not go too far beyond his course and yet, within reason, he might deviate sufficiently to attempt a rescue. In the main, his chief duty would be to get out to his area as quickly as possible and relieve the other destroyers that had been tossing in the storm out there for over a week.

Incidentally, there is always a storm, ten months out of the year, on the big acrostic. As soon as he reaches the high seas on his path to his post the commander must know that sharp eyes are covering every inch of the tossing waters about him. The latest German periscope is, speaking roughly, shaped like a greatly elongated beer bottle, with a neck only an inch and a half in diameter. The neck is glitteringly nickel-plated so that, with the submarine lying in the path of the sun, the nickel takes on the sheen of the waters and can hardly be discerned; while on a dull day it mirrors the flat hues of the surrounding water, taking on its dull colors of camouflage. It is a telescoping tube that can be thrust gently half a foot above the surface by the German submarine commander without any great stir of the water. Eyes must be searching the waves for this six inches of metal. With wreckage visible in many directions this task is doubly hard, and, in line with the good American motto of "Safety First," many of the periscope alarms proved false in those early days. Other eyes, gazing further asea, must be watching for life-boats containing shipwrecked seamen.

Saving the Victims

"Oh, God! How they do beckon!" said an American destroyer commander to me, in telling of some of his rescues. Once an American destroyer came across a life-boat containing two British ship officers and nine Chinamen. One white man and two Chinamen were dead. The Chinamen, with Oriental fatalism, had given up the struggle and were waiting to die. They wouldn't even seize the rope which was thrown down to them. The white man, saluting courteously, grasped the ship's ladder and started to ascend; he seemed as cool as if he had been merely boarding the ship in harbor. His first few upward steps were strong and sure. He stopped a minute; then his hold loosened. He had used his last strength. Like a bag of sand he fell into the water, face first, dead. From the Chinamen, who were lifted to the deck in swings, the Americans discovered that the boat had been adrift six days, without food or water, which explained the Englishman's death at the moment of rescue. The rule is now, as the result of this and similar incidents, to descend into the life-boat and fasten ropes under the arms of the life-boat occupants. There's no time to send the ship's doctor down to ascertain the physical strength remaining in the bodies of the sea-drifters. The stories of these rescued drifters are always fascinatingly interesting to the American destroyer men; they outdo, as Stanton Kalk wrote to his mother, all the magazine stories ever written. In one life-boat the American boys picked up a rugged American seaman who had been torpedoed and had taken to the sea in life boats eleven different times; the matter-of-fact way in which he took his rescue made an impression on the young Americans that has extended throughout the destroyer fleet.

"Weren't you afraid you wouldn't be picked up?" a navy man asked him.

"Hell, no. I'm always picked up. I used to worry some at first, but I know, by this time, that some one'll always come along and get you."

And still other eyes must range farther to the horizon for smoke. Out there, on the wave-jagged edge of the world, a ship may be lying in distress with her wireless useless. And you must know all the ships that are amove in your part of the sea. They must prove themselves friends, either by wireless, by flag-signal or by the hoarse megaphoned voice of the skipper.

The Periscope Eye

Eye-work is perhaps the biggest part of submarine hunting; and it has its evils and penalties. Woe to the man on a destroyer who is gifted with that strange, unexplainable talent of being able to see by night. There be such. His is almost a twenty-four-hour-a-day task. And he finally gets the "periscope eye" and is sent ashore to get well, if he can. His eyes weep tears of pus by day and, after sleep, his lids are glued together with granulation. It is a new disease of this mad century.

"You keep looking through those high-powered binoculars like an old lady reading through her spectacles," one of the boys explained to me, "until finally they seem to be pulling your eyes out of their sockets."

And so, whispering sparingly, now and then by wireless, because the submarines have wireless ears, scanning the water by human eye-power, reading the chart and locating the disasters that are being told off in the cries of the sea, the destroyer makes its way to its station. Somewhere in the square miles in that area it must find the destroyer it is to relieve. This done, it goes on watch. To be on watch in one of these spaces in the great acrostic means to range the district back and forth, like a hound. The weather doesn't count. No undamaged American destroyer, up to the time of this writing, has ever come in to shelter from a storm. It stands on the records of the British Admiralty that, one time, they were told by wireless to seek shelter, but the storm was so bad that they all decided it would be safer to stay out!

There is always a storm out there. Ninety miles an hour of wind is not uncommon. When waves are so high that a destroyer can lean over one hundred and seven degrees on a wave side and still roll back to safety, you've got some wave!

It takes five and a half seconds for the average American destroyer to complete a roll. That is, in that space of time it will roll to one side, come back to erect, roll to the other side and then return to erect. If the sea is not bad, the five-and-a-half-second roll is fairly gentle. But in a high sea those five and a half seconds are full of motion; the rolls are lightning like in their speed. No matter how far the sea wants her to go over, she must go over that distance, swing back almost a corresponding distance to the other side, and come to erect, all in five and a half seconds. She is built and weighted so that she must make this rolling time. When the seas are high, the end of each roll has the effect of the snap of a whip. There are chances for broken legs in her and death from broken necks when the storms are high.

There's no eating at table, though I have had a destroyer man say to me: "Some of us get pretty good at sitting at table, after a lot of experience." Dishes on a table, even in racks, are like stones in a boy's whirling sling. If the cook is able to cook anything at all, he does it in pots and pans lashed to the hot stove. If he enters the ward room with a tray of eatables and suddenly looses his hold on them and leaves them momentarily in mid-air while he, in the midst of the accompanying crash, grabs the nearest immovable object, the incident passes without comment. The code on the destroyer is, "When she rolls, grab."

On the bridge the officers prop themselves in corners, wedging themselves in with their elbows. Now and then one of them is snapped across the bridge. He grabs at the first thing he can seize. Officers, under such circumstances, have unwittingly seized the whistle rope and blown the siren. One officer, seizing the nearest object, got his hands on the telegraph that started one engine backing at full speed while the other was going full speed forty miles an hour forward, converting the destroyer into an ocean-going top.

There is no real bathing even during the average roll that accompanies the ten-month storm in these parts.

"You'd drown in a bathtub, because the water climbs on top of you," explained one American, "and if you try to go under the shower, you can't dodge around fast enough to keep under the stream. Why, I've had to chase a shower-bath stream clear out of the bathroom into the gangway to stay under it."

The first thing destroyer men do on reaching port, therefore, is to rush to a bath house. Sleeping is difficult. Most of the boys remove the springs from their berths and place their mattresses on the boards. This increases the height of the side board and permits them to wedge themselves in more securely by the use of their knees. But it's difficult to sleep.

"Your innards jerk around so much, even if your body is relatively stationary," explained one. Days pass when no one undresses.

The Seasickness Test

There are days of this incessant rolling; days on end. It takes a youth blessed with a God-given immunity from seasickness to endure it. Some have been made sick, almost to death. The rhythm of their heart beats are lost and their internal machinery fails to operate in coordination. Then they themselves and every one else knows that they were not made by nature to be destroyer men. They must go to some other branch of the Navy. Some of our destroyers have tried out as many as two hundred boys who couldn't stand the seasickness test.

It is a job for youth, and handpicked youth at that, with perfect organs and oaken hearts, this destroyer work.

For five days, six days, ten days, as the case may be, the destroyer plows its beat. It must not go too far afield. Every now and again it comes to the boundary of its square and must right about in another direction. No matter how high the sea and how deep the trough of the waves, it must put its side to them, in turning, and lay over on the waters while it makes the shift.

And all the time, in the olden days of submarine supremacy, there were the cries of the sea coming by wireless.

"Is that in my square? Or is it near enough to my square to justify my going to the scene and leaving my own station unprotected for a time? Or will some other destroyer answer them?"

These are questions which the destroyer commander must answer for himself every time a cry of the sea comes to his bridge.

His orders from the admiral are, as we remember: "Don't ask me for instructions. Use your own judgment. Do a thing and then tell me you have done it."

Life for him, with all the storm and the danger, is, in reality, a matter of making hourly decisions which may mean life or death for himself, his crew or hundreds of submarine victims. The soundness and the common sense of these quick danger-time decisions by these young American destroyer commanders—they average in age around thirty—has elicited the highest respect of the European naval commanders. Quick thinking and right thinking are coming to be known abroad as American naval characteristics.

Defensive submarine warfare by these American destroyers consists of escorting ships for convoys. It has excitements of its own, very different, in the main, from these of the offensive submarine hunt.

In this defensive submarine warfare, the submarine, strangely enough, is not the danger which the young destroyer commanders fear most.

"The first fear is that you won't find your convoy. The second fear is, that, after you've found it, you'll lose it again. The third fear is the submarine itself," was the fashion in which an American commander described the worries of escort work.

He thereby drew the background of a new life of the seas—a twentieth-century war-time life—that has never been told either in fact or fiction.

"Go out to a certain place in the ocean and pick up a convoy," appears, to the layman, a simple order, easy of accomplishment. But let us follow half a dozen of these speed monsters out to sea on such a quest.

From the moment they leave, there is the eye-work to be done; every square inch of the waters must be scanned for the enemy. Castaways in life-boats must be picked up, on such a trip, even though the destroyers are running on schedule to their rendezvous. Any submarine that shows its signs must be hounded to death, if possible, and still the destroyers must be at their meeting-place on time.

"Meeting-place" is highly indefinite. Some of the great liners, supposedly following a given pathway across the ocean, may be as

far as twenty miles out of their line, in one direction or the other, a
variation of forty miles. The wireless is hushed. Lights are out, if it
is night. Human eyesight is the only means of finding the ponder-
ous slow-going ships that come from America with their precious
loads of American soldiers and war supplies. The destroyers, at full
speed, range the likely areas until the quick, tireless signal goes out
from some one of them that the convoy has been found.

Then comes danger in abundance. The destroyers line themselves up at various stations around the great ships. Nothing is left
to chance here. Greenwich time[16] is given to the commanders of the
big ships, by signals. Every body's clock is set right. And then, by
the clock, the zigzag begins. With great hulks like these and priceless loads of men and supplies, such dangerous work as zigzagging
can not be left to the whim of each individual commander. At just
a certain tick of the chronometers all the commanders of the great
ships must change their courses each in a prescribed direction and
send their huge flock veering from its line. When this is done in
the black darkness of a winter night, the seamen concerned may
safely be described as performing the most dangerous evolutions
known to the sea.

There are no lights. Safety lies only in catlike eyesight, in following the very ticks of the clock, and in blind luck. In the early days
of the war the dangers were enhanced by the independent spirit of
the commanders of merchantmen who were disinclined to yield to
navy leadership and instructions.

Guarding the Convoy

All around the veering flocks of ships dash the destroyers. Their
dashings, however, are more or less methodical, like hunting-dogs
scouring the fields, but always returning to their master. Moving
at a far higher speed than their convoy, they too have their own
zigzag schedule. For every new direction taken by the transports,
they must form themselves into new geometrical designs in relation
to the convoy. Like football players changing their formations for
each new play, or like baseball players shifting from their own positions into another's field in order to give assistance and supports,

---

16. Until 1972, Greenwich Time was the worldwide time standard, fixed at the Royal
Observatory at Greenwich, England, and used for navigational calculations.

so the destroyers in the pitch blackness, at every certain number of clock-ticks must, at full speed oftentimes, turn in their courses and take new places. If everybody else in the convoy has followed his clock faithfully, all is well. In the pitch darkness of a stormy night the destroyer men can go only by faith, trust and luck. Not even eye sight is of avail. And if somebody has gone wrong and got into some area not his own at the wrong time, a deadly collision is inevitable. It is blind sailing.

"As far as seeing anything around you was concerned," said a commander of one of the dozen destroyers that I have in mind, "you might as well have closed your eyes. Perhaps, now and then, if there was a little clear spot in the sky somewhere, you might catch just a glimpse of the dark hulk of one of the big ships and guard it. But I have speeded for hours in a group of many ships and destroyers and not seen a single one of them."

In the seventeen-hour nights that fall on the northern seas in winter the nerve of these destroyer men as well as of the big ship commanders is strained almost to the endurance point.

"You get jiggly and superstitious, if you aren't careful," one of the destroyer men told me. "You may try to run your destroyer by hunches. One night, for instance, while I was on the bridge, just at zigzag time, something told me to throw my helm over and put her at full speed. I don't know why I did, but I gave the order. And right behind us, just where we had been a minute before, dashed another destroyer, out of her course. We'd been cut in two if she had hit us.

"'You were dead-right in doing it,' my commander said to me, when he hurried up to the bridge a minute later and saw the white wake of the other boat; 'but what I want to know is: why did you give the signal? You couldn't see her coming in the darkness, could you?'

"'Don't ask me, sir,' I said. 'I couldn't see her or hear her, but something told me to get out of her way and I did.' He put his hand on my shoulder and said: 'Keep at it, young man. You're learning how to be a real destroyer man.'"

The commander who said that fear of not finding the convoy came first, was speaking from the view-point of personal pride. The supreme danger in the convoy work comes from possible collision. With a stormy sea, filled for many square miles with huge zig zagging ships, and with a night so black that human eyes are useless, every moment abounds in danger.

And yet these boys of the destroyers have brought dozens and dozens of these great convoys through a submarine zone without a loss or even a light collision.

The Great Moments

There are high moments, worth living a lifetime to pass through, that come to the destroyer men now and then. Months of dull, drab strain, heightened only by picking up occasional survivors, or getting two or three days' leave ashore where the Y.M.C.A. huts[17] and soft unrolling beds await, are dotted with high spots that atone for all the dreariness and strain.

The supreme moment, of course, is getting a submarine.

Depth bombs are at hand on a destroyer. There isn't anything among the weapons of the navy, except the great shells, that has the explosive power of the depth bomb. They are more powerful than torpedoes.

"I knew I was right over a submarine. I had calculated it to a 'T'," said one commander, who shortly is to have a British decoration for bravery. "I dropped one depth bomb and hurried out of the way. Say! Did you ever see a heavy object fall on ice? You know how it powders the ice just where it hits, and how the cracks run out from the center in every direction. Well, sir, that depth bomb went off so hard that it seemed to turn the water into a solid mass. That water had that same powdered center and the same cracks that you see in ice. I swung around and hurried back to the same place and dropped another. Then I went off, because I was in charge of a convoy.

"The next day some of the destroyers saw oil floating in that spot. For days, every ship that came in from that direction reported oil on the water there and two weeks later, when I got a chance to steam over that way, the water was still greasy. That moment of dropping those bombs was worth all the hardships of a year."

The destroyers themselves, with their high speed, have little to fear from torpedoes. The *Jacob Jones* is the only American

17. Facilities for recreation and religious services in the war zone, provided by the Y.M.C.A.

destroyer that has been hit by a submarine. It was a thousand-yard shot, and pure luck.

"They fired her on the top of the water," said a young man who had stood on the deck of the destroyer at the time. "If they had fired her at the usual depth, a dozen feet below the surface, she might have gone under us. She came bouncing like a porpoise. Whenever she jumped out of the water she sounded like, the Twentieth Century Limited,[18] because of the roar of the escaping compressed air. They had aimed her to the millionth of a second, I think. It killed fifty men when it hit us, but the rest of us were rescued, after a while, from our life-rafts."

The worst storm in the history of that part of the world struck the submarine zone in December of 1917. It lasted seven days. In desperation several of the American destroyers, badly damaged, made for the coast of Spain. Two of them sighted it in the height of the storm, but internment for the duration of the war would have been the price of safety in a neutral port. And so they went fifteen hours farther in the storm, to the shores of Portugal, where they found a pro-Ally welcome.

Yarns of the Patrol

The hardships of the submarine hunters do not get into the cold official reports that find their way back to Washington and the Navy Building. It's just the tale of bare, unadorned achievement that is told in these. And none of the lightness and fun of the life gets into these reports, either.

By the spinning of yarns alone the whole story is told. Here are a few, hit or miss:

"You should have seen us Christmas Eve on our destroyer," yarns one young officer. "We were sent eighty Christmas packages and we had a hundred men. We sat up all night undoing those packages and remaking them so that there would be enough to go round. And we were in a storm, too, with a terrific roll. But we had a great Christmas the next day, even if the officers did look sleepy."

"One time, in the Bay of Biscay, we came across a life-boat with thirteen men in it and a black cat. What do you think of that for a

---

18. The *20th Century Limited* was a famous express passenger train that operated between New York and Chicago.

bad-luck combination?" said another yarner. "Well, sir, not one of them was in bad shape and the black cat was the smartest of them all. It knew it was rescued. How it ever did it, we never could figure out, but as soon as we got alongside, it climbed right up the side of our destroyer. Seemed to fasten its claws in the paint. It made itself at home right away and we've had it for a mascot ever since. We put our dog mascot ashore, because he used to get terribly seasick and he couldn't hold on to the decks with his claws. Our cat is the best mascot afloat, we think."

"We saw an oiler afire one day, on our beat, and we hurried to it as fast as we could go. A submarine had set her afire with shells and had then departed. We raced an English torpedo-boat to the scene, but she had the start and got there before we did. She picked up the survivors and just as we were going away we saw that they had missed one castaway. It was a little black dog, swimming around in the water. The Englishmen saw it, too. Neither of us dared stop dead still, and we couldn't rescue the dog while we were moving because he couldn't grab a rope like a man in a boat.

"'You circle around us to protect us and we'll pick him up,' signaled the Englishmen. So we circled at full speed while the English destroyer got out a boat and saved the dog. A dog that you pick up that way makes the best good-luck mascot in the world."

A valuable dog, that. The power of forty thousand horses was used in saving his single dog-life, and by the standards of sane youth, it was worth it.

There are other heroes asea in the American Navy, besides the destroyer men. Some of them are as young as the destroyer men, averaging less than twenty-three for the crews, and some are older. They steam and hunt and fight in ships of other sorts than the gaunt, high-powered, jewel-mounted, oil-driven destroyers and they have their places on our honor-roll of the sea.

I have taken the destroyer men for my theme because they conduct the dramatic submarine patrol in the northern seas, and because, in telling of America's new glory on the sea, the yarns grow far too long if spun in all its hundred-sided aspects.

Chapter 6

⟡

⟡

⟡

⟡

⟡

In the Air

Introduction

Threhe air war gave America its first war heroes—before America even entered the war. Although many Americans volunteered with the armies of all the belligerent countries, they served in virtual anonymity. Only those Americans who flew for France received coverage in the press. Some had volunteered at the outbreak of hostilities, some later when the glory found by pilots motivated them to join. In a war fought on so massive a scale, with staggering numbers of soldiers and casualties, the novelty of aerial combat captured the public's imagination. It glorified the daring pilots, "modern knights" of the air, who engaged in individual combat. In 1916, the American aviators volunteering with France were organized into their own distinct unit known as the Lafayette Flying Corps, and their exploits received even more publicity.

The United States entered the war unprepared in the area of aviation. It did not have a sufficient number of trained pilots, and it had not kept pace with the rapid evolution of fighting aircraft during the war. The U.S. spent the entire war flying in Allied airplanes.

Initially, they also relied on veteran French pilots for training. In "France's Flying School," Henri Bazin described his visit to the air training school in Avord, France, in July 1917, while the first American pilots were beginning their training under French instructors. Many of these early American novice flyers had seen service with the French army, the Foreign Legion, or had driven for the American Ambulance service. Now, under Uncle Sam's banner, they chose to fight in the sky.

At Avord, Bazin encountered the African-American pilot Eugene Bullard, who had been the subject of news articles while serving with the French Foreign Legion and the French air service. It's hard to overstate what an anomaly Bullard was. He was the lone black combatant to be featured in news stories prior to U.S. entry in the war. He was the only African-American pilot to fly in World War I; ironically, he did not fly for the United States. Although he applied to serve in the U.S. Army Air Service, which desperately needed experienced pilots, he was rejected because of his race. A grateful French government would eventually award him fifteen decorations for his service.

The downing of the first German plane by an American pilot made headline news in the spring of 1918, as did the loss of the most famous American flyer, Raoul Lufbery. Lufbery had earned his "ace" status flying for the French, but after the United States entered the war, he transferred to the Aviation Section of the U.S. Army Signal Corps to pass along his combat experience to American aviators preparing for their first action. Hundreds of American soldiers and French civilians witnessed Lufbery's dramatic death in aerial combat.

By the time George Seldes wrote about the day he spent at an American aerodrome in July 1918, American aviators were fully involved in the air war. In "Modern Knights Who Ride to Battle in the Air" he captures the hectic daily schedule of combat flyers protecting their sector of the Western Front.

In the final article in this chapter, America's top aerial ace of the war, Eddie Rickenbacker, writes about his chivalrous feelings towards a German pilot he encountered in the skies.

American Fliers in Training

"Send would-be fliers for the cause of right to Avord.
And send them in shiploads."

Henri Bazin
"France's Flying School"
Evening Ledger (Philadelphia), July 26, 1917

Together with a number of journalists and writers I have been the guest of the French War Office at Avord, the aerie of Allied aviators. There I saw 600 young men, war fliers in the making, every man jack as fit as a fiddle and eager for his pilot's brevet.

The great majority were, of course, French, but with them were Russian, Japanese, Italian, Serbian, Rumanian, Belgian and Portuguese youths, and last, but not least, seventy-two boys from the United States.[1]

They come virtually from every State in the Union, with a brave showing of twenty from Pennsylvania, of whom ten are from Philadelphia or suburban points a few miles away. Their names are Charles J. Biddle, Andalusia, and Julian C. Biddle, Leo J. Brennan, Lewis Leslie Byers, James A. Connelly, Joseph Flynn, Upton S. Sullivan, Archibald G. McCall and Stephen Tyson, all of the Quaker City, with Charles Kerwood, of Bryn Mawr.[2] I am honored in being permitted to here inscribe their names, and I pray every reader of this article may make them a silent salute.

Avord is in the Department of Cher and about 150 miles due south of Paris, being thus virtually in the center of France. Before the war it was a village hardly to be found on the map, although a small aviation school had existed there from 1912. Today it is the largest and most important aviation school in all France, with a population of 4000 people. It is a vast camp of flying men, mechanics, sleeping quarters, shops and hangars, with vaster fields as flying, starting and landing points. Six hundred machines are in use and over 1000 motors. From 12,000 to 15,000 gallons of gasoline are used daily. Expert mechanics, in the main from French colonies, quickly repair, adjust and put together motors

---

1. All countries at war with the Central Powers (Germany and its allies).
2. Under most circumstances, censorship restrictions prohibited the naming of individual soldiers. However, that was not the case for aviators.

as well as virtually rebuild the machines when necessary. There is a hospital and a fire department and all the adjuncts of a city. The buildings are of wood and cement, solidly constructed and in no sense temporary. They are, it goes without saying, in the simple good taste prevalent everywhere in France.

Like a Flock of Birds

We who were privileged to see witnessed a never-to-be-forgotten sight within an hour after our arrival, 250 flying machines being sent into the air at one time for our benefit, the purring of their motors resembling a great roar in different notes of a scale, and the machines themselves a huge flock of birds which flew not in flock formation but seemingly haphazard in every direction under the lovely blue of June. And after dark, amid a starlit, moonless sky, 100 flew again, each with a starboard and larboard light, as a ship. About a third of this number performed thrilling stunts as their lights indicated, while others executed such maneuvers as are usually only to be seen at the front, dropping bombs upon imaginary foes, shooting Lewis shells at imaginary Boches, discharging graceful rockets as used in Zeppelin attack and defense. It was altogether an unforgettable sight, demonstrating the full worth of this important branch of a service that has become an heroic reality and a stern necessity of modern warfare.

The American boys were marshalled in three squads at different points of a vast field, 1000 hectares square. Two of the squads were photographed, among them five of the boys from Philadelphia. It was my pleasure to shake hands with each of them, and to note their eager, modest vigor and youthful manliness. If signs count for anything, these boys will be heard from.

More Than 200 Americans Trained

It is and was at Avord that 222 young Americans were and are being entrained as members of the Lafayette Flying Corps[3] of the French and now the American army. Twenty of these young men are members of the Lafayette escadrille, flying the Stars and Stripes on the western front. Six are in French escadrilles, and

---

3. A unit of American volunteer pilots who flew for the French Air Force prior to U.S. entry into the war.

two in Allied army escadrilles. They rank from captain, the title in the French army held by Bert Hall, of Kentucky, to simple pilot. Seventeen have received the Croix de Guerre, and four the Military Medal,[4] truly the proudest distinction of the French army. Three are aces, having brought down five or more enemy planes. Nine have given their lives for the cause, and one is a prisoner in Germany. One hundred and six are now at Avord, and eight at other schools in France. Of the Avord 106, twenty-seven are men with front experience, being temporarily detached to the school as instructors and interpreters.

Fully 20 per cent have seen service of six months or more in the American Ambulance, and eleven boys have served in the Foreign Legion[5] or various branches of the French army during the last two years. Of these, Eugene Bullard, twenty-six years old, of Columbus, Ga, is the only negro from over the sea. He is as black as the proverbial ace of spades. Bullard, whose physiognomy is full of intelligence, has Roosevelt[6] beaten forty blocks on white teeth. This boy has served forty months in the Legion and was twice wounded. In each instance he was reported killed and the news telegraphed to America as the first black man from the United States to give his life for France. He wears the Croix de Guerre, the Military Medal and the smile that won't come off. He is a qualified pilot on all types of machines save the fighting plane, in which he is taking final instructions. Finally, he has the distinction of being the sole representative in any Allied army of the millions of negroes in the United States. As such he is very proud—and lonely.

Remembering he had been reported killed, I said to him just before the photograph was taken:

"The next time you are going to die, Bullard, send me word in advance. And if your courage is as good as your skin is black, you'll be some flier."

As I reached for his hands with the words, he replied:

"I am proud to have served France, and now more proud to serve the United States. The only part of her that will be 'in

---

4. The *Croix de Guerre* and the Military Medal were French and British medals awarded for bravery.

5. Prior to U.S. entry into the war, some Americans volunteered to fight with the French Foreign Legion or to drive ambulances in support of the American Hospital in Paris. Some of these volunteers eventually became pilots with the Lafayette Flying Corps.

6. Former president Theodore "Teddy" Roosevelt was famous for his toothy smile.

Eugene Bullard was the only African-American pilot and he was credited with two unconfirmed kills. He served with the French Foreign Legion, the French Army, the French Air Service, and Lafayette Flying Corps, but was rejected for the U.S. Army Air Service, because they only took white pilots. Bullard flew with a mascot, a Rhesus monkey named "Jimmy," pictured here. *Source:* U.S. Air Force.

the air' is the bunch that will fly for her. And won't you try to get some more black men over there to come over and help on the job."[7]

French, Belgian and Italian Machines

The machines used at Avord are of the Farman, Coudron, Volsin, Bleriot, Spaed, Nieuport and Caprona types,[8] being thus French, Belgian and Italian, some with one and others with two and three motors, and serving in the varied branches of observation, photographing, bombthrowing and fighting. Upon our arrival every machine in the outfit was drawn up as if on parade before their respective hangars, looking for all the world like so many gigantic insects. And as more than a third took the air, the sight was one of wonder and admiration.

Before we left for Paris, Director Groh, who has truly fathered the American Ambulance and Lafayette Flying Corps, gathered all the American boys together about us and spoke feelingly of and to these brave youngsters whose faces we could hardly make out in the night, saying that they were the real advance guard of a great American army, and that those who had entered the school and the service before American entry were entitled to special honor for serving their hearts as well as their country. And as we entered our cars, some youngsters yelled out: "Boys, give a real cheer for the little old U.S.A." It came from their youthful throats with a vim and a will that sounded like home.

Avord Aviation School is in charge of Captain Max Boucher, of the French army, and under the direction of Lieutenant Colonel Girod, Inspector General of Aviation for France. Since America is going in strong for aviation, and since, too, aviation is playing and destined to play a tremendous part in the war which must, in the main, end through American arms, the more American boys that can come to Avord, the better. It might be fully possible to secure entire control of Avord School and make it virtually a purely American base for aviation pupils from the United States.

7. This July 1917 article appears to have captured Bullard after he had applied to serve in the U.S. Air Service but before he had been rejected because of his race. It makes his call for other African-Americans to serve all the more ironic, since the racial prejudice that existed in the U.S. Army prevented any black Americans from serving in combat. Two divisions of African-Americans did fight with the French Army.

8. Different varieties of aircraft.

For here are the machines, the shops, the instructors and all the accessories that would permit teaching the game of flying more quickly and to better advantage than at any school existing or to be constructed in the United States. Certainly it is undeniably true that at Avord a thoroughly experienced, progressive, methodical course of instruction is given, as is evidenced in the record of 300 able fliers turned out monthly. This means that for purely or almost purely American purposes Avord means more than words convey in American future air glory. Here are all the needs for manufacturing heroes, whipping into shape intrepid soldiers of the air, who take their lives in their hands to a degree impossible to any land or sea soldier, no matter how brave and true. Here more than 5000 aviators could be turned out in a year, and twice that number at less expenditure than 1000 in any school for aviation in any part of the United States.

Send would-be fliers for the cause of right to Avord. And send them in shiploads. Every man of them would be full welcome, and what's more to the point every man of them is needed.

First AEF Air Victory

"He looked me all over and then asked me in good French if I was an American."

Lieut. Alan F. Winslow
"Tells How He 'Got' First Enemy Plane"
The Sun (New York), June 16, 1917

The following personal diary of Alan F. Winslow, Aviation Section, Signal Reserve Corps, of Chicago, the first American aviator of the American Expeditionary Forces to bring down a German plane, is made public by the War Department.

It was not written for publication, but is given out on account of its historical and descriptive value.

On Sunday morning, April 14, I was "on alert" from 6 A.M. till 10 A.M, that is, I with Lieut. Douglas Campbell of Harvard and California (since designated as the first American "ace"[9]) were on emergency call duty. We were sitting in the little alert tent, playing

9. Pilots with at least five air victories.

cards, waiting for a call. Our machines were outside, ready at a moment's notice. I was patrol leader.

At 8:45 I was called to the phone and told by the information officer, who is in direct touch with all batteries and observation posts, that two German airplanes were about 2.000 meters above the city, which is only a mile or so from here. We were told they were going east. We were rushed down to our machines inside cars and in another minute were off in the air.

Meets German Almost at Once

"Doug" started ahead of me, as I was to meet him above a certain point at 500 meters, and then take the lead. I gave him about forty-five seconds start and then left myself, climbing steeply in a left hand spiral in order to save time, I had not made a complete half turn and was about 250 meters, when straight above and ahead of me in the mist of the early morning and not more than a hundred yards away I saw a plane coming toward me with huge black crosses on its wings and tail. I was so furious to see a Hun directly over our aviation field that I swore out loud and violently opened fire.

At the same time to avoid bullets he slipped into a left hand reversement[10] and came down firing on me. I climbed, however, in a right hand spiral and slipped off, coming down directly behind him and "on his tail." Again I violently opened fire. I had him at a rare advantage which was due to the greater speed and maneuverability of our wonderful machines.

I fired twenty or thirty rounds at him and could see my tracers[11] entering his machine. Then in another moment his plane went straight down in an uncontrolled nose dive. I had put his engine out of commission. I followed in a straight dive, firing all the way. At about six feet above the ground he tried to regain control of his machine, but could not, and he crashed to earth. I darted down near him, made a sharp turn by the wreck to make sure he was out of commission, then made a victorious swoop down over him and climbed up again to see if "Doug" needed any help with the other Hun, for I had caught a glimpse of their combat out of the corner of my eye.

10. An aerial maneuver consisting of a half-roll and a half-loop.
11. Tracer bullets carry a small pyrotechnic charge that allows the pilot to follow their course and determine where his shots are hitting.

Campbell Downs Foe in Flames

I rose to about 300 again to see "Doug" "on the tail" of his Boche. His tracer bullets were passing throughout the enemy plane. I climbed a little higher and was diving down on this second Hun and about to fire when I saw the German plane go up in flames and crash to earth. "Doug" had sent his Hun plane down one minute after I had shot down mine.

Mind you, the flight took place only 300 meters up. In full view of all on the ground and in the nearby town, and it took place directly above our aviation field. Furthermore, mine dropped about 100 yards to the right and "Doug's" 100 yards to the left of our field.

These are remarkable facts, for one of our Majors, who, with the French army since 1915, has shot down seventeen machines, never had one land in France—and here we go, right off the bat and stage a fight over our aerodrome and bring down two Huns right on it. It was an opportunity of a lifetime—a great chance.

When we landed only our respective mechanics were left in the "drome" to help us out of our flying clothes. The whole camp was pouring out, flying by on foot, bicycles, aide cars, automobiles; soldiers, women, children, Majors, Colonels. French and American all poured out of the city. In ten minutes several thousand people must have gathered. "Doug" and I congratulated each other, and my mechanic, no longer military, jumping up and down, waving his hat, pounded me on the back instead of saluting and yelled: "Damn it! That's the stuff, old kid!" Then Campbell and I rushed to our respective Hun wrecks.

Prisoner is Amazed

On the way there—it was only half a mile—I ran into a huge crowd of soldiers—blue and khaki—pressing about one man. I pushed my way through the crowd and heard somebody triumphantly say to the surrounded man in French: "There he is; now you will believe he is an American." I looked at the man—a scrawny, poorly clad little devil, dressed in a rotten German uniform. It was the Hun pilot of the machine I had shot down.

Needless to say, I felt rather haughty to come face to face with my victim, now a prisoner, but did not know what to say. It seems he would not believe that an American officer had brought him down.

He looked me all over and then asked me in good French if I was an American. When I answered "Yes," he had no more to say.

There was a huge crowd around the wrecked plane, and the first man I ran into was our Major—the commanding officer—and he was the happiest man in the world outside of me and "Doug." A French and an American General blew up in a limousine to congratulate us—Colonels, Majors, all the pilots, all the French officers, mechanics—everybody in the town and camp. All had seen the fight.

One woman, an innkeeper, told me she could sleep well from now on and held up her baby for me to kiss. I looked at the baby, and then felt grateful to my Major, who pulled me away in the nick of time. I had my mechanics take off everything available—the machine was a wreck—and I got some splendid souvenirs. The big black German crosses from the wings, his rudders, pieces of canvas with holes from my bullets, in them, all his spark plugs, his magnets, his mirror, clock, compass, altimeter, his clumsy signal revolver, &c. It is a great collection.

"Doug" had set his Hun machine on fire at 300 meters and it had fallen in flames, rolling over three times and then completely burning up. There remained but a charred wreckage, like the sacrifice of some huge animal. The Hun pilot had been thrown out and was badly off. His face, hands, feet, nostrils and lungs were all burned, while one leg was broken. He is now in hospital and my Boche probably is commencing his job of ditch digging for the rest of the war.

They got much valuable information from my man—the other couldn't speak. He was a Pole, said he was not an officer because he was a Pole, although he had been an "aspirant" and a pilot at the front for two years. He said to me with a sort of sigh of relief, throwing up his hands at the same time, "Alors, la guerro est fini pour moi!" (The war is finished for me!)

That afternoon my wrecked Hun plane and the charred result of "Doug's" good work were exhibited in the public square of the town, surrounded by an armed guard and overlooked by a French military band. It was a great day for the townspeople and has had a good moral effect. You can imagine it when you realize it took place above their rooftops at only 300 meters and that they were able to see the whole fight. The Americans are indeed welcome in the town now, and "Doug" and I can buy almost anything half price.

An amusing incident was this: the flight was so near to the earth that bullets were flying dangerously all about the ground. No one was hurt save a French worker in the field, who received a hole through one ear from one of my bullets and is very proud of it.

Top U.S. Ace Killed

"Lufbery jumped from his flaming machine when 800 yards above the ground."

Associated Press
"Lufbery Killed by Leap from Flaming Plane"
New York Tribune, May 28, 1918

With the American Army in France, Sunday, May 19. Major Raoul Lufbery,[12] who had been regarded as the best aviator in the American service, was shot down in flames and killed this morning by a big German triplane which he was attacking. Lufbery jumped from his flaming machine when 800 yards above the ground. He had seventeen victories to his credit.

It was about ten o'clock this morning when a German triplane suddenly descended from the clouds, apparently because of engine trouble, until it was only some 1,500 metres over the city of Toul. The American flyers were on the alert and some of them headed for the fighting line to await the enemy on his return.

Lufbery and the pilot of another machine made after the German, who quickly ran away from the direction of the line, the two American machines following him. Eight miles away from the enemy's line Lufbery was seen to attack from under the tail, but then he drew off, as if his machine gun had jammed. Two minutes later he attacked again from the same position, and almost immediately his machine burst into flame.

---

12. Like some other American pilots, Lufbery served in both the French Air Force and the U.S. Army Air Service. With sixteen air victories while flying with the French, he was already a legend when he joined the U.S. air unit. He used that experience to train American pilots.

Renowned air ace Raoul Lufbery was born of a French mother and an American father. Beginning in 1914, he flew in the French Air Force, then in 1916 transferred to the Lafayette Escadrille, the group of Americans flying for the French. In late 1917, he joined the United States Army Air Service. He is credited with seventeen air victories. *Source:* Prints and Photographs Division, Library of Congress, LC-USZ62-101970.

Body Falls in Flower Garden

The Americans on the ground and hundreds of French men and women going to church along the country roads were horror-stricken as they saw the airplane, like a ball of fire, plunging earthward. Suddenly they saw the form of a man leap from the machine.[13]

Lufbery's body fell in a little flower garden, while his airplane, still burning, dropped to the ground 400 yards away. By the time the first Americans had reached the spot the body of the famous flier had been taken by the French to the little city hall, where it was covered with the French tri-color and great piles of roses and wild flowers.

The German machine which brought Lufbery down, which was armed with two machine guns with an operator for each piece, apparently escaped.

Lufbery's only wound, aside from those received when he fell to earth, was a bullet hole through the thumb. Apparently the same bullet punctured one of the gasoline tanks of his machine.

The German machine was under heavy anti-aircraft fire several times both before and after the air fight, and one explosion of a shell upset the enemy plane, but it managed to straighten out again.

Major Lufbery was known throughout the American army and in the French air service as "Luff" and was one of the most popular flyers on the front. He was a daring aviator, but noted for his coolness as well as his dash.

Cuts Short His Leave

Lufbery had just returned from visiting his godmother at Brest. His sister lives there also.

Lufbery came back from Brest before his leave had expired because he thought his help was needed and had made three flights since his return in his Nieuport pursuit machine before his fatal flight. He had been engaged in writing a record of his life since he became an aviator for some little time previous to his death.

Lufbery never missed an opportunity to attack an enemy machine, frequently taking desperate chances to add to his victories.

13. A subsequent investigation determined that Lufbery was thrown from the plane rather than jumped. His plane flipped over in flight. Lufbery, who had unfastened his seat belt so he could clear his jammed machine gun, was thrown from the plane.

It was only yesterday that Lufbery remarked jokingly:

"You fellows can't get all the easy pickings. I heard how you were knocking them down and decided to hurry back and get some myself. Let 'em all come, the more the merrier."

The air service has lost more than a crack aviator in Lufbery. It has lost a first class instructor of young airmen just coming to the front who looked to him for pointers on the little tricks of the trade which in the pinch may mean life or death to an aviator.

A Day at an American Airfield

"He had torn off the German's rudder, and the German went spinning to destruction beneath him."

George Seldes
"Modern Knights Who Ride to Battle in the Air"
The Sunday Star (Washington, DC), July 21, 1918

An American battle plane base, France. July 11, 1918.[14]

For our fighting aviators, the fighting day begins at 4 o'clock. Promptly the orderly came into the room and touched the two sleeping lieutenants. They yawned, dressed and went out.

"Hate to make the supreme sacrifice so early in the morning," said one.

"What's the use of getting a boche now, when there's nobody awake to credit you with it," said the other.

So they both laughed and started for the hangars.

Ten minutes later there was a roar of motors and a whistling of wings. The grass on the aviation field was tossed about like the waters of a lake in a hurricane. Stray things flew out in the wake. The planes sped along the earth their allotted distance, rose, circled for altitude, and away to the north.

There was no more sleep for me. I got up and went to the field to wait for the return of my roommates. Thanks to the invitation of Lieut. J-----, whom I had known in New York city. I had been

---

14. Feature articles, such as this one, which were not time sensitive, were typically mailed back to the newspaper rather than cabled, which would have been too expensive. That explains the ten-day difference between the dateline and the publication date. With magazine articles, the time delay could be several months.

invited to spend a week with this fighting unit, and although 4:30 is an unearthly hour for the beginning of the day's work, it was my purpose to record here, with neither additions nor subtractions, multiplications nor divisions, what happened on a real day in the real history of one of our real aviation squadrons. So 4:30 it was.

In one of the hangars the flight recorder, a lad from San Francisco, having noted the accent, was holding a conversation with a mechanic who once worked on Grant boulevard, Pittsburgh, on the one eternal subject the pride of resistance, and the other early risers were tinkering with the planes within the shed.

It was yet too early for the clouds to sculpture themselves, vast and brilliant, on the indefinable heavens. For a little while peace and light mist enclosed us. Then, from the north, the sound of a gun, followed rapidly by a series of three sounds and then the noise of barrage. The mist and the sky were perforated in a straight line. Gigantic black bubbles seemed to be bursting.

"German Archies,"[15] said the recorder; "our aviators have crossed their line."

At 6 o'clock, with the day clearing, we heard the droning of motors, two of a flock of crows which never flap their wings, came over our field, one circled, made a "renversement," or turn on his wing, and landed. His mate followed a minute later. Both "taxicabbed" from the landing spot to the hangar, got out, removed their leather helmets, fur coats and electrically heated shoes, picked up their canes, adjusted their overseas caps, said "breakfast," rubbed their hands together and started for the mess hall.

"See anything?" asked the flight recorder.

"Fritz[16] never gets up this early," was the disappointing reply.

At 6:30 two aviators appeared and their machines were tuned up for them. One was Lieut. Eddie Rickenbacker,[17] who once raced an auto, and the other my host. On Rickenbacker's wing he had pasted a liberty loan poster. My host explained it to me.

---

15. "Archie" was a colloquial name for anti-aircraft fire, which would burst against the sky like "black bubbles."

16. "Fritz" was another of the common names used for German soldiers/flyers. It did not carry the same derogatory tone as either "boche" or "Hun."

17. Rickenbacker already had six air victories by the time this article appeared, making him an ace.

"You see," he said. '"Eddie gets up there in the air and looks down on his wing. He sees the poster and reads: 'Fight or buy liberty loan.' Well, he looks around, and he can't buy any liberty loan up there, so he puts his hand on the machine gun and just fights."

At 7 o'clock the recorder's telephone rang. Book in one hand and glasses in the other, he came from the hangar to where two more aviators were sitting in the shadow of the tent and announced:

"Three Albatross—forty-two Bingvillers—going south." Forty-two was altitude in hundred of meters, Bingvillers the town. The two aviators sprang into their clothes. Six Signal Corps mechanicians had their two machines ready the same moment. Then New York and Elgin, San Francisco and Altoona and Pumpkin Center, U.S.A., engaged in the following conversation:

"Essence, s'il vous plait," from the aviator.

"Essence," replied the mechanic at the propeller, and the gasoline ran down.

"Contact," from the aviator.

"Contact," from the mechanic.

Then, round went the propeller, the aviator made his tests and a wave of the hand was the signal to remove the wooden blocks placed under the landing wheels.

And, if the motor missed, the conversation would be extended into:

"Coupe l'essence, s'il vous plait."

"Coupe."

All of which is simply the French style for "switch on" and "switch off." It was explained that in aviation the French terms were always used because they are so precise that no mistake can be made. And, besides, the men like it.

At 7:45 there was a greater thrill. A plane was circling our field, and as it came lower, it did not shut off its motor, but began landing with the propeller whirling its best. Neither did it flatten out, but as it came within good eyesight we saw its left upper wing, the canvas torn in strips, some of it flapping behind, the wing itself bent and broken. Mechanics, the recorder, the officers on the field rushed out of the hangar, ran from their magazines and letters and work places, stopped on the edge of the field, and, with strained eyes and short breath and quickened beatings of the heart, awaited the landing.

"Number Xteen—it's Rickenbacker," the recorder whispered.

Still flying chiefly on its right wing, the plane made the last circle and, motor still roaring, dipped into the field. It seemed inevitable that the right wing would catch the earth and the plane would crash.

But Rickenbacker knew his plane. Although he had only 40 per cent of his canvas on his left wing, he did straighten out just before the landing gear hit, shut off the motor which alone had saved him, rolled fully across the field and stopped without so much as a heavy bump on the rolling ground. When the mechanics helped him from the bus, the sweat was pouring from his face and he could hardly speak. After a while he told us.

He had collided with a German aeroplane. He had attacked three, and was shooting one down, but a second got over him and was diving at him when he noticed his danger. He dived immediately, but a fraction of a second too late. The planes crashed. Rickenbacker's left wing had a strip eight inches wide torn off, one crosspiece in the wing torn off, three broken and the canvas ripped. But he had torn off the German's rudder, and the German went spinning to destruction beneath him. He himself fell 4,500 feet, straightened out, and, relying on his right wing carrying through with his motor on full, he started for home.

The rest of his day was a series of congratulations.

At 8:15 the telephone announced that Maj. X. would send a biplane photographing machine out in ten minutes to take photos behind the German lines and wanted two "chasse"—battleplane—protectors.

At 8:25 a large machine circled the field and fired a colored rocket, which hung in the air a minute amid a deep purple smoke cloud. Two of our squadron who had prepared, arose, circled for altitude, and, taking their places on the flanks, the formation went north.

"Wonder where Jay is?" said Rickenbacker, meaning my host. "We got separated over the forest of Y-----."

"Probably calling on friends," someone answered.

In the intervals between our own starts and landings, goings and comings, "alarums and excursions," other squadrons near and far away were sending up their men, and they flew over us, low and high, so that there was never a period of ten minutes of the day without citizenship in the world overhead.

At 9 o'clock one of the planes commonly termed "flying battleships" made a quiet landing on our field, and pilot and observer got out. On the fuselage of this warrior the American flag was painted boldly and its wings bore the red, blue and white centered cocarde. That, too, is American, for the British and French having preceded us into the war and their colors being red, white and blue also, we have had to make a change in the order of the colors in our rosette.

The newcomer came from an observation unit and his mission was "reglage," or spotting for the infantry. He was equipped with a wireless, a Vickers machine gun above his propeller and two Lewis machine guns over the rear seat. The pilot and observer had a little talk with two of our fighters and a few minutes later three planes went out over the battlefield to help our batteries in registering on the German positions.

A little while later we saw the puffs of German shrapnel again and knew our work was under way.

At 9:45 the three chase planes returned, our men landed and the observer went home. A few minutes later we saw a machine fall in the distance.

My host had left the field at 6:30. At 9:45 it was apparent that I was not the only worried man on the field. When a motor cyclist appeared with a rumor that a plane of the type our squadron flies had been brought down in flames, an era of anxiety began for us.

At 10:20 our intelligence department brought definite word that Lieut. B----- had been in battle with the Germans. He had been wounded severely, but had succeeded in getting back to our lines. When near our field he had fainted from loss of blood and his machine had fallen a short distance, causing additional injuries. An ambulance company had extricated him from the broken plane and he was in hospital.

Still no news from Lieut. J-----.

At 10:25 several of our planes escort two photographing biplanes.

10:30—Alert sounded. Two of our planes go up.

11:10—With several of our machines engaged in various missions, the telephone announced six Albatross at 6,000 meters at W-----.

11:11—Again the recorder received a report from a post a mile away from W----- announcing four Albatross.

"Four low. Two high, for protection. Let's go," said the commandant of the squadron.

Five planes went up. A minute later the protecting planes of the photographic mission returned. Five minutes later the two which answered the 10:30 alert arrived. One aviator had seen nothing; the other reported an encounter.

"Got on the tail of a couple of Albatross" he said, "but the birds fled before I was near enough to shoot. I went after the tail and they got four more damned birds to help them, two high ones and two low ones, and they got after me. I got in five shots when my machine gun stuck, and, believe me, I beat it for home."

The recorder asked the direction. It was W-----. "The major ought to have some good pickings," the recorder observed and the aviator agreed.

Our number at the noon mess was very small and the talk was largely speculation. But speculation turned into narration as by twos and singly the missing men came in, some with tales of encounters, all with something to say. As more men arrived, those who had eaten went to the field to relieve the aviators on duty, and soon everyone was accounted for but Lieut. J-----. We talked about him. We also talked about Capt. James Norman Hall, missing for many days, and but recently cited by Gen. ----- of the French army as "dying gloriously in combat with four German monoplane machines."

"Jimmy isn't dead. He isn't dead. I haven't any proof, but I feel it," Hall's pal, Capt. M----- said. Just as he had said every day since Hall's disappearance.

The major came in, followed by four who took the air with him when the six Albatross were signaled. To the upturned faces that questioned plainly "did you get anything?" he replied:

"They went back to Germany the minute we got one shot at them. They won't stand up and fight unless they have two guns to our one."

The major took his place at the head of the table. His four companions sat down.

"The major did knock a boche out," one of them said. "Force him into a vrille[18] after giving him about thirty shots, but the duck straightened out near the ground and the six of them beat it."

At 1:15 went up to protect an artillery regelage biplane.[19]

At 1:20 an alert took Capt. D.M.K. Peterson out for a chase after a German biplane.

---

18. An aerial maneuver in which the pilot makes a nose-first spinning descent.
19. An airplane that identifies targets for the artillery.

At 2:10 a double-motored biplane belonging to an allied squadron which had a base many miles away, began descending on our field and as is usual when visitors arrive via air, everyone stood up to give them welcome.

The biplane made what seemed a perfect landing, but no sooner had the wheels touched the ground than the tail came down heavily and the landing wheels, at the next unfortunate moment, went into a gully. The tail of the plane then slowly but seemingly with irresistible force, poked itself upright, and as the machine came to rest the tail made the complete turn over and the pilot and observer were pinned under the bus.

From every hangar the mechanicians rushed forward.

"Six men, six men," shouted the major, who was at our hangar, as he took charge.

Six men of those who had started running continued. From the edge of the field we could make out an arm or leg moving under the overturned plane. I do not know what the men about me felt, but I know that I missed several heart beats when the accident occurred, and that I had that indescribable sensation of witnessing violent death, when-----.

"There they go," said an officer at my side, "feet over appetite, as usual."

And the major and the lieutenants and everyone except myself laughed.

"Don't look like a mourner at a funeral," the lieutenant then said to me. "This is happening every day. About the worst they've done is smashed their propeller and probably broken a wing."

And sure enough, as our men lifted the plane, the pilot and observer untied their safety belts and crawled unscathed into the field.

At 2:12 Capt. Peterson landed and reported to the recorder that the German biplane which had probably attempted to photograph our front had decided to return to Germany when he approached.

"Anything heard from J----- yet?" he asked.

Every man who went up in the next hour asked the same question on returning. I was no longer the only worried man on the field.

At 3 o'clock the clean blue sky was cut with a silver roulette. In formation which told of magnificent strength that showed not only power but majesty and beauty, twelve great planes went by more than a mile above us, and the golden sun in their wings.

The commandant of our squadron stood up and recognized them, and with a wave of his hand in their direction, he said, with enthusiasm and solemnity:

"Go to it, little old England, go to it."

That evening a British aviator visited us with the news. The formation had divided into sixes. One group had bombed the works and the bridge of a Rhine city, the other had done likewise to Cologne, and it was the "broadest broad daylight of the year," he said. Several German machines of the scores which attacked them were destroyed. The British had no losses of machines, and the only casualty was the wounding of one of the gunners.

Our men could not say enough in praise of the British air service.

At 3:15 the telephone in the hangar carried the voice of Lieut. J-----. It brought relief to us all. My host, having separated from Lieut. Rickenbacker, had found a German Rumpler on our side of the line. They attacked each other, played for position, exchanged shots for a while and when Lieut. J----- got two or three bullets through the wings of his adversary Rumpler fled.

But he did not cross the line. He flew over it many miles, and Gude, in his desire to complete his attack, followed. Finally Rumpler crossed into Germany, and with his gasoline gone, Gude was forced to land. He came down on a French farm, close to the line, and had to walk many miles to a village which possessed a telephone.

A 5:25, despite the imminence of the dinner hour, Capt. Peterson went out for a "joy ride"—meaning that he went for a trip over the German line unaccompanied and with no definite object in view except shooting down such sundry Germans as he might encounter.

Peterson is a new American flier. In his manners and methods, from what I saw of him in a week spent with the squadron and from what his companions say, he is surely of the Lufbery type. He has the same quiet smile. He has the same alert eyes. He is the same modest, the quiet-spoken, quick and strong young man.

Pennsylvanians should remember Capt. Peterson well. He is a native son in every sense, for he was born and spent most of his life in that state. Let Honesdale, Pa., be proud of him. Scranton, the nearest large city, should honor him, too. He knows Philadelphia well, for he was in the metropolis for many years, and before he became an aviator he spent some time working for the Gillespies on Neville Island, Pittsburgh, and has many friends in the city of hills and steel.

Peterson fights by himself. As a patrol leader they say he had no equal. Like Lufbery, he is of the type that does not make friends easily, but when he does it is real friendship. He is a commander that not only gives his men confidence, but inspires them.

At 6 we had dinner.

At 7:15, coming back to the field, we stopped on the path to let a plane land. The aviator who got out of it gave his flying clothes to a helper, said a few words to the recorder, and came toward us. It was Capt. Peterson.

"Anything left to eat?" he asked.

"Raisin pie," someone said.

"See anything?" another asked.

"Had a little fight," he answered and went on.

At 7:35 a French balloon observer gave us official confirmation. He had seen one of our men attack two German biplanes, and one of the big machines crashed, four miles behind the German lines.

It was Capt. Peterson's fifth victory. He had become an ace.

At 7:45 two men made an evening patrol.

At 8 o'clock Lieut. J----- got out his cigar box violin and someone played the piano in the assembly room. Several of the men in their pajamas, including my two roommates, who had the 4:30 trick that morning, went across to the barracks for a shower.

At 9 everyone had retired, some to read a bit or write a letter, others to rest for the next morning's work.

At a little after 10 we heard loud and many motors. We went outside. Above, but low, and with lights burning, to signal us, groups of planes were flying toward Germany.

"There go those British raiders again," said the major. "Gad, I wish I was with them."

At 10 we went to bed.

And so ended the flying day. I have tried to picture it faithfully, but in this game no two days are alike, and the story of yesterday may have been sadder and tomorrow may bring us greater victories. Ultimately, our flying men hope to help win the victory that America wants, for their way in the air is the way of the American eagle.

Rickenbacker Duels in the Sky

"The gun fired two shots and jammed. There was nothing to do
but zoom off home."

Eddie Rickenbacker[20]
"Gab of the Gimper; Speed King of the Air"
The Daily Gate City (Keokuk, IA), August 9, 1918

With the American airmen in France, July 10—(By mail.)—
"There's a certain German airman I'd like to meet after the war, if
he lives and I do," said Lieut. Eddie Rickenbacker, American ace
and former auto racer.

"If we meet in the states, I'll buy him an ice cream soda and if it's
in Germany, I'll expect him to buy us both beers. He flies number
16 in a certain German squadron. His machine is an observing and
fighting type combined. For a German, he is an exceptional sport.
We had four days successive rendezvous together without result
and it was real fighting all the time.

"The first morning I hopped into the can and went up to a pink
tea, looking for anything in general and nothing in particular. I soon
spotted number 16 and he spotted me. We jockeyed for position,
both of us trying to get the blind spot in front of the sun.

"Finally I got under his tail, after half an hour of maneuvering
this way and that, and let him have it. The gun fired two shots and
jammed. There was nothing to do but zoom off home, which I did.

"Next morning I went up at the same hour over the same spot.

"There was Heinie[21] number 16, escorted by two German
fighting planes. He was higher than them, but I was higher than
they, so I jockeyed for position. Again the gun jammed, and I fell
into a vrille to get out of his range.

"When I zoomed away, I got the gun working again, and again
jockeyed for position with Heinie, whose two fighters had been
driven off by other Americans by now. He began shooting out of
his belly at me and I zigzagged to dodge his bullets, which were
whizzing by me.

20. When Rickenbacker wrote this article in August 1918, he was already an ace, but
had only six victories to his credit. When the war ended three months later, he would be
America's top ace, with twenty-six victories.
21. Yet another slang name for a German fighter.

Eddie Rickenbacker, with 26 aerial victories, was America's most successful fighter ace during the war. *Source:* National Museum of the U.S. Air Force.

"Then we began playing around and kept it up for three-quarters of an hour, each trying to get a bead on the other. Finally I got in the blind spot and started down on him. Again my gun jammed and of course he had the edge on me.

"Instead of running, which would have been more dangerous, since he had the altitude after I dived past him, I again jockeyed for position, though I knew my gun wouldn't shoot. I wanted to fox him and make him think I was still in the fight.

"It worked, for after a few minutes more of maneuvering, he decided it was enough for the day, since neither of us could get position. So he fired two shots wild as a good-bye, waved his hand, and went home. It was a good thing for me, because my motor went cuckoo a minute later and I struggled home on a glide, barely making it over the lines.

"The boys had seen me come down and my mechanics were beginning to figure their Eskimo wasn't coming back, when I finally got in, travelling most of the way in an ambulance.

"Next morning I had to borrow a plane, since mine wasn't repaired yet. I went out looking for Heinie Number 16. He was there at the given spot, but very, very high. I maneuvered for all I was worth, but couldn't make my plane reach him. It was out of the question for I had one with two guns and the weight kept it down.

"Heinie had an exceptionally good plane and I saw him directly above me, several times. But he didn't shoot—that is, with his gun. I saw him take a picture of me with his camera, and finally he went off while I tried to get position close enough to shoot.

"Next morning I again borrowed a machine and went after him with two guns. He was there, taking pictures. We began maneuvering for position and finally I got it and let him have it. Then one gun jammed. Before I could get a bead on him with the other, he was letting me have it. I vrilled and came back at him still higher.

"Finally both our guns jammed, and both of us knew the other couldn't shoot, though we tried to repair the guns. But no luck. So we wobbled each other goodbye with our flappers and both departed. Next day I was sent away for a few days and the boys said Heinie Number 16 wasn't there either. Some day we'll settle it, and a lot of bets that were placed on us by the mechanics."

Chapter 7

✦

✦

✦

✦

✦

In the Trenches

Introduction

L ong before America entered the war, trench warfare had
become symbolic of the murderous futility of fighting on
the Western Front. It had populated the language with
phrases resonant of death and suffering, such as "over the top,"
"no man's land," "trench fever," and "trench raid." It gave rise to a
new class of weapons designed for close fighting, such as the hand
grenade, trench mortar, trench knife, flame thrower, and poison
gas. And it all played out on a shell-blasted landscape of mud,
corpses, barbed wire, snipers, and vermin.

When America sent its own sons into this lethal environment,
the public was understandably anxious to know how they fared.
Veteran reporter Herbert Corey was on the spot. He had been
covering the war since 1914 and covering the AEF since July 1917.
It was said of Corey that "he can take an incident that the ordinary
person would hardly notice and make a column story out of it that
clergymen will read from pulpits." Corey's account of a night-time
patrol into No Man's Land—that deadly, free-fire kill zone between
the opposing trenches—introduced readers to one horrifying form
of trench warfare.

During February and March 1918, while doughboys in the
trenches were still a novelty for readers, many American

correspondents visited the front lines to report on what the boys were experiencing. In his feature article for *Collier's Weekly*, James Hopper paints an evocative picture of his night-time visit to the American trenches. As he moves progressively deeper into the trench system, he passes destroyed villages, learns to use a gas mask, tromps through flooded shell craters, catches the spectral flash and boom of distant artillery, and hears the crackle of machine gun fire. Until he finally comes upon that solitary, young soldier keeping lonely vigil in the most forward of the trenches. Hopper sees him as the "guard over humanity's spiritual treasures, over Beauty and Kindness menaced by Ugliness and Insane Cruelty."

Martin Green provides a more light-hearted report on one of the trench tricks learned by American fighters. His article "Eight Months at the Front With the American Army," shows that American fighters were slowly becoming veterans by applying some inventiveness to the challenge of trench warfare.

Americans Get Their Piece of the Line

"Boys become men overnight in battle."

Herbert Corey
"Uncle Sam's Boys Take Up Trench Life"
Evening Star (Washington, DC), March 6, 1918

With the American army, January 20—Today there is an American "front" in France in the war against Germany.

Not much of a front, perhaps. Only a pin point on the 500-mile long line[1] the allies hold in the west. The troops engaged are but a handful compared even to the army of Belgium, which has been four years at war. Serbia was stamped out in the first year, but Serbia has more men fighting on the hills of Macedonia than the United States has in France after being ten months at war. Nevertheless we have a front. We are in line at last.

Because this is to be a story of a day which will be remembered in American history, I propose to write it without flapdoodle and

---

1. The Western Front ran from the Swiss border to the North Sea, a length often given as 440 miles.

flag waving, if I can. It would be an easy matter to write it in Fourth of July style.[2] It may not be so easy to tell the plain story of events, and yet make plain through all that story the pride I felt in the youngsters who went into the trenches yesterday.

Started Trench Training in October

It is impossible to indicate upon what point in the French line the American troops have been stationed. Because it seems to me that a recent statement by Mr. Secretary of War Baker[3] to the effect that "we have a fighting army in France," may be misconstrued in the United States as it has been in France. I wish to make this preliminary statement:

In October a small detachment of American troops was sent into the French trenches to be trained in trench warfare.

The Germans raided their trenches. There is no evidence that they knew they were raiding American trenches. The affair was one of the petty attacks that take place every night on some point of the front.

Shortly afterward the Americans were withdrawn from the trenches. Approximately two months passed, during which no Americans were in the trenches at any point on the front. An American engineer regiment worked with the British and during this period was caught in the German attack at the Cambrai[4] break through.

Other American engineer regiments have been with the French in the Verdun sector and have been more or less constantly under fire there.

But none of our soldiers were in the trenches until last night. They moved in about 6 o'clock, relieving some French colonial troops.

U.S. Unit Under French Orders

To be technically accurate, the United States has not even yet a "front" of its own in France. The men who are in line now make

2. No need to resort to exaggerated images of patriotism, when the reality of the men in the trenches is real patriotism.
3. As Secretary of War, Newton D. Baker presided over the U.S. army's involvement in World War I.
4. The Battle of Cambrai, November 20–December 7, 1917.

U. S. INFANTRY & MACHINE GUN MEN ASSIGNED IN TRENCHES ©C.P.I.   4606

American infantry and machine gunners in the trenches, under the supervision of a French soldier, visible in the background. *Source:* George Grantham Bain Collection, Prints and Photographs Division, Library of Congress, LC-B2-4606-12.

part of a French army. Although they are under the immediate command of their own officers, the unit is subject to the orders of the general of the French army.

The British army made its entrance in trench warfare in France under similar conditions. After the retreat from Mons,[5] in which so large a part of the British professional army was wiped out, a new army was hastily thrown together to aid the French to hold the line.

This formed a part of a French army for a time, in that it was under the command of a French general. The arrangement was only a temporary one, however. As soon as the British were able to send enough men to France to create an independent army a separate command was set up. Precisely the same thing will be done with the American forces.

5. The first major action by the British Expeditionary Force, August 23, 1914.

For the time being the liaison between the French and the American forces will be very close. When the men went into the trenches last night they found French officers waiting for them.

Officers to Guide Newcomers

Each French company which was relieved left behind one commissioned and two non-commissioned officers to guide the newcomers.

This is usual when troops who are new to the sector are sent in "en relieve." The officers who wait behind inform the new arrivals on the peculiarities of the enemy opposite and of the terrain. Sometimes the German troops may be Bavarians, who have a liking for storming at night.

Sometimes they are Prussians, the stiffest and hardest fighting men in the German army, but so thoroughly disciplined that initiative has been crushed out of them. If they begin a charge they may be depended on to carry out that charge to the bitter end. But if a new trick can be played upon them it breaks them up. They are especially helpless if their officers are shot down.

The officers left behind are there to instruct the incomers on the kinks of the no man's land, which lies between the two lines of wire. One sees almost nothing through the periscope during the first day of watching under such conditions. Lanes of wire, shell holes, earth piles, perhaps bodies—in the distance the brown line of enemy trenches.

Learning "No Man's Land"

The second day the watcher sees more, and with each succeeding day vision is granted to him. His memory becomes photographic. If the leg of the particularly unpleasant corpse ten feet to the right of the shell hole near the "dud" shell seems to have changed position during the night investigation is made. Perhaps the corpse is now the camouflaged shelter of a sniper or of a close-up observer. The watcher becomes familiar with the very blades of grass in his field of vision. That is why men are kept in the front-line trenches ten or twelve days sometimes—until physical weariness forces their withdrawal. They have become specialists on forty feet of uptorn ground.

The company officers will remain with the Americans but a day or two. By that time the strangers may be supposed to have become sufficiently familiar with no man's land to do their own watching. The case is different with the artillery. French observers and gunner officers will remain with the American guns for at least a week, and perhaps two.

Enemy Known as "Jerry"

The same reason may be assigned, however. The Americans, moving into a new sector, are not familiar with the ranges and marks, although several of their officers have been studying the ground for days past. The French officers will wait until their new aids have become tolerably well acquainted with the best way to drop shells on Jerry.

"Fritzie" is passe, by the way. No well informed soldier ever speaks of the enemy as "Fritzie." Jerry is his name today.[6]

The Americans are solely responsible for their sector, both for the trench-holding and the artillery. They have been told how to do it by the French, and if there are better soldiers than the French they have not been developed in this war. War cannot be taught by slate and book, however. No doubt the Americans will make mistakes and mistakes are paid for in blood. All the other armies have made mistakes.

But an education is quickly gained under such conditions. If there is "liveliness" on the American front, the boys I saw march toward the trenches yesterday will be veterans long before this story is read. Boys become men overnight in battle. On the streets of French towns one sees mere striplings—their rosy cheeks hardly stained by the first fuzzy beard of adolescence—who are yet matured men. Courage and competence radiate from them.

A Fight in No Man's Land

"Germans began to yell and throw bombs."

Herbert Corey
"Meet the Tactics of Boche Veterans"
Evening Star (Washington, DC), March 26, 1918

---

6. More of the many names given to German soldiers: Huns, Boche, Fritz, Heinie, Jerry.

With the American army of the field. February 1—When the last fight "on the wire" ended the Americans were still "taking it to" the Germans who had ambushed them.

The fact is the single one of significance, as it seems to me, in the story of this little battle at night. The fight itself was of no importance, as fighting goes in this war. Such tiny affairs are of nightly occurrence on the 500 miles of western front. Only twenty men were engaged on the American side, against an unknown but much larger number of Germans. Half the Americans were killed or wounded and the wounded were taken prisoners. But the Yankees were on their toes.

In Fight With Veterans

In reading the tale of the fight on the wire it must be remembered that the Americans were all greenhorns at war and the Germans were veterans. The division which opposes the American sector in the Vosges[7] came not very long ago from the testing fires of Verdun.[8] They had been well banged up there, according to the information at hand, but that only made them better soldiers. It may be admitted that they are not the Huns of 1914. The universal comment in the west is that the physical material of the Germans has deteriorated in almost four years of fighting.

"The boches we fought in 1914 were he-men," was the recent comment of an officer who has fought through the war. "The boche of today is a runt. He likes to kill, but he hates like thunder to stand up and fight."

The Americans were just the same clean-limbed, clean-minded youngsters who may be seen today on the streets of any American city.[9] They are not a meek and namby-pamby lot, but they are not quarrelsome. They have been hardened and toughened physically by the hard training of the last few months, but they have not yet been made into warriors. They do not yet know the technique of fighting. The use of the fist is more natural to them than that of the bayonet. They have yet to learn that instinctive use of arms that is natural to the skilled fighter.

---

7. A range of low mountains in eastern France, near the border with Germany.
8. The epic Battle of Verdun ran from February to December 1916, with an estimated 700,000 casualties.
9. Many news articles characterized the American troops with positive comments about their character or appearance.

Into "No Man's Land"

"I wish I was in front of the cigar store back home," they probably whispered to one another when they crawled over the trench parapet that night to go on patrol.

"No Man's Land" is perhaps 300 yards wide at the point where the fight took place. The opposing trenches are guarded by wide belts of wire and between these belts is an open space, muddy, mucky, incredibly dark on a moonless night. The chill of the Vosges is a different cold from that we are used to in America. It goes straight to the bone through the warmest wool and is moist and foggy. On clear, moonlit nights "no man's land" is never patrolled. The enemy would cut a patrolling party to bits with their machine guns. On dark nights constant watchfulness is needed. Otherwise a raiding party might bomb a trench section and get away clear.

Officer Goes First

The officer in command went first, of course. That is a point of honor. Back of him crawled the twenty men of his patrol, one after another, trying their best to be silent. At such moments the slightest sound is magnified by the strained nerves. Once an officer leading such a party ran head-on into the barbed wire entanglements. Ten minutes afterward the patrolling party re-entered its trenches. The officer was called on to explain:

"Holy mackerel!" he said, astonished. "Didn't you hear that tin hat of mine when it hit the wire? It rang like a bell. It must 'a' waked every boche in a mile."

On the night of this latest fight the patrolling party had been sent out to examine the wire. The night before it was suspected that the Germans had been trying to cut it. In the hollows the men walked, half bent over, in Indian file, trying to keep even from breathing. Sometimes they crawled in the cold and gummy mud.[10] A slight drizzle had been falling and it was so dark that as they crept on no man could see the boot heels of the man ahead.

---

10. Mud was so pervasive in the trenches and on some battlefields, and mentioned so often in news articles, that it took on a character of its own, a force of nature as aggravating as the enemy, with its own dangers.

At last the officer in command stopped. The word was passed down the line:

"Silence."

He had heard—or sensed—something in the darkness. The men stopped in their tracks, crouching, the fingertips of one hand on the ground. In the other each held his rifle. There was a moment of complete silence. Then, before an order could be given by the American officer, all hell broke loose. Out in the open, away from the wire, Germans began to yell and throw bombs.[11] Some of them fired their rifles at the stooping figures shown by the flare of the first grenade. The Americans had not even had time to straighten up. The Germans had been given the order to pull the firing pins of their bombs by nudges, probably, so that no word need be spoken.

After that first burst of bombs the Germans charged.

Then the Boche Battle Cry

The Americans were undoubtedly bewildered. Their mental state must have been that of the man wakened from a sleep by the cry of "Fire!" But they reacted quickly. They stood there in the darkness, not daring to attack for fear of striking a comrade, but thrusting with their bayonets at the sound of the clumsy figures that grunted toward them through the darkness. Some of the unseen foes shouted their German battle cry. They yelled "Kamarad!"[12] They hoped, no doubt, that it might fool some chivalrous foeman into standing still to be murdered safely.

Then the Germans ran. They took with them some wounded Americans. This is known, for the men who stood elbow to elbow with them in that unseen battle line in the dark had heard their friends cry out as the steel entered them, or had seen them fall when the bombs were thrown. As the Germans hurried back toward their own lines the Americans carried along were heard

---

11. Hand grenades.

12. The word "Comrade" was used by surrendering soldiers to indicate a plea of friendship and mercy. The suggestion here is that it was used as a ploy to make an attacker fatally hesitate.

groaning. Perhaps some of the Germans had likewise been hurt in that brief scrimmage, but no one may say definitely.

School for Green Soldier

In spite of the loss of life such an affair need not be taken too tragically by the folks at home. It is by such fighting that green soldiers are made into good soldiers. The men who still live in that raiding party know the trick now and all their comrades know the trick. By and by they will be devising tricks of their own. The all-important thing is that they held their ground and they want to try it over again. Every one of the bunch wants to try it over again. He feels he is beginning to know the game.

After what was left of the patrolling party had been called in, one man—who had once been counted—was again missing. By and by he came in by himself, to explain that he had stayed out there to hunt for his bunky. His ancestors did not come over on Mayflower, but he's none the less a good American.[13]

His name is Sorenson.

A Visit to the Front-Line Trench

"A sort of dim phosphorescence was on No Man's Land."

James Hopper
"In the American Trenches"
Collier's Weekly, June 8, 1918

We went along a bit farther in the limousine. Just as a cowboy will mount his pony to go from the saloon to the post office across the street, so does the war correspondent stick to his limousine to the last extremity. It was now an automobile without horn or lights,[14]

13. This seems to be a reference to the wartime mood against "hyphenated Americans," especially to a May 31, 1916, speech by Theodore Roosevelt. "I stand for straight Americanism unconditional and unqualified, and I stand against every form of hyphenated Americanism .... If the American has the right stuff in him ... I care not a snap of my fingers whether his ancestors came over on the Mayflower, or whether he was born, or his parents were born, in Germany, Ireland, France, England, Scandinavia, Russia, Italy or any other country."

14. Vehicles traveling near the front line trenches at night did so without lights so as not to attract the attention of enemy artillery.

though, mute and blind, groping along a black road, furtive and muffled, all its insolence gone. The road was camouflaged; when our eyes had become accustomed to the darkness we could see, thanks to the vague milkiness which filtered from the moon through heavy banks of cloud, a sort of high screen to our left, made of long poles twined with twigs and leaves; and once, when we stopped to make sure of the way, my electric torch, winked for a moment, lit up a sign which said—or whispered—"Attention: l'ennemi vous voit" ("Beware: the enemy sees you"). This meant that from some observation post the German held this part of the road under his eye—my electric torch went out abruptly. We turned to the left, by the immobile shadow of a traffic policeman, looking exactly like the one at Forty-second Street and Fifth Avenue if you'll whelm that one in night and silence and helmet him mysteriously, and after a moment entered a village. The limousine stopped, and this time we left it.

"How Fast Can You Get Your Mask On?"

It was the most empty, the most silent village. We were on a wide main street; as far as we could see before us, and to the right and the left, there was not the smallest point of light, the slightest squeak of any sound—not the eyes of a cat nor the scurry of a rat. The stone houses had queer, distorted attitudes; they seemed to wring their hands and to scream voicelessly. Going up to them, we could look, through holes that had been windows, right up into the sky through holes that had been roofs; the houses were mere ghosts, the village a wraith. A chapel drew me by its apparent solidity. But it was the same. Standing in the Gothic arch of the entrance, at the head of the half-pulverized steps, and looking upward, I could see nothing but the sky—the heavy dome of cloud vaguely phosphorescent with moon—and where the altar had been there was a bush, almost as big as a tree, with one branch that looked like a witch astraddle.

We had left the machine up against a wall for shelter, and the chauffeur had vanished into the earth—into a dugout, I surmise, where he had friends (chauffeurs have friends everywhere). The limousine, now, in that tenuous village which seemed suspended in a state between life and death, looked fantastically solid and sacrilegiously out of place; but also it looked very lonesome, and it seemed wrong to leave it thus alone. We did, though; we had come to the utmost limit allowed to machines; it was afoot that we made for the other end of the village. And while in a little solid group, as incongruous as the limousine, we tramped through this unreal scenery, reality and the moment suddenly reasserted themselves. Deep somewhere in the night, something boomed heavily, followed by a clearer, nearer crash. The sound spread, was taken up and imitated; a half-lazy, half-interested artillery game began—big guns, startled for some reason or other, baying, but without much conviction. There would be dull booms, then clear, vicious cracking detonations nearer, and once in a while something traversed the sky above like an invisible rocket, with a long hiss which seemed to travel from horizon to horizon. It was as if Old Dame Slaughter, deep asleep in the middle of the night, had stirred vaguely with mutterings of a bad dream.

At the end of the street we dived into a dugout—a deep, solid little place, snug and warm, where we found the intelligence officer—a captain—who was to guide us on our onward journey. He said: "How fast can you get your gas mask on?"

I have said that you can tell if you are getting toward the front by the villages you go through and by the houses of the people you visit. You can also tell by the concern displayed toward your mask. When you leave on your trip, someone or other will say carelessly: "You'd better take a gas mask along." You take it along, and throw it at the bottom of the limousine, and forget it. At some stage of the journey someone says: "You had better string your gas mask on," and you sling it on, loosely, letting it hang upon your hip. Further on you are told to place it at the ready, and you hitch it up to its place beneath your chin. Then you get to a place where an officer says: "How fast can you get your mask on?"

I answered I had never had one on; that last time I was at the front they had not been invented.

Our intelligence officer put on an air of exaggerated horror, and said: "I'm going to give you a little lesson in putting it on." Upon which I was made to practice a while. I found the art more difficult than I thought. The mask is a rubber contrivance, with two goggles, and it covers your whole face. Once you have it on, your only communication with the outside world is through a rubber tube connected with the little reservoir, filled with filtering material soaked in neutralizing chemicals, which hangs still on your chest tightly; you take the end of the tube between your teeth and breathe through that, your nose meanwhile being closed by two little pieces of wood, connected by a spring, which pinch your nostrils together. That is, they are supposed to. But they didn't hold mine. I didn't know till then what a stubborn nose breather I am. At my first attempt the little piece of wood flew off my nose violently; I took a deep breath through my indomitable nostrils and exhausted, of course, what little air was in the mask, which immediately sucked in flat against my face. For the next breath there remained no air—I began to drown, right there in that place without water, while everybody laughed. Even then I didn't breathe in by the tube held between my teeth: I had to snatch off the mask, purple-faced. Well, the captain held me practicing till I had got the hang of the odious instrument, then said consolingly: "That mask of yours doesn't fit, anyway; it's much too small; it would let the gas through."

The Chatelain of the Castle

After which the captain took us to see his maps. These were in an old chateau nearby, one of the rooms of which he had made his office and work shop. We stood in the ruins of a garden a while, listening to the cannonade—dull boomings of heavy guns, resonant arrivals and, now and then, that long, ripping sound as though of a rocket hissing from horizon to horizon and tearing in two a sky made of paper—while in the distance, to the north, the east, and the west, flares of an incredibly violent whiteness of light rose in the darkness, hung long, then died slowly out with a few last luminous crumbs. We then entered the castle, groping blindly behind our guide across a large hall with stone flooring, our feet striking now and then resonances of huge vaults, then up a stone stairway with balustrades of marble, stepping carefully, to the words of warning of our leader, over strange voids, holes, and missing steps. Upstairs was a long corridor, along sashless windows. The captain opened a door, and we entered his domain—a large room with a Gothic fireplace at one end. It was lighted by one guttering candle, and in its poor light a young French soldier, a boy with large brown eyes and curly hair, was working, bent over a long table. As a matter of fact, he was working on a map, but he seemed to have been here forever in this old castle, toiling upon an urgent, minute, and interminable task—the chatelain of the castle, bewitched. The old place had been gutted of furnishings, but the many maps upon the wall rustled like tapestry to invisible currents of air, and small cavalcades of rats passed overhead. A battery of heavy guns nearby let loose suddenly; the whole pile rocked and shook to its deep foundations.

Following Mercury

When the intelligence officer had shown us, on his maps, to what point of the front-trench system we were going, we started on the last lap of our journey. We passed through the village again, and by our limousine, which looked very lonely and vulnerable there against its wall, and then went out into open country. To the right and the left plains spread dimly, houseless, treeless, untenanted and dead, unstirred even by whir of wing or squeak of small rodent. The melted snows, the rains, had converted them into a sea of mud, and across this sea the road went straight, narrow, and hard as a causeway, and so empty that it seemed impossible anyone could ever have traveled it. Once in a while we plumped into a shell hole, icy water above the knees; the strange half-light, passing through heavy clouds, transformed all shapes into deceitful semblances. The cannonade was gradually ceasing, and giving way to the intermittent stuttering of machine guns, and ceaselessly, now on one side, now on the other, now before us, the very lights hung themselves above the horizon, violet-white, violent, and spectral.

We came at length to the headquarters of the colonel of the regiment. This was among the stumps and vestiges of a murdered hamlet. The lower part of the one chaumière,[15] the outer skin of which still stood, had been heavily rebuilt into a low shelter of heavy beams and concrete. Just five minutes before our arrival, we found, a big shell had passed through a corner of the old roof and had fallen into what once had been the peasant's cabbage patch. We viewed the very respectable hole made in the much-fertilized soil (the shell seemed to have turned and turned in it like a dog preparing his bed), and then were invited inside.

15. Cottage.

The room, low and heavily beamed, was filled with tobacco smoke and fragrance of hot coffee; two small lamps, half smothered, threw gleams on strong faces above a rough table; the colonel and his staff were here (no one sleeps at night in the first-line positions), close to the telephones—their eyes caved in with long vigils, their clothes coated with the mud of frequent inspections. A runner was ordered for us, and when he had reported we went on again, following him.

A runner is a soldier who is used because of his instinct of direction and his knowledge of the trenches. In peaceful moments he guides staff officers on their visits through the intricacy of the narrow guts or reliefs coming in or out. But during an attack or a raid, when the telephone wires have all been cut and the rockets signal wildly, he is the last resort, the last means of communication between the front line and the commanding post, and it is he who, link in the running relay, bears urgent messages—calls for help or rigid orders—through barrage fires, through very hells of fire and destruction. The runner walking ahead of us with a long, elastic step was very young—a slim lad built on greyhound lines. The long rubber boots which he wore to the hips, the sleeveless, tight leather jerkin above, defined his athletic slenderness—and suddenly something I had sought in my mind for several hours came to me: I knew what he looked like, what so many young lads I had seen this day looked like under their small, straight-brimmed helmets. He—and they—looked like the god Mercury, Mercury of the winged feet—or, rather, like pictures and statues I had seen of him (I've never seen the real Mercury).

For a little while longer we followed the road, at first with a few stumps of destroyed houses to right and left, then with only the immensity of the spongy plain. The batteries were going back to sleep one by one—a lone boom once in a while—but the very rockets, now nearer, lighted up the whole earth at intervals with an unearthly light and our faces as well. Machine guns too were stuttering. Tat-a-tat one would say and then abruptly stop, then another Tat-a-tat-tat and another Tat-a-tat-tat-tat-tat-tat, while a last one unrolled its whole belt in sudden, frenzied decision. Then insensibly we left the road and took to a path by its side, and insensibly the path sank itself into the earth, and before we knew it the path had become a trench, a communication trench. First we were

within it up to our knees, then to our thighs, then to our necks—
and to an observer outside (but, thank the Lord, there wasn't any)
we would have looked like a line of heads solemnly sliding along
the surface of the plain. Finally our eyes too sank beneath the
level of the earth, and we proceeded narrowly imprisoned to the
right and the left, with just one opening to take, a narrow slit of
an opening, ever ahead. From the manner in which a leprous spot
of sick light, which marked the moon behind the clouds, shifted
now to the right, now to the left, we knew our way was a winding one, but most of the time our attention was entirely taken up
with the problem of merely proceeding, of following that diabolical
runner who led the way so lightly. The gut we followed had been
dug through a land soaked and re-soaked. Whenever, losing our
balance, we put out a hand against one of the walls, that hand sank
in something cold and clammy; whenever a shoulder struck, great
flakes of diluted earth fell to the bottom. That bottom was much
worse than the sides. Three-quarters of its width was taken up by
a narrow walk of slats. Sometimes this little walk was out of sight
all together beneath a two-foot layer of liquid mud. Sometimes it
was vaguely visible, humped over a bit of firmer stuff, and then one
slipped from it as from the back of a greased pig and landed with
a ploop into the drainage ditch at the side. At other times again it
was visible, but that was because it floated across a little lake. You
stepped with mistaken confidence upon the nearer end of a section
of slats, and abruptly found yourself in water to the hip, while the
whole section, uprearing, came up to the perpendicular and slapped
you in the face. Soon we were balls of mud, painfully waddling,
and every once in a while, what with the necessity for silence,
we would have to group close to control a mad fit of laughter and
keep it down, through mutual severity and exchanges of warning,
to smothered chucklings that hurt our poor ribs. And with some
stupefaction we thought: "Here we are, come from the far States
across the sea; here we are, in the midst of the greatest convulsion
of all times; here we are, in one of the foremost bastions of the
greatest war of all times—and we are laughing like fools!"

The P.C.

After a long time of this the communication trench became a fighting
trench. We dived into a hole right in its side, crawled down
a few rough steps, and found ourselves in the P.C.—the post of

commandment; in other words, the captain's dugout. The captain was sitting on the upper of the two bunks, and two of his officers were sharing the bunk with him. The reason no one was using the lower bunk was that, from its earthen wall, a thin stream of chocolate-hued water was ceaselessly dripping. The fluid collected on the floor and floated its slatting. The huge-beamed ceiling was so low one had to be bent all of the time, and between the bunks and the small table against the other wall was just man width. The whole place, filled as it was with tobacco smoke, reeked nevertheless with another and more powerful smell—that penetrating odor of deep, wet earth which is so loathsome to man because so suggestive of his last habitat.

We had coffee there, in the dugout—coffee offered by a mysterious hand which emerged from a sort of low tunnel, the beginning of some abandoned sap, in which evidently were lodged the cook, the strikers, and the kitchen. Then the captain dressed to go out with us by the simple act of leaping down from his bunk into his big rubber boots, which stood at the ready on the floor below. A captain in a trench never sleeps nor undresses at night—nor in the day, with the possible exception of a little two hours' nap. I liked that captain. He seemed very young; he looked like the captain of a football team, and he had the same simple, calm, and alert efficiency which one finds in a good captain of a good football team. But he had been now seven days in the trench, and there were lines in his face which one doesn't find in the face of the captain of a football team.

A Wedge

We went out with the captain and, winding, reached the very first-line trench. We picked up on the way the lieutenant of the platoon. *His* home was a sort of little dog niche, just wide enough for a bunk, scooped out of the wall of a short gut between the first and second trench; he rose from it like a jack-in-the-box—a tall young fellow with head shaven under the helmet. As may be seen, our excursion had been in the form of a wedge, penetrating always farther toward the boche and narrowing ever from organization to organization—from army to corps, from corps to division, from division to brigade, from brigade to regiment, from regiment to company, from company to platoon. We were now with the platoon.

Well, we visited thoroughly the bit of France held by this platoon. It was all trench, of course. In spite of the darkness, through our sense of touch and the dim ghost of light that came through the clouds, we could see that the ground was bad. We were in the water all the time now, and the trenches were shallow, hardly higher than one's head. There were places where cave-ins had occurred, and the fresh trace of shovels recently used could be seen; sometimes sacks of sand had restored a fallen wall; and there were places so narrow through slips that even as we scraped through we imagined the walls—like the walls of the torture chamber in one of Poe's fantastic tales—to be slyly approaching each other to catch us like worms. Every once in a while we stopped, and raised ourselves to a firing step, and peered over the parapet. We could see, on the level with our eyes, a few blades of frozen grass (at first we would think they were trees), then, perhaps, a little farther, the pickets of the barbed wire, then nothing—nothing at all except something we knew must be the No Man's Land, but which, soon merged in shadow, did not even seem solid, seemed vaguely to undulate like the sea.

Our Boys

And then we kept meeting our soldiers, our boys. We would come upon them singly or in little groups, motionless and wrapped in shadow. It was thrilling and strange. They came from our own land, maybe we knew some of them, maybe here was the gay grocer boy of my small town, he who before the war flitted about all day atop his delivery Ford like a swallow catching bugs—but we could not find out. They stood immobile in the dark, and silent, helmeted, booted, and jerkined, changed as though by enchantment, mysterious and grim and impenetrable, and so, as we passed by them, we whispered merely: "Good night, boys," and they murmured back huskily: "Good night, sir." Some stood watch by little piles of grenades—small objects that looked like toys, like pretty toys; others stood by a sheaf of rockets—at the slightest menacing movement from the enemy one of those rockets would go high up in the sky, and to the signal the artillery behind would instantly transform the fluid and vague No Man's Land into a hell of steel and fire; each and every one had his duty apportioned, and waited, vigilant and attentive.

We stopped quite a while at a gabionade,[16] a small half-lunar redoubt giving toward the German trenches. We rose on the firing step, and stood half emerged, our waists even with the plane of the earth, protected only by the night, and tried to take in and absorb a larger view than that given in the interminable narrow galleries. The German trenches were before us; we could not see them at all, but their unseen presence, thus, in some way, was all the more impressive. Ahead we could see only the dim barbed-wire pickets, with their strange shapes, sometimes of crouching men, but to the right and the left, as far as the eye could command, white flares were rising and bursting, illuming the horizon long with their savage white light before they died, leaving behind them drooping white tears. The night was wonderfully silent. That is, what noise pierced it was of that quality and intermittence which gives silence its utmost power. The artillery exchange of the first part of the evening had ceased, and only at very long intervals, very far away, there sounded a dull booming, more like the pulse itself of the night than a detonation. Then upon a large slice of silence would come the chatter of a machine or rapid-fire gun. Tat-tat-tat, one would go, then stop abruptly, as though it said: "No, no, I'm mistaken; there's nothing there." But another would say: "By Jove, I don't know, it seems to me there *is* something there—tat-tat-tat-tat-tat- tat-tat-TAT-tat." And a third: "Oh, my—I'm getting *so nervous!* I can't hold on any longer! I'm going to let go—oh-oh, here goes!" and he would fire off its whole belt.

We resumed our walk along the first-line trench, and after a time noticed that we were passing, at regular intervals, little curtains hung seemingly against the wall of the parapet. I raised one of these—and it was not an earthen wall which was behind, but a space hollowed within it. My eyes immediately were attracted in this darkness by the light of a loophole, and then almost at the same time I became aware of a head close by, between me and the loophole, but a little to the left. I dropped the curtain; with the curtain up, that head probably showed in silhouette from the German trenches. The captain was at my elbow by this time. "Go on in if you want to," he said; "but close the curtain quickly."

So I went in, snapping the curtain shut behind me. The place was small and dark; boards were beneath my feet not mud.

16. A defensive construction made of wicker.

The loophole irresistibly drew the eye; from the profound darkness of the place, through the loophole the sky, the horizon, were
extraordinarily light, and a sort of dim phosphorescence was
on No Man's Land, making it luminous yet vague for perhaps a
hundred yards—when it lost itself finally in a fantastic fluidity of
black and opalescence. Within, to my right, I could just make out
a recumbent figure upon a bench—a young soldier, asleep, and to
my left was the man whose head I had first seen. He sat on something I could not discern—a high bench or high stool—and before
him was a steel thing which in the obscurity seemed half great
quadrant and half gun—a rapid-firer, no doubt. He was a slim lad;
he sat very erect and watchful, motionless, his eyes peering fixedly
through the loophole. We were very close; we almost touched.
I said softly: "Hello," and he, without turning his head, said softly:
"Hello." I whispered: "What are you doing?" and he, his eyes never
leaving the loophole, whispered back: "From here I have a *fine*
sight across there." Then, as some slight movement brought me
nearer, I felt that he was trembling—trembling with eagerness and
fine vigilance.

"Go On Over There"

I knew now that I had come to the apex of my journey; through
army corps, division, regiment, company, platoon, to this lone
sentry, to this boy from the States, forefront sentinel on guard over
humanity's spiritual treasures, over Beauty and Kindness menaced
by Ugliness and Insane Cruelty. The great German offensive[17] was
just at its eve. This boy, although he did not know it, had said to
some soldier of France: "Go on over there, feel free to go; go there
where the threat is greatest. I am still young and untried; before
you I am humble; but soon I will be able to be wherever you are,
to feel your ribs against mine in the hells to which you are accustomed. Meanwhile go and feel free and easy; I will take your place.
And be sure that over this place no one shall pass." That is what
that boy had said. Only he did not know it, and so, when I asked:
"What are you doing?" he answered simply: "From here I have a
fine sight across there."

17. Germany launched a major offensive in the spring of 1918. Bolstered with troops
from the Eastern Front, where it had just settled a peace with Russia, the Germans hoped to
capture victory before the full force of American men and materiel could be fully deployed.

The captain clutched at me through the curtain. "Come on," he murmured; "you're being left behind."

Soldiers of Canvas and Papier-Mâché

"'Jimmy Casey'—Exhibit A in the report of how a sniper was located and silenced."

Martin Green
"Eight Months at the Front With the American Army"
The Evening World (New York), September 28, 1918

In the mist of early dawn on a day last spring, German soldiers in outposts opposite one of the American fronts in Lorraine[18] saw three columns of ghostly figures rise out of the ground in no man's land and advance slowly but steadily in perfect formation toward the German trenches. The forms of the soldiers were shadowy, indistinct, but there was no doubt that an attack was on, for here were Yankee soldiers coming across without the warning of a barrage or artillery shelling of the German trenches.

The outpost sentries sent back the word. Rifles popped all along the German trenches on the front line. Occasionally one of the advancing soldiers dropped, but the columns moved on steadily, sometimes hidden in the floating, steamy clouds of mist. All at once, from a position in a wood on a hill at the right of the advance, machine guns opened up. Streams of whining bullets flowed over the field, and every figure in the advancing line disappeared.

Just one minute later a large, energetic American shell landed in that clump of trees on the hill, and in the next five minutes a hail of heavy explosives dropped there. The machine gun fire ceased and the shelling of the wood slackened, but for the rest of the day and all the following night an occasional American shell exploded in the position.

As soon as the machine gun opened and the shadowy forms which had been moving toward the German lines disappeared soldiers in the front line American trenches began to pull vigorously on ropes which passed over the top, under our wire and out into

18. In April 1918, American troops occupied trenches near Seicheprey, in Lorraine.

no man's land and soon there came tumbling into the trench what appeared to be sections of stage scenery.

The American soldiers laughed uproariously as they folded up the sections of wood and canvas and carried them to a communicating trench where other laughing soldiers started with them toward the rear. Some distance in the rear an American Colonel in an observation post picked up his telephone receiver.

"This is Col. -----" he said. "Connect me with X. Y. Z. 4-11-44."

There was a grin on his face as he began to talk.

"Yes," he said, "it worked. We put over a Chinese charge on them and they opened up from their new machine gun nest enfilading us on the right. From the way it looks from here we have blown up the position with our artillery and we can keep them from locating there again. General, it was actually funny."

In this instance the military property room, far removed from the battle line, had furnished to the fighting forces trick material which had revealed a concealed enemy machine gun position without the loss of a man or a shot. For the soldiers the German sentries had seen advancing through the mist of the dawn were not real soldiers. They were silhouette, soldiers of canvas and wood, mounted, by a hinged arrangement, on platforms which could be manipulated by ropes from the American trenches.

During the night, at intervals when German star shells[19] were not illuminating no man's land, a few American troops had pushed under our wire entanglements three long, flat, irregular arrangements to which were attached numerous lines. They were left lying on the ground in front of our wire and at the morning hour when the east began to give warning of approaching sunrise and the valley was heavy with fog and observation was apt to be faulty the lines hanging in our trenches were pulled and a certain number of silhouette figures, representing American soldiers carrying rifles with bayonets set, popped up stiffly and stood motionless.

An officer at a firing post, looking through a powerful night glass, whispered to a runner crouched on the firing step at his feet. "The Chinese soldiers are all on the job," he said. "Tell the Captain to start them on their way."

---

19. A star shell was an artillery shell that contained a magnesium flare on a parachute. As it descended to the ground, it would illuminate no man's land.

The runner disappeared and in a moment reported to the Captain in charge of the work. Whispered orders passed along a certain sector of the trenches, and soldiers began to pull steadily on certain lines hanging over the parapet and away from our wire and out into no man's land moved the canvas advance. When the plop, plop, plop of the machine guns was heard the soldiers at the ropes gave a grand heave at lines which had been touched only occasionally before and the canvas soldiers fell flat on the movable platform to which they were fastened.

Two days later the canvas troops which had fooled the Germans into revealing their machine gun position got back to the property room. They were sieve-like in appearance. Machine gun bullets had riddled them and in many places the wooden supports were splintered. They were sent to a workshop, where artisans and artists patched them up and painted them over, and before many hours had passed they were ready for duty again, somewhere at the front.

"Good old life savers," remarked the officer in charge of the camouflage plant as he passed through the workshop and looked over the work of repair.

"Chinese soldiers," as these pieces of war property are called, are used frequently in trench warfare to trick the enemy into revealing positions which cannot be located by air observation or talks with prisoners. They are used in many different ways and under many different circumstances and they are nearly always effective against selected backgrounds or under selected weather conditions it is impossible to tell them from real soldiers. Even in daylight, so perfectly are they cut out and mounted and painted, they are deceptive at a distance. Incidentally, the Germans use them too.

One hot afternoon last summer a German sniper was making things mighty uncomfortable for the occupants of an American front line trench. He was concealed in the ruins of a village back of the German lines, and so skillfully concealed that our observers could not come anywhere near locating his hiding place. Frequently he sent a bullet into our parapet dangerously near to one of our observation posts. One of his bullets had passed through a crevice in our sandbag protection and dropped on a soldier sitting in the trench writing a letter.

A steel helmet on top of a rifle barrel was passed along a short sector of trench where it was necessary to stoop almost double to keep out of sight. A bullet from the sniper whizzed over, struck the helmet, was deflected and slightly wounded an officer standing at the door of a dugout twenty feet away. Other helmets were passed along the same place, but the sniper refused to shoot at them. The Lieutenant in command sent back to headquarters for a "Jimmy Casey."

That night "Jimmy Casey" arrived and the next morning, while there was still a mist on the ground, although the sun was shining brightly, the head of "Jimmy Casey" was cautiously raised over the parapet. At first only the top of his helmet appeared. He ducked, and in a minute or two the top of his helmet appeared again. There was desultory machine gun firing all along the line. For the third time "Jimmy Casey" showed himself for a reconnoiter of no man's land. This time he popped up quickly, showing not only his helmet but his face and one shoulder. Zing! A bullet went through "Jimmy Casey's" head and down he tumbled into the trench.

Immediately the Lieutenant and another officer and an expert rifle shot jumped on "Jimmy" and held a post mortem. His position when he showed his head over the parapet had been carefully marked. The wound allowed that the bullet had struck him in the left eye, passed through his head and emerged just back of his right ear. The Lieutenant had a map of the trench positions on both sides on the ground before him. On top of the map he placed a compass. After making some calculations in pencil on the margin of the map he drew a line from the position in the trench which "Jimmy Casey" had occupied when he was shot to the marks on the map indicating the ruins of the village back of the German lines. After this he went to his observation post with the map and carefully studied the village ruins through a glass.

By reference to his map he established that the line he had drawn passed, for purposes of his observation, through what was left of a roofless stone structure that had served the village women in days of peace as a community wash house. There they had gathered to scrub and pound their clothing on the edge of a stone-lined pool. The pool was still full of water, covered with green scum. That there was water in the pool had been shown by photographs taken by our aeroplane observers.

"Heinie," said the Lieutenant to himself, "is in that pool, probably up to his neck in water, with his ammunition on a dry shelf in front of him, sniping at us through a hole in the wall."

He called a runner and scribbled a message which he sent to the rear. In about fifteen minutes a shell from an American 75[20] landed a little beyond the wash house. Another landed a little in front of it. A third struck it fair. Other shells landed in the same spot. After that no more bullets came from the sniper and the papier mache head and torso of "Jimmy Casey" was sent to battalion as Exhibit A in the report of how a sniper was located and silenced. "Jimmy Casey" is a product of the property room of the war.

20. American troops used the French 75 mm artillery piece.

Chapter 8

♦

♦

♦

♦

♦

Battles

Introduction

Amerlca had been in the war for over a year before its fighters participated in their first real battle. During that long wait, they had been in training, served in the French trenches, repulsed German raids, and exchanged artillery fire with the enemy—all this under the nurturing care of veteran French soldiers.

On May 27, 1918, the German army launched a large-scale offensive (the Third Battle of the Aisne), in a last attempt to win the war before the buildup of American troops could affect the outcome. Initially, the offensive met with dramatic success. America's first battles of the war came in response to this crisis, as they aided their French and British allies to stop the advance.

First at Cantigny, and then within days at Château-Thierry and Belleau Wood, Americans fought to help stop the German advance. By any measure, in the wartime landscape, that first battle, at the little town of Cantigny, was little more than a skirmish, but symbolically it carried all the weight of Allied salvation. Americans got their noses bloodied, but they fought well, achieved their objective, and demonstrated to their war-weary allies that America was ready to take its place in the front lines. The Battle of Cantigny

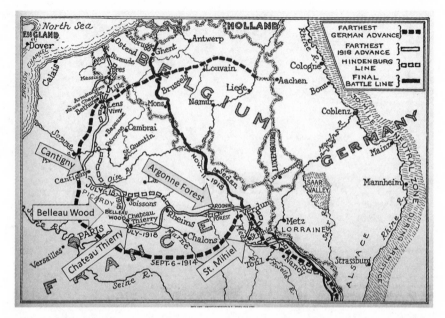

The major battles of the Western Front in which the AEF participated. *Source:*
Adapted from *Forward March*, by Frank J. Mackey, Chicago: The Disabled American
Veterans of the World War, Department of Rehabilitation, 1934, 17.

(May 27–31) got extensive coverage in the American press. In
the first article in this chapter, Herbert Corey styles the Battle of
Cantigny as the occasion "When We Made Good."

Days after Cantigny, Americans were pressed into emergency
service along the Marne River. The German advance had moved to
within fifty miles of the French capital. It was a frightening replay
of the opening days of the war when the Germans came so close to
capturing Paris. This time Americans played an important role in
helping to halt the Germans at the Marne River town of Chateau-
Thierry (June 3–4). Edgar B. Hatrick and his filmmaking team
worked to capture the unfolding battle on film for the U.S. government's Committee on Public Information (CPI).[1]

The CPI's influence on the news was pervasive. It encompassed
nineteen sub-divisions, devoted to different forms of propaganda
that supported the American government's official position on the
war. Its Division of News distributed thousands of press releases

1. The Committee on Public Information was an independent agency of the federal
government created to influence American public opinion towards supporting U.S.
participation in the war, using as its primary tools censorship, public relations, and
propaganda.

of war news. It recruited famous writers to do feature articles for its Division of Syndicated Features. Its Division of Films created motion pictures such as *The Kaiser: The Beast of Berlin* and *Pershing's Crusaders*, that were enormously popular. Hatrick's movie, *America's Answer to the Hun*, fit this mold.

The name of *Chicago Tribune* war correspondent Floyd Gibbons is forever associated with one battle: Belleau Wood (June 6–June 26). Traveling into the action with a unit of Marines, Gibbons was shot three times, but lived to tell about it. War reporters often found themselves in the thick of the action, but seldom did they charge into the fighting with the soldiers. Gibbons's article, "Devil Dogs," glorified the role of Marines at Belleau Wood, but more famously it also chronicled his own experience in that battle, giving readers an up-close description of what it was like to be shot.

By that summer, German fears were realized. American fighters were arriving in Europe at the rate of 250,000 a month and General Pershing could create the United States First Army, a force that would operate independent of French command to plan and carry out its own campaigns. In the article "Story of Great Victory Is Thrillingly Told in Cable to Evening World," correspondent Lincoln Eyre paints a picture of the Battle of St. Mihiel (September 12–16), the first campaign of the war that was planned, commanded, and carried out by the American army.

Much war reporting was done anonymously by journalists working for one of the press syndicates, such as the Associated Press or United Press. An AP or UP story would appear in thousands of newspapers throughout the country. The AP story included here provided a post-Armistice summary of the Battle of the Argonne Forest (26 September–11 November 1918), the final, largest, and most costly American battle of the war.

Cantigny—America's First Battle

"Cantigny was the touchstone that proved the worth of the American soldier."

Herbert Corey
"When We Made Good"
Everybody's Magazine, November 1918

It was "H hour"[2] and in front of Cantigny. The gently rolling land in advance of the American trenches had for an hour been bubbling and steaming with bursting shells. Their dust-filled craters looked in the mist of dawn for all the world like the little pot geysers that bubble and steam on a volcanic flat. Around a half circle four hundred guns were concentrating their fire upon the German batteries. The gun crews worked single-mindedly, dripping with sweat through which black powder fumes were smeared. They had ceased to think of anything but speed. They tore the breech-blocks open, jammed in a shell and hurled the steel gates shut. Sometimes, they bawled to each other, at the top of their voices. The roar of the guns had reached a high level which was quite unbroken by any peaks of sound.

Twelve tanks left their hiding-places behind the line and began to waddle and slip and clank down the hill. A tank would be absurd except in war. The absurdity of war normalizes it. They reared at obstacles and crossed or crushed them and nosed blindly into ditches. A curtain of dust and smoke was drawn across the volcanic flat ahead. The rolling barrage[3] of the seventy-fives had begun. Somewhere back of the American line sixty-four machine guns began to tat-tat-tat. The thin air of their bullets passing over the trenches was precisely that of the wind in the lighter cordage of a ship at sea.

American soldiers climbed unemotionally out of the jumping-off trenches and began to plod across the flat behind the tanks, under the protection of the curtain of dust and black smoke, which from time to time made fifty-yard leaps ahead, in time with their progress. They walked stiffly, with a peculiar, flat-footed, laborious cadence, for they were heavily laden. They walked in little groups, each man behind his leader. As they moved on the groups began to thicken up. Second lieutenants shepherded their platoons. In such a charge, officers do not run and wave their hands, in spite of the war artists. Each had crooked his left arm before his face and eyed his wrist-watch intently. Now and then they waved their men to a slower pace or imperatively beckoned them to hurry. The men watched them from the corners of their eyes.

2. The hour at which the battle is set to begin.

3. A "rolling barrage" or "creeping barrage" was a continually moving curtain of exploding artillery shells designed to move forward ahead of advancing infantry to force the enemy to remain undercover rather than fight off the attackers.

Overhead an air-plane methodically signaled the progress of the advance to the regimental post of command. It flew very low, sometimes not more than fifty feet above the ground. In this way the observer could locate the German machine gunners who had been nested in this field across which the Americans were moving. Now and then one would pop up, deafened and shaken by the shells, blinded by the dust, to sprinkle that advancing curtain with bullets. They knew that behind it the Americans were coming. Sometimes the advancing men stumbled on them and there would be a little fight with two or three on the one side and the stuttering machine on the other. Always the line moved on.

A second and then a third wave of Americans left the trench behind and began to plod heavily and unhurriedly across the flat. Each in its turn had been brought to the jumping-off trench when its occupants started across the volcanic flat. Behind them at intervals came groups of others. There were angry carriers strung about with canteens and other angry carriers with bundles of wire and screw-end stakes,[4] and still other angry carriers with ammunition and grenades. Carriers are habitually angry because they are forbidden to get into the fight except in case of necessity. Yet their risk is as great as the others. Stretcher-bearers came, too, and hospital orderlies with first-aid packets, and the military police.

At headquarters they say the affair at Cantigny was a mere straightening of the line, it would not do to brag before the French— the heroes at Verdun and the Aisne and the Marne—of such a pinprick to the Boche! No doubt headquarters is right. There are— there were—only a chateau and twenty-odd houses at Cantigny. The careful documents of the French war office specify them in the schedule which was prepared for the taking of the place. One reads that Machart's house was built upon a vault and the Fontain's cellar was thirty feet deep and that Hennique's home was underlaid by a chain of caves in which the Boche would shelter himself.

But if one considers the attack at Cantigny from other than a purely military angle, the story is worth the telling. It was here that the American Army made its first gain of ground in the war

---

4. A type of stake for holding barbed wire that has a cork screw base, designed so it could be quickly and silently implanted in the ground.

against the German in France. It was the first offensive planned and carried out by the Americans alone. It is true that French tanks and French guns helped. It is also true that there had been much American fighting in the Vosges and Lorraine, but this affair at Cantigny was something more than mere fighting. Small it may have been, but such as it was, it was a battle.

Most of all, the taking of Cantigny was the touchstone that proved the worth of the American soldier. The French onlookers declared he was magnificent. A week later an American division was thrown into the breach made in the French lines before Château-Thierry in the fight on the Marne. The German advance was stopped short when it ran into the Yankees who helped hold the road to Paris. They would hardly have been given the chance if their mates had failed at Cantigny the week before.

Cantigny

While it is true that Cantigny was a little place, it was a most irritating little place. First the French held it and then the Germans took it and the French regained it and the Germans got it again. It had been mauled about and pawed over until it had ceased to be a village and became only a dangerous point on the military maps. In front of the little place the Germans had thrust an obtuse V—a salient,[5] in military language—right into the Allied front. Headquarters recognized that as a good jumping-off place for a German offensive. The town was held by the 271st and 272d German Reserve Regiments. They were not the best German troops, but they were very good.

The men in the observation posts on the hill used to watch Cantigny as scientists might examine under the microscope a nest of bugs. The little town glistened in the yellow light of the French spring against its background of green hills. Sometimes a gray figure hurried from one pile of white chalk ruins which had been a house to another pile of white chalk ruins which had been a house. If the figure loitered, someone sniped at it with a piece of artillery. There was one gunner who had an allowance of fifty shells of six-inch caliber each day for sniping only. Sometimes he sniped the crossroads, where the ammunition wagons passed, but he preferred to snipe at singles in Cantigny. The game required more skill.

---

5. A protrusion of the line that is surrounded by the enemy on three sides.

Between times other gunners would drop shells into Cantigny, and columns of white chalk-dust would spurt into the air. The gray cloud would hang about for half an hour afterward, so thoroughly had Cantigny been pulverized. The shells were mere evidences of dislike on the gunner's part, for everyone knew the gray figures lived underground and were safe as safety goes in war. Tunnels crossed and recrossed from the cellars of the houses. A tunnel seventy yards long led from the cellar of the chateau. Some of the ruins which had once been houses had been starred on the secret maps as doubtful.

The Underground Village

"A prisoner," the notations ran, "says that a machine gun is hidden here. The post of command is believed to be under the château. Look out for Robillard's house. A prisoner thinks there is a new observation post hidden there."

When the Germans looked out from Cantigny toward the American line the view must have been about the same. There was a no man's land of rolling green, bounded at one end by a swamp and at the other cut across by a ravine. On the hills behind were other piles of sparkling white chalk which had once been houses and more muddled blotches which had been villages. Patches of wood had been frazzled into stubby brushes. There were shell-holes which had been made into strong points and here and there a puny bit of trench. Neither side bothers to dig trenches in open fighting.

An American division had been sent to the Montdidier sector. Its men say proudly that they are "old regulars." They are not, of course. There is no American regular army any more.[6] But the regimental numbers in this division were those of "old regular" regiments and here and there is an old regular officer, and there are leather-faced old non-coms who are its regimental souls. There are no traditions in such a regiment as these. One hears of fights, at Mindanao and China and where-not, and forgotten names crop up in the talk at mess.

"Take Cantigny!" was the order that came to the division. "Straighten out that kink in the line! Get rid of that salient."

6. The American "regular" army was that which existed prior to the war. By this point it had been blended with National Guardsmen, volunteers and draftees, and thus lost its individual identity.

One day three regiments suffered heartbreak when they heard the fourth had been given the assignment to take Cantigny. The lucky regiment became unbearably chesty. Its men talked vaguely of incidents in its past which had led to its selection for this honor. The other regiments hinted darkly that there was favoritism somewhere and that if Black Jack[7] knew of this outrage he would fix somebody all right, and there were dissensions and shoulder-hitting. Someone brought the news that the Germans knew the Americans were opposite Cantigny and had laughed about it!

"What do we care?" the Boche had asked. "The Americans are no good. Soft, you know!"

Every time the division heard that the steam rose in the divisional gage. The officers of the three regiments invited the officers of the fourth to dinner and told them, in the kindest and most insulting fashion in the world, of little dodges they had picked up which might be of use and offered to ride over some day and show'em. And the officers of the lucky fourth regiment told in a superior way how they were giving their men a special training for the fight. They thought the general planned to have the other three regiments look on some day. It would do'em no end of good.

Rehearsing a Battle

When there is time to spare such affairs are rehearsed as carefully as any other great modern spectacle. Not a "Queen of Sheba" herself, with her fireworks and adjuncts, could be given more minute drill. Miles in the rear an area had been found which duplicated that of Cantigny as nearly as possible, and on it the stage-managers did themselves proud. Both enemy positions were marked off, and the enemy gun emplacements indicated by stakes and flags. The town itself, or what remains of the town, and its streets and houses and tunnel exits and dugouts were carefully plotted out.

A sand-table[8] was even built, twenty by thirty feet in size, on which every house was built to scale. Then the regimental and then the battalion and later the platoon officers were rehearsed in the parts they were to have in the new play. They were kept at

---

7. A nickname for General Pershing acquired from his command of a unit of African-American soldiers in the Spanish-American War.

8. A sand-table is a model of the battlefield terrain, constructed for planning and training for a battle.

it until they were letter perfect on every detail. They knew where they were to jump off from and where they were to go to. They knew the compass bearings of their prospective routes, and each had marked down a landmark to follow. At last, on "J three" day, the whole regiment was rehearsed.

"J three" is three days before "J" day, which is the day on which a planned fight is to happen. On "J three" the regiment as a body moved forward behind men waving tree branches, which represented the protective barrage behind which they were to make the assault. It was a most distressing performance. Officers and men got tangled and forgot and were frankly bored and lost their way. They were stupid and slow and careless. Yet when "J" day came, that dull regiment went through on its toes like so many ballet-dancers. There was not a single mistake.

When "J" day came twenty thousand Americans sustained the sort of painful excitement one used to feel about the climacteric game of a World's Series. It is true that only thirty-four hundred were to be engaged in the fight, if all went well, but the rest of the division was ordered to stand by. Cantigny was to be taken, for the commander-in-chief himself ordered it. If the lucky regiment failed the three others were to put their men in the attack. "H hour" was 6:45 A.M. and for four hours before it sounded there were groups of men before every divisional telephone. One found them in dugouts and first-aid stations and posts of command. They might have been waiting for the election returns or a flash from the ringside at Reno. Between times they kidded each other:

"They've detrucked," was the first of the messages to come in.

That is one of war's new words. The men who were to fight had been brought up to a point near the jumping-off trench in camions.[9] It was a warm, starry night in the last quarter of the moon. As they marched forward there was a sentimental reaction. Some of the platoons sang, one repeated over and over and over— that its "Bonnie Lies Over the Ocean." Another sang *Madelon*,[10] this season's French march song, with great feeling and an atrocious accent. Others harmoniously scattered themselves among other

9. The term is being used here to refer to trucks, but it was also used to refer to the tens of thousands of heavy wagons that clogged to roads of France, transporting munitions and supplies to the front lines.

10. The song *La Madelon* tells the story of a soldier flirting with a waitress in a tavern. The song was popular throughout the war and remains popular in France today.

songs, but almost every platoon sang the *"Marseillaise."*[11] Not one sang a hymn, although every village-reared private in the regiment knows a hymn or two.

Waiting

The telephones were silent for a long time. By and by reports began to come in. Companies C and G and I had found their places and settled down for the wait. At half past three o'clock only one company was still straying about in the darkness that had begun to grow gray and wan before the advancing sun. The men at the telephones worried. They discussed the character of the company commander and the company's past history. At 4:57 A.M. the bells shrilled again along the divisional line.

"Fifty-four-forty," came the report from the regimental post of command. That meant that every company was in place and ready. The men at the telephones began to ask each other for the makings and to twist cigarets busily. Waiting became a nervous business. Yet only three casualties had been reported on the march up. The company officers had avoided the areas which the methodical German was in the habit of shelling. Down in the jumping-off trench the men propped themselves up against their packs and began to smoke. Noise was discouraged, but they were permitted to talk in low tones. They might even smoke cigarets if they kept their heads below the trench parapets. Many of them went to sleep, for they were tired.

The Bombardment

There had been little shelling during the night. From time to time an American heavy had registered on the battery it was to smash later on. When the gunners had found their target they stopped firing. It was not the intention to alarm the German, and induce him to start active counter-battery work. A little play—a little camouflage—was put on instead. The night before the Germans had raided the American lines with some slight success. They might have had more luck except that Captain Frey, wounded to death by the fragments from a high explosive shell, had leaped on the lip of the trench.

11. The French national anthem.

"Come on, boys!" he had cried when he saw the round-topped helmets of the enemy through the morning light. "Come on; give 'em hell!"

That is a good American war-cry, Frey's men broke that German charge inside our wires and Frey knew that they had broken it before he died. It was but natural that we should try for a little revenge for such a raid, and the Germans no doubt expected it. The American guns fired just enough that night to make it seem like a reply to the previous night's affair, and not enough to alarm an enemy who reads signs as well as an Indian tracker reads a twisted leaf. As morning came on, the firing thickened up a little, but not much. The German batteries replied from time to time. Down in the dugouts and chalk caverns the telephone-bells began to whir. A voice at regimental headquarters said over the wire: "Five o'clock forty-two minutes—three—five forty-four—"

No one heard it say "five—forty-five." That was the hour at which the bombardment was to begin. The guns went off with a crash. There was to be an hour's work on the German batteries before the charge was ordered, in order that the charge might be accomplished in comparative safety. There are heavies and super-heavies, and mediums and lights.[12] All blazed away at the top of their voices. The sky above had paled before the morning, but it glowed above this jerking fire. Over on the German side a tangle of flashes showed where the shells were bursting. They made one think of the signal lights of a fleet at sea. The Germans replied feebly at first. Then they became almost silent.

Timing the Attack

The confronting positions followed the configuration of the land. Neither side had much in the way of trenches, but had built strong points to be defended in an attack. At places the lines waved toward each other so that they were hardly more than one hundred yards apart. Elsewhere four hundred yards separated them. If the attacking troops had "hopped over" from the front line, the distances to be traveled would have been unequal. Some must have stuck their noses in the barrage, as the French say, while others must have run breathlessly to catch up with that moving curtain of fire and smoke.

12. Different calibers of artillery, with differing range and explosive power.

Therefore a jumping-off trench had been built, a kilometer and a half long, in the rear of the American positions and roughly parallel to the German line. Each American would in this way have approximately the same distance to march that each other had. The watches of the platoon leaders had been synchronized, so that they might march with the march of the barrage. They must put their men just one hundred yards from the jumping-off trench within two minutes from the jump in order to get under cover of the friendly curtain. Every man of the three waves must be out of the trench and grouped two hundred yards away within ten-minutes of the jump-off. An exhaustive inquiry into the Boche's mental processes and battery speed had led to the conclusion that it takes him just ten minutes to lay his barrage down from the time of alarm.

They're Off

An intelligent enemy hides himself when he is being vigorously shelled and does not come out until his watchers tell him that the attack has started. At 6:43 A.M. the officers in the jump-off trenches nodded to their men. "On your toes," said they. At 6:44 A.M. the leaders put their hands on the trench lip and prepared to climb out. At 6:45 the men at the telephones along the line nodded at each other. Their synchronized watches told them the move had started, but their ears would have done them the same service. The tanks were clattering on like so many threshing-machines in travail. The note of the bombardment had changed. The seventy-fives were tack-tacking the barrage down.

"I want you to show me that new three-inch machine gun," said a serious-minded German prisoner after the fight. "That is very new. We did not know a three-inch gun could be fired so fast before."

The men plodded ahead under their sixty-pound loads rather slowly. Each had two canteens of water, two hand grenades and one rifle, grenade, some empty sand bags, a pick or shovel, two hundred and twenty rounds of ammunition, two days' iron rations and a shelter half. Each kept his eyes on the ground on the lookout for stray Germans in ambush, much as quail-shooters watch for birds. Now and then they took snap-shots at those they saw. The photographs taken by the air-plane observers at this time show groups of bodies, spouting out of unsuspected hiding-places and running away. Only here and there a pair or trio stayed to fight.

"There were three machine guns we overlooked on the Advance," said an officer who went through it. "The Germans hid themselves. It was not until we passed them by that they pulled their guns out of the holes and turned them on us."

The line went on calmly, in spite of this itch of bullets at its back. Maybe the men did not know that the gunners were there. The noise of passing shells had become that of a great siren, of which the inflections varied but in which the ear could not detect a separate note. A lieutenant who eight months before had been an undergraduate at Harvard detached a few of his men and ordered them to clean up the gunners. The line went on. By and by the men caught up to it, panting and wet with sweat. The gunners were piled in odd heaps over the saddles of their guns. From a little distance they looked like piles of old, gray clothes.

One thinks of a charge as a peculiarly deadly affair, and yet this at Cantigny was safe as churches—at least as churches are in a German war. Not more than a dozen casualties were later reported, and some of these were occasioned by fragments from the friendly barrage. There are always casualties of that sort to report, but it is always better for the men to keep close to their curtain. When the edge of Cantigny was reached a few more men fell from the bullets of the Germans who had learned what was going on. They were beginning to clamber out of their holes and begin their defense. They are not to be blamed, even by the All-Highest War Lord, for their tardiness. The Americans had covered in twenty-five minutes ground which by a German schedule should have taken them forty-five minutes to march over. It is always interesting to know the enemy's method of thought.

"What came next?" I heard a colonel ask one of the men who went through the fight.

"Well," he said vaguely, "we ran around—I don't know."

Mopping Up

No man tells the same story of what happened after the Americans entered Cantigny. Our guns stopped playing on the village, once our men were in it, and began on the batteries behind. Having kept the Germans underground during the charge, it was their part to reduce the activity of the German batteries upon a town that in twenty-five minutes had become actively hostile. The men of the two sides found innumerable little actions in which one man or two or three would combat as many enemies. There is none of the parade and show of war in such a fight as this. The duty of each man is to kill.

"We never saw men fight so angrily," the German prisoners said after the affair ended. "They seemed to hate us. They hit us with the butts of their guns."

It is rather incomprehensible, but that inherited trait of a nation of woodsmen seems particularly to fret the German soldier. To be shot or stabbed with a bayonet or to have the butt of a gun thrust in his face may be unpleasant, but it follows the rules laid down in the text-books. These thin-hipped Americans, their ridiculous iron hats lopping over one ear and then another, their eyes flaming, leaped at the Boche and swung the gun by the muzzle. Wherever a butt landed one of the Kaiser's unsafe folk went out of business.

Hand to Hand

The tanks slipped and slathered about in the dense obscurity of the dust and smoke. Outside of Cantigny the day was a bright one. The hills were gilded by the sun. The air-plane photographs show that over the town itself a heavy cloud hovered, as though the funnel end of a cyclone were twisting there. At the forward end of each tank a man peered through the tiny slits and swung his gun pointblank on the German groups. From either side machine guns clacked away. In the rear walked the men of the tank *liaison*. Their duty is to keep the men inside in touch with the events of the insane world without and only to fight if forced. Each carried a grenade in his right hand.

The most vivid description of hand-to-hand fighting I have ever heard came from a man who was there, and yet could recall no incidents at all. He painted a scene of utter, mad confusion, through which men ran and yelled and shot aimlessly, as it seemed. A German and an American, running madly, heads down, met each other full on, breast to breast. They reeled from the shock, glared at each other for a moment, and each ran on. A German ran howling through the fetid mist. His trench knife in his right hand was red and his arm was red to the shoulder. He tripped and fell.

"Then he sang," said the observer. "Just sat there in the middle of that madness and sang. Some one killed him."

Other Germans ran away. He reported a curious optical illusion. "The Germans seemed about knee high," said he, "and their legs seemed to pump up and down very rapidly, as in an old 'chase' film, and yet they did not make speed. Do you understand me? Their effort was prodigious but unavailing. Their clothes looked floppy, somehow. The Americans seemed about fifteen feet tall and advanced by huge leaps, I stood there and laughed like hell."

Once again a German sergeant-major at the head of a group put up his hands in token of surrender. He smiled as he did so. "He was rather a handsome man," said the man who saw it, "blond with big blue eyes and an open, candid expression." An American lieutenant advanced to accept his surrender when the blond man hurled a grenade. It struck the lieutenant fair in the breast and he died.

"I'll say this for the blond man," said the American. "He knew what was coming when he threw the grenade and he died game. But the other men of his group whimpered."

A wounded German was being led to the rear by a wounded American. They were leaning upon each other, amicably enough, it seemed. They whirled apart, and, bleeding as they were, thrust at each other with the bayonets they had drawn from their belts. The American killed his man and then sat down and wiped the perspiration from his forehead. A captain came by:

"Gee, I'm tired," said the wounded man simply.

Once a group of Germans tried to surrender. They walked about with their hands up, crying "Kamerad." No one paid the least attention to them, busily hunting other Germans out of the underground hiding-places with bombs and flame-throwers, and shooting at those who appeared. In despair the weak-hearted crowd ran toward their own lines. They were on the outskirts of the little town, without guns or canteens or any of the other impedimenta, lacking which a soldier seems stripped and bare, when a tank saw them. One after another, as they ran, the machine gun dropped them.

Time drew on. The tanks swung around and started for the safety to be found miles back of the line. A tank is helpless in the open against artillery. There was an effect of duck-like agitation as they squattered down the road. The surface of Cantigny was being cleared. Stretcher-bearers had carried the wounded to the rear or into the caverns in which the odor of blood and death mingled with the heavy stench of burned petroleum. Dead were everywhere, their blank faces turned up to the sun that was now appearing through the clearing clouds of smoke and dust.

Squads of prisoners were being trotted to the rear by the same military police with the green bands on the left arm that one sees now at so many roads in France. The mopping-up parties were clearing the tunnels of the bodies of those they had mopped up, for Americans must live in those tunnels now. A minute—hours—had passed. No one can say.

Hot Work

Men did not stop even to wipe the perspiration from their foreheads. There was too much to do. The men of the first wave were frantically turning the shell-holes in the edge of what had been a town into a "line of surveillance." Those of the second wave were digging trenches. Those of the third were building three tiny strong points for defense against the anticipated counter-attacks. Carrying parties staggered up from the rear with screw-poles and wire—and the odds and ends of organization. The American artillery fire upon the German batteries was slackening, for the guns were getting too hot to work. A stream of walking wounded was reaching the first-aid posts where the surgeons waited. They were chattering anew, like magpies;

"You'd oughta seen me mop up that big Heinie, Doc," one said.

"Lie still," said the surgeon.

"Yes, Doc, but listen," said the soldier, sitting up on the stretcher. "He was coming at me, and I said to myself——."

So it went on. Every man had his story to tell. The litter-bearers not only worked like heroes—a man must be a hero to be a litter-bearer—but like the giants in an iron-furnace. Their khaki clothes were black with perspiration. Not one of them slept for forty-eight hours and during those forty-eight hours they worked constantly. It is impossible to understand how men could do what they did, for flesh has its limitations of strength and a soldier is extraordinarily heavy when carried in a litter.

The wounded clamored to get away from the hospitals and back to the fight:

"I'll come back to-morrow, Doc," man after man promised. "Honest to God, I will. But the boys need me over there to-day."

Holding Fast

The spectacular event was over. The men at the distant telephones hung up the receivers with thankfulness and went about their work or sought sleep. Then the real tragedy of Cantigny began, for the German batteries, relieved of the steel pressure of the American guns, began to shell the little town. The single trench which had been dug was only three feet deep. The tiny strong-points were mere targets for the Boche gunners. The Yankees held the trenches under a concentrated fire that time after time filled it, or uprooted it, or turned its shallow lengths into bowl-like depressions. They might have sought safety in the tunnels, as the Germans had done; but if they had done so they would have lost the town to the first counter-attack.

For two hours the Boche guns dumped shell into the town unopposed, for during that time the American guns could not fire. The one really worth-while counterattack of the battle was launched at this period. The Germans were beaten off by rifle-fire. Some unidentified officer had told them to be calm. "Go easy, boys," he ordered. "Don't fire until you are sure of your man." Four other counter-attacks were sent to Cantigny in the four days during which the men of the "lucky regiment" held it. Not one reached our lines. The Americans went without food and water, because neither food nor water could be brought up under the German fire. They lived on raw bacon and sweet chocolate and grit. After four days they were relieved.

They came out—those who did come out—tired; impossibly, incredibly tired. They stumbled along dully. They were just able to carry their rifles. Lines were cut deep in their faces and sweat had run in them and dirt had dried black in them. They were thin and tattered. They only looked at one if they were addressed and they did not speak if the effort could be avoided. But they were happy.

"Do you know what the Germans call us now?" asked man after man, smiling with stiff lips: "The Blacksnake Division.[13] And I guess Heinie knows why."

----

13. The 1st Infantry Division, which would later become more commonly known as the Big Red One, for the red number 1 on its shoulder patch.

When the Americans "Saved Paris"

"One could hear the hushed whisper 'American,' and a grateful
look would come into their eyes."

Edgar B. Hatrick
"How Our Soldiers Turned the Tide at Chateau Thierry"
Washington Times, September 28, September 29, 1918

Gettysburg, Bunker Hill, Yorktown, Trenton, Manila Bay, Santiago,
are some of the names dear to the hearts of all Americans. At each
men fought and died for the cause of liberty. In many cases,
however, it was not the military significance of the battle that
made the place live in history, but the great moral effect that the
result had on the people. After the battle of Bunker Hill, although
the American troops suffered a defeat, it succeeded in arousing the
entire country. The heroic fight made by the New England troops
attracted the attention of all the colonies and did more than any
other single factor up to that time toward uniting them in their
struggle for independence.

To this list of places is now added another, which will be dear,
not only to the hearts of all Americans, but to the people of every
nation in the Allied ranks—Chateau-Thierry, the beautiful little
French city only fifty miles from Paris, where the Germans for the
first time felt, on June 1, 1918, the real force of American arms.

We had been in the war for over a year. Our troops had been
in the trenches since October, 1917, and in all the sectors which
they had occupied they had given a good account of themselves.
But our engagements with the enemy had been of a limited character. At no place on our front had the Boches made a spectacular
drive, and our work consisted principally of holding the line, and
now and then making a slight dent into the German ranks for the
purpose of letting them know we were on the job.

This condition lasted all through the Winter and Spring. Then
came the great German drive against the British in the north of
France, when the Hun was within a stone's throw of Amiens. Some
of our troops were sent up with the French in the early part of
April, but it was several weeks before they got into action, and,
while they gave an excellent account of themselves, they were by
no means the controlling factor in the situation.

Simultaneous with the March drive the Germans started the bombardment of Paris with their long-range guns,[14] and, while this weapon did very little material damage, it did serve to increase the anxiety of the French people.

Then came the second drive, which began May 27, when the Germans broke the line between Soissons and Rheims, captured Soissons and started down for the Marne valley. Within three days they advanced about thirty-two miles, and brought about the most critical situation since the early days of 1914.

To help stem this advancing horde the American troops were called in, and two divisions, numbering approximately 54,000 men, were thrown into the section around Chateau-Thierry on June 1. One side of the city had already been occupied by the Germans, but that portion on the south bank of the Marne was being held by French infantry, and American machine gunners of the Third Division were thrown into the breach. This was the high-water mark of the German drive. Here the Hun was stopped and later on hurled back, and from all indications it is the closest he will ever be to Paris.

The effect of this was electrical throughout France. The French people for the first time realized that American aid was not limited to dollars and cents and a few divisions of troops, and that we had at last arrived with plenty of men and that our boys were holding the most critical point on the battle front in conjunction with her own troops.

It was my fortune to be present at Chateau-Thierry when our troops were thrown into the line. In company with C.J. Hubbell, I arrived in France the middle of March on a special mission for the Committee on Public Information. The purpose of our trip was to make a motion picture of the activities of the American Expeditionary Forces to show the allied and neutral countries what we were actually doing in the prosecution of the war. We had visited every active division in the line, and had also, with the help of the Signal Corps,[15] secured films showing the great construction work going on behind the lines for the purpose of maintaining

14. The German's long-range "Paris Gun" could fire a projectile 75 miles. It was employed against Paris from March to August 1918.

15. The U.S. Army Signal Corps' responsibilities included all ground communications, but also photography (ground and air), as well as meteorology, cryptography, and the Army's air program.

World War I was the first war to be recorded by the motion picture camera. News organizations, private cinematographers, army units, and government propaganda agencies used the movies to bring the war to the public. *Source:* National Archives and Records Administration photo, courtesy of the Newseum.

an enormous army at the front. By the latter part of May our picture was about completed, and on Decoration Day we made a trip to the American headquarters in order to make pictures of the Decoration Day ceremonies.

It was a beautiful morning in May, and as we drove along it was hard to imagine that the world's bloodiest war was being waged only forty miles away. We reached the little French village about 9:30 a.m. where the ceremonies were being held in a little churchyard on the outskirts of the town. The cemetery was a waving mass of French and American flags, and a row of freshly made graves marked the resting places of some of the American boys who had already given their lives in that far-off country. Two companies of stalwart marines stood attention, while addresses were delivered by the French and American military officials, and after the firing of the salute over the graves the procession filed back to the town.

Hubbell—he was better known as Joe at press headquarters—and myself started for general headquarters to get our passes renewed for the month of June. While there we ran into Colonel C-----, attached to the Intelligence Department. He had taken a great interest in our work from the start and was very anxious to know how everything was coming alone. I told him the picture was about completed, but we hadn't had anything real exciting as yet.

"You come inside," said the Colonel, and drew me into his private office. Taking me over to the wall he pointed to a military map.

"Do you see this line." said the Colonel, indicating a line running from Soissons to Rheims. "Yes," I answered. "Well, the boches broke through here night before last, and they are coming down toward the Marne Valley as fast as troops can possibly move. We are sending some of our boys up there to try to stop them, and if you want a real show that's the place to get it."

I told him we were ready to go if he could give us a fast car and our old conducting Officer, Lieutenant D-----, of New York. To this the Colonel quickly assented. He couldn't give us any information as to the exact spot where we were to go, but said we should head for Chateau-Thierry, and get as close as possible. "But look out for Boche cavalry," were his last words as we started out the door.

Two hours later our party left press headquarters on that memorable trip. Sergeant M----- driving the eight-cylinder touring car, license No. U.S. Cent dix huit; Lieutenant D----- in charge of the party; Sergeant Duff, the world's greatest still photographer; Joe and myself. That night we stopped at one of the large and important business centres in France. The whole city was filled with an air of suspense and suppressed excitement. There were crowds in front of the bulletin boards of the telegraph and newspaper offices waiting for the official communiques.

The following morning we resumed our journey, and after a two-hour drive ran across the first signs of the German drive—refugees. We rounded a bend in the road and stretched out before us, as far as we could see, was a conglomerate mass of animals, carts and humanity moving slowly toward us. It was the vanguard of the army of refugees fleeing before the advancing Germans. But what an army—old men, women and children! This tragic column was headed by two cows and as many women with white handkerchiefs covering their heads, driving the cattle along the road. Ox carts followed filled with all the material belongings that the family could gather together in their hasty flight. Helpless old men and women sat on top of the household goods and held the babies, while the mothers trudged slowly along the road driving the horses and oxen. Within twenty-four hours these people had been deprived of all their earthly belongings, had been compelled to abandon their homes and flee for their lives. But they took it philosophically. There was no weeping or wailing in the vast throng. They plodded along the road resigned, and as Joe's movie camera clicked off the record of the tragic scene one would occasionally smile and call out "Ci-nee-ma."

Now and then the refugees would crowd to one side of the road as French soldiers would come by with several hundred boche prisoners—moving a camp to the rear.

By two in the afternoon we had traveled too far into the fighting zone to run across any more large bodies of refugees. Here and there we would meet some stragglers plodding along, but the main body were well on their way to the rear. The town of M-----, only a short distance from Chateau-Thierry, presented the first signs of actual battle.

This place had been entirely evacuated by the civilian population. Having learned that Chateau-Thierry had already been partly occupied by the German troops, we surmised that our boys might detrain here to go into the line, so we hurried to the station.

Here there was plenty of evidence of actual battle. The station yard was a mass of wounded French and British soldiers stretched out on small cots and some lying on the ground. Two American women, Miss Helen Wiborg, of New York, and Mrs. Herbert O. Squires, attached to the French Red Cross,[16] were making their way among the sufferers and ministering to their wants as best they could. Not only the station

---

16. Through the Red Cross, American nurses served the French army, before and after U.S. entry into the war. Unlike Britain and the United States, France did not have professionally trained nurses, relying instead on nuns.

yard, but the interiors of both the freight and passenger stations, were covered with wounded. At the request of Miss Wiborg our car was pressed into service to hurry some of the more serious cases to the Evacuation Hospital.

Shortly after our arrival, British ambulances put in their appearance, and then a French hospital train arrived.

While the work of attending the wounded was going on we heard the shrill shriek of a French locomotive, and looking down the tracks we saw a long trainload of khaki clad boys coming toward us. It was the advance guard of the American troops. Within a few minutes the train pulled into the station. There was no cheering or flag waving. This was no day for receptions, and besides, they weren't expected. A smart looking bunch of young officers jumped off the train, and after a few hurried commands, the work of detraining started.

A husky young captain walked up to me and said: "Say, fellow, do you know where we are?"

"About ten kilometres from Chateau-Thierry," I answered.

"Well where is that?" he asked.

"Just over the hill." I answered, "and from last reports the Boche have occupied one-half of the town."

Then glancing around at the wounded soldiers, he said with a smile:

"We haven't been in the trenches as yet, and expected to go into a quiet sector, but it doesn't look very quiet around here." Then without waiting for a reply, he continued: "Well, this bunch will give the Hun all he is looking for!"

And they did.

An hour later a machine gun battalion marched through the little station yard between the rows of French and British wounded. It was a magnificent and historical sight. The Tommies and Poilu that were physically able raised their heads from their stretchers, and, although they were too feeble to give any welcome cheers, the look in their eyes was all that was needed to greet the boys from across the sea.

Down through the lanes of wounded they marched, up the hill, through the little village and out on the highway to Chateau-Thierry. Three hours later they had taken up their positions in the city with the French infantry. There were no trenches, but they had their machine gun emplacements camouflaged by vines in backyards, in ruined houses and any hasty shelter that offered itself. The Boche got no further. He had only an advance guard in the other half of the town, but his advance to Paris was stopped. By the time his reinforcements came up, our entire division was in the line at the apex of the drive with another division, including the redoubtable marines on the left flank, and the road to Paris was closed for all time.

When the history of the future is recorded it will undoubtedly give full credit to the machine-gun battalion of the Division, troops that had never before been in the line, but whose heroism and pluck stopped the Hun drive on Paris and planted the American Flag at the turning point of the present war.

That night we slept on the floor in a room of what was the town's leading hotel. There were no lights, and all night long we could hear the guns roaring and see the flashes in the sky.

The following morning we started for Chateau-Thierry, and all along the road we passed our infantry plodding along to take up their positions. There were no bands playing, no flags flying and no cheering throngs. The only sound was the dull thud of the hundreds of hob-nail boots, interspersed now and then with a sharp command, as these modern steel helmeted warriors marched to take up their grim business.

We soon passed the advance guard, and veering off to the left started for Chateau-Thierry. About five minutes' ride brought us to the crest of a hill with a sharp slope, and another hill ahead of us. We couldn't see anything or anyone, so we proceeded cautiously until we reached the top of the next incline. Suddenly to our left and right we heard the sharp bark of the French seventy-fives from their shelter among the trees and the shells go screaming through the air. We continued along the top of the bill, and just as we started the descent we emerged from behind a clump of trees, and there stretched out below us was Chateau-Thierry, the town destined to become famous, not only in American history, but in the history of the world.

A boche observation balloon hovered over the opposite hill, and fearing that he would catch sight of our car we stopped and backed it into the woods. We then started out on foot with our camera equipment, and after proceeding about two hundred yards found an excellent position under a fruit tree in an orchard, where we commanded a good view of the town.

A small fire was burning in the eastern section, probably started by a bursting shell. With the exception of an occasional shell screaming over our heads from the French batteries everything seemed peaceful and quiet.

But we hadn't long to wait!

The Hun had evidently seen some movement in the lower part of the town and started a show for us that lasted most of the afternoon. He began pumping shells into the lower part of the town, while we sat under the tree on the hill with Joe cranking the camera and recording every shot. Soon the town was covered with a thick haze and it was hard to see bursting shell through the smoke. While the firing was at its height a boche plane hovered over the town and dropped to within 200 feet of the ground. Two French planes came after him and for a few minutes a battle royal was waged almost in front of us, but the Hun managed to elude his pursuers and fly back to his lines.

The following day we started for General Headquarters and reached there late at night, where we were informed that another division, under the command of Major-General Bundy,[17] had gone in on the left, so we started back as soon as we had made preparations for developing our film.

We reached the town of M-----, slightly to the northwest of Chateau-Thierry where Division Headquarters was located. Strung out on all sides in the woods, fields and on the roads were guns, and they were all firing. One could see that they had been brought up in a hurry, as there were no permanent emplacements and very little attempt to camouflage—in fact some were firing from the open road. It was a gala day for the movie man.

Joe had been on the lookout for a boche helmet, not the kind one purchases in a souvenir store, but one taken from a real Hun ivory dome. Now the opportunity presented itself. A short distance ahead of us we saw three German prisoners trudging along the road followed by a French soldier. One of them was wearing a helmet, and as soon as Joe spied it he whispered a few words to Mac, the driver. The next we knew Joe was leaning out over the side and

17. Major General Omar Bundy

as we whizzed by he lifted the helmet off the German's head. The boche threw his hands into the air. and when he found his helmet gone his face broke out in a grin.

We proceeded to a smaller village where some of our machine gunners were located, and while standing there by one of the buildings a squadron of fifteen boche planes appeared overhead. Joe stood the camera out in the street with the idea of getting a picture. He had cranked several seconds on it, when an officer yelled out of a window of one of the buildings: "Get out of the street, you, or they'll be dropping something in a minute." We didn't need a second warning.

On our way back, along the road we saw one of our observation balloons brought down, by an enemy aeroplane. There was a burst of flame from the bag and in a few seconds the observer came sailing through the air in a parachute. We were too far away to see him land.

Not finding any place to sleep in this sector, we ran around to the position of the other division, where we found quarters in our old hotel.

The position on the hill overlooking Chateau-Thierry from the south had given us one good picture, so we started out the next morning to see if we could duplicate it or get something better. But no such luck. We stood our car among the trees and then started down to our old position in the orchard about two hundred yards from the car. The shells from our own and the French batteries were screaming out over our heads on their way to the boche lines. The same old balloon, or his twin brother, hovered on the other side of the hill.

We had no sooner taken up our position on the hill, when we heard a shell coming in. It was an entirely different sound, and when it burst about fifty yards from us, I knew the observer in the Hun balloon had sighted us, and was sending in his calling card. Ten seconds later another came along and burst a little nearer. We started back for the car on a run, but about every twenty yards would drop to get out of the way of another bouquet from our friends on the other hill.

I don't know how many came in, and we weren't waiting to count them. We reached the car and didn't wait to climb inside, but started down the road as fast as we could go to get out of range.

That afternoon we went around to the division with which the marines were brigaded. It was June 6, the day our boys drove the

Hun out of Boureches and Torcy, and got a firm grip on the apex of the salient that was so menacing to the French capital.

We reached division shortly after noon. Here things were moving swiftly. Orderlies were dashing in and out of the small building which had been taken over by the division staff. Lieutenant D-----, our conducting officer, felt sure something out of the ordinary was doing, and after talking to some of the officers at headquarters we started ahead. We had not gone more than three hundred yards down the road when the show was started by the French and American batteries.

Judging from the sound, Joe felt certain that all the guns in the world were in that vicinity. The screaming of the shells on their outward journey was continuous and this was accompanied by the sharp bark of the 75's and the booming of the guns of heavy calibre. The country for the greater part was an open one with here and there a small copse of woods that afforded shelter for the batteries.

This was so-called open warfare, but to the "movie" man, who is always on the lookout for the picture, it was decidedly disappointing. It was impossible to see any of the guns, unless one was on top of them, and as the flashes from the muzzles were not discernible for any distance, and there was no smoke, the sight from the picture standpoint was exceedingly disappointing.

One incident along the road furnished an opportunity for a picture with some war color in it. This main road was filled with motor trucks and transport wagons drawn by the old-fashioned Missouri mule, hauling ammunition and supplies to the infantry lines a few kilometers ahead. The road in a great many places was an open one and under plain sight of the enemy's observation balloons, but there was very little activity on the part of their guns that afternoon.

As we were moving along the road a wagon drawn by four mules was approaching from the other direction. Suddenly a French battery of 75's, stationed alongside the road under some trees, opened up. The mules stood up on their hind legs, and finally rolled over on the ground. Within a few minutes the road was a mass of horses, men and automobiles, while the guns alongside kept blazing away. It would have made quite a mess if a boche shell had dropped on the road about that time.

We continued on to headquarters of a marine regiment. It was in front of this that our infantrymen and marines had taken up their positions in the grain fields and the woods, in whatever shelter they could get, as there were no trenches in this section and no time to dig any. The barrage kept up all afternoon until about 6 p.m., clearing the way for the advance of our men on Boureches and Torcy. I don't know how many Huns were killed by it, but when our infantrymen advanced it did not take them long to clean up the few stubborn machine gun positions.

A few days later the two American divisions—the Third, which had been thrown in front of the Hun at Chateau-Thierry, and the Second, which had attacked him on the left—effected liaison. The boche got no further on his way to Paris. At that time, however, his fighting spirit was still high. It was only his advance guard that was stopped at Chateau Thierry, and he still felt certain of continuing his drive to Paris as soon as he brought up the bulk of his troops and his heavy artillery. But Fate—and two American divisions—had decreed that Chateau-Thierry would be the high water mark of the drive, and probably of the war.[18]

It was the morning of June 7 that we were standing at a field hospital when two motor trucks rolled from the line filled with wounded marines and infantrymen. They were hurriedly checked off and started for the rear. Those able to sit up were placed in large trucks, and the more serious cases were placed on stretchers in the Red Cross camions. We followed them back several miles to the Evacuation Hospital, which was being filled as rapidly as it was being emptied. While our wounded were being loaded into the camions for their journey to the base hospital several women clad in black stood weeping in the corner of the yard, in front of a file of French holding their guns at attention.

The door of the hospital opened and several French soldiers came out bearing the body of a French aviator. "Give me my dog," was the cry we heard as this mournful procession passed before us and, turning around, we saw an orderly carrying a dog to a wounded marine officer lying on a stretcher in the yard. They placed the mascot on his chest, and as they lifted the stretcher aboard the ambulance, the young officer's arms came up from the covers and enfolded his pet.

---

18. U.S. troops played an important role in turning back the Germans at Château-Theirry, but American news coverage tended to overstate the case, making it appear as though U.S. troops had "saved Paris." For various reasons, the French allowed their new ally to take the credit.

We followed this procession of wounded all the way to the base hospital in Paris. As we approached the outskirts of the French capital, the sight was one never to be forgotten. As the ambulances rolled along the streets a shutter would open and an anxious face peer out. The women and children in groups of twos and threes would emerge silently from the doorways and stare anxiously at the ambulances as they trundled by. Children in the gutters stopped their play and gazed solemnly at the procession. They had seen these sights before, and knew only too well that another battle was on, and this time near the city. Then one could hear the hushed whisper "American," and a grateful look would come into their eyes. They realized then, as never before, that America was in the war not only with her money but with the best blood in her country.

It was only a little over two weeks later that the official American Expeditionary Force picture "America's Answer to the Hun," was presented for the first time at the Gaumont Palace in Paris. The house was crowded with French and Americans, including such celebrities as Marshal Joffre, Ambassador Sharp, Lord Derby, the British Minister, and many French Senators and Ministers. One portion of the house was allotted to the wounded marines, who were brought to the theatre in huge motor trucks, and the ovation they received was tremendous.

During that period, all France, and especially Paris, had come to realize that the Hun had been stopped, and that the Americans had played an important part in the fight. The picture, which depicted the enormous effort that America had put forth, both in an industrial and a military way, was received with the greatest enthusiasm.

When the German advance was stemmed at Chateau-Thierry the first week in June it furnished the opportunity for Marshal Foch to prepare for his great counter-offensive the middle of July. In conjunction with the French, these two American divisions held the positions for several weeks, which gave the French Generalissimo an opportunity to bring up his reserves. Among these were at least three veteran American divisions—the First, under General Bullard;[19] the Forty-second or Rainbow,[20] under General

19. Major General Robert Lee Bullard, commander of the First Infantry Division. He would achieve the rank of Lieutenant General when given the command of the Second U.S. Army in October 1918.

20. The 42nd Division came to be known as the Rainbow Division because it included soldiers from many different states.

Menoher,[21] and the Twenty-sixth, or New England, Division under General Edwards.[22]

These divisions had been in the line in other sectors since early last Fall. The arrival during April and May of thousands of American troops gave the French commander an opportunity to draw these veteran divisions from the comparatively quiet sectors they were then occupying and fill their places with the new troops from across the seas. The plans were well laid, and by the first week in July American troops were to be found from Rheims along the southern line of the salient to Chateau-Thierry, and from the latter place along the western side of the salient to Soissons.

When the Hun resumed his drive of July 15, with about half a million troops, everything was in readiness for him. In some places he was permitted to cross to the south bank of the Marne before the counter-offensive started; but when it did; his retreat was quickly turned into a rout.

Since that time Marshal Foch has not given the German commanders an idle moment. He has continued his hammering tactics, first in one sector and then in another, until the German troops have been compelled to retreat along the whole line.

While the end of the war is not in sight, it is safe to say that Chateau-Thierry marked the beginning of the end, and historians of the future will record the daring and spirit of the two American divisions who stood like a stone wall between the Hun and Paris and sounded the death knell of German militarism.

Into the Action with the Marines at Belleau Wood

"I did not know yet where I had been hit or
what the bullet had done."

Floyd Gibbons[23]
"Hottest Four Hours I Ever Went Through"
American Magazine, March 1919

---

21. Brigadier General Charles T. Menoher.
22. Major General Clarence Ransom Edwards.
23. Like other famous war correspondents, Gibbons got a lot of mileage out of his war stories. He was a correspondent for the *Chicago Tribune*, but also published stories in some of the largest—and best paying—magazines of the day. This same story also appears in his 1918 war memoir *And They Thought We Wouldn't Fight*.

Just how does it feel to be shot on the field of battle? Just what is the exact sensation when a bullet burns its way through your flesh?

I always wanted to know. As a police reporter I "covered" scores of shooting cases, but I could never learn from the victims what the precise feeling was as the piece of lead struck. But now I know! For three German bullets, which violated my person, completely satisfied my curiosity.

It happened on June 6th just to the northwest of Chateau-Thierry in the Bois de Belleau,[24] which the French have renamed "The Wood of the Americans." On the morning of that day I left Paris by motor for a rush to the front. I knew that American divisions were in this section; and that was my reason for hustling out there.

At Montreuil, then the headquarters of the second United States Army division, I learned that two of our infantry brigades, and also the marines, were fighting in the line, just four miles away. And accompanied by Lieutenant Oscar Hartzell, who was in the Intelligence Department of the Army, I went a mile or two farther on, to the headquarters of Colonel Neveille of the Fifth Marines.

Reaching there about four o'clock in the afternoon, Lieutenant Hartzell and I announced to Colonel Neveille our intention of proceeding to the front line.

"Go wherever you like," was the reply; "but I want to tell you it's damn hot up there."

An hour later found us in the woods to the west of the village of Lucy le Bocage, in which German shells were continually falling.

The ground under the trees was covered with bits of white paper. I could not account for their presence until I examined several of them and found that these were letters from American mothers and wives and sweethearts; letters—whole packages of them—which the tired, dog-weary marines had removed from their packs and destroyed to ease the straps that cut aching grooves in their shoulders.

On the edge of the woods we came upon a hastily dug pit in which were two American machine guns and their crews. The field in front of the woods sloped gently down some two hundred yards to another cluster of trees. This cluster was almost as big as

24. Belleau Wood.

the one we were in. Part of it was occupied by the Germans. Five minutes before five o'clock the order for the advance across the field reached our pit. It was brought there by a second lieutenant, a platoon commander.

"What are you doing here?" he asked, looking at the green brassard and red "C" on my left arm.

"Looking for the big story," I said.

"If I were you I'd be about forty miles south of this place," said the Lieutenant, "but if you want to see the fun, stick around. We are going forward in five minutes."

We hurriedly finished the contents of the can of cold "Corned Willy"[25] we were eating. The machine guns were taken down and the barrels, cradles and tripods were handed over to the members of the crew whose duties it was to carry them.

And then we went over. There are really no heroics about it. There is no bugle call, no sword waving, no dramatic enunciation of catchy commands, no theatricalism—it's just plain get up and go over. And it is done just the same as one would walk across a peaceful wheat field out in Iowa.

But with the appearance of our first line, as it stepped from the shelter of the woods into the open exposure of the flat field, the woods opposite began to cackle and rattle with the enemy machine gun fire. Our men advanced in open order, ten and twelve feet between men. Sometimes a squad would run forward fifty feet and drop. And as its members flattened on the ground for safety another squad would rise from the ground and make another rush.

They gained the woods. Then we could hear shouting. Then we knew that work was being done with the bayonet. The machine gun fire continued in intensity and then died down completely. The wood had been won. Our men consolidated the position by moving forward in groups, ever on the watch-out for snipers in the trees. A number of these were brought down by our crack pistol shots.

At different times during the advance runners had come through the woods inquiring for Major John Berry, the battalion commander. One of these runners attached himself to Lieutenant Hartzell and myself and together the three of us located the Major

25. Canned corned beef.

coming through the woods. He granted permission for Lieutenant Hartzell and me to accompany him and we started forward, in all a party of some fifteen, including ten runners (messengers) attached to the battalion commander.

Owing to the continual evidences of German snipers in the trees, every one in our party carried a revolver ready in his hand, with the exception of myself. Correspondents, you will remember, are non-combatants and must be unarmed.

At the bottom of the slope there was a V-shaped field. The apex of the V was on the left. From left to right the field was some two hundred yards in width. The point where we came out of the woods was about one hundred yards from the apex. At that point the field was about one hundred yards across. It was perfectly flat and was covered with a young crop of oats between ten and fifteen inches high.

This V-shaped oat field was bordered on all sides by dense clusters of trees. In the trees on the side opposite the one on which we stood were German machine guns. We could hear them. We could not see them but we knew that every leaf and piece of greenery there vibrated from their fire, and the tops of the young oats waved and swayed with the streams of lead that swept across.

Major Berry gave orders for us to follow him at intervals of ten or fifteen yards. Then he started across the field alone at the head of the party. I followed. Behind me came Hartzell. Then the woods about us began to rattle fiercely. It was unusually close range. That lead travelled so fast that we could not hear it as it passed. We soon had visual demonstration of the hot place we were in when we began to see the dust puffs that the bullets kicked up in the dirt around our feet.

Major Berry had advanced well beyond the center of the field when I saw him turn toward me and heard him shout:

"Get down everybody!"

We all fell on our faces. And then it began to come hot and fast. Perfect withering volleys of lead swept the tops of the oats just over us. For some reason it did not seem to be coming from the trees hardly a hundred yards in front of us. It was coming from a new direction—from the left.

I was busily engaged flattening myself on the ground, when I heard a shout, so I lifted my head cautiously and looked forward.

The major was making an effort to get to his feet. With his right hand he was savagely grasping his left wrist.

"My hand's gone!" he shouted. One of bullets had struck his left arm at the elbow, tearing away muscles and nerves of the forearm and lodging itself in the palm of his hand. His pain was excruciating.

"Get down. Flatten out, Major!" I shouted. And he dropped to the ground.

"We've got to get out of here," called the major. "We've got to get forward. They'll start shelling this open field in a few minutes."

I lifted my head for another cautious look.

I judged that I was lying about thirty yards from the edge of the trees in front of us. The major was about ten yards in front of me.

"You are twenty yards from the trees!" I shouted to the Major. "I am crawling over to you now. Wait until I get there and I'll help you. Then we'll get up and make a dash for it."

"All right," replied the major. "Hurry along."

I started forward, keeping as flat on the ground as it was possible to do so and at the same time move. As far as it was feasible, I pushed forward by digging in with my toes and elbows so as to make as little movement in the oats as possible. I was not mistaken about the intensity of fire that swept the field. It was terrific.

Then it happened. The lighted end of a cigarette touched me in the fleshy part of my upper left arm. That was all. It just felt like a sudden burn, no larger than one made with a cigarette.

At the time there was no feeling within the arm, that is, no feeling as to aches or pain. There was nothing to indicate that the bullet, as I learned several days later, had gone through the bicep muscle of the upper arm and had come out on the other side. The only sensation perceptible at the time was the burning touch at the spot where the bullet entered.

I glanced down at the sleeve of my uniformed coat and could not even see the hole where the bullet had entered. Neither was there any sudden flow of blood. At the time there was no stiffness or discomfort in the arm and I continued to use it to work my way forward.

Then the second one hit. It nicked the top of my left shoulder. And again came the burning sensation, only this time the area affected seemed larger. Hitting as it did in the meaty cap of the shoulder, I feared that there would be no further use for the arm until it had received attention, but again I was surprised when I found upon experiment that I could still use it.

So I continued to move toward the major. Occasionally I would shout something to him, although, at this time, I am unable to remember what it was. I only wanted to let him know I was coming.

And then the third one struck me. In order to keep as close to the ground as possible, I had swung my chin to the right so that I was pushing forward with my left cheek flat against the ground and in order to accommodate this position of the head, I had moved my steel helmet over so that it covered part of my face on the right.

Then there came a crash. It sounded to me like some one had dropped a glass bottle into a porcelain bathtub. A barrel of whitewash tipped over and it seemed that everything in the world turned white. That was the sensation. I have heard that when one receives a blow on the head everything turns black; but in my case everything became pure white. I remember this distinctly because my years of newspaper training had been in but one direction—to sense and remember. So it was that, even without knowing it, my mind was making mental notes on every impression that my senses registered.

I did not know yet where I had been hit or what the bullet had done. I knew that I was still knowing things. I did not know whether I was alive or dead but I did know that my mind was still taking notes on every second.

The first recess in that note-taking came when I asked myself the following question: "Am I dead?"'

I didn't laugh or didn't even smile when I asked myself the question without putting it in words. I wanted to know. And wanting to know, I undertook to find out. I am not aware now that there was any appreciable passage of time during this mental progress. I feel certain, however, that I never lost consciousness.

How was I to find out if I was dead? The shock had lifted my head off the ground but I had immediately replaced it as close to the soil as possible. My twice punctured left arm was lying alongside my body. I decided to try and move my fingers on my left hand. I did so and they moved. I next moved my left foot. Then I knew I was alive.

I brought my right hand up toward my face and placed it to the left of my nose. My fingers rested on something soft and wet. I withdrew the hand and looked at it. It was covered with blood. As I looked at it I was not aware that my entire vision was confined to my right eye, although there was considerable pain in the entire left side of my face.

This was sufficient to send me on another mental investigation. I closed my right eye and—all was dark. My first thought following this experiment was that my left eye was closed. So I again counselled with myself and tried to open my left eye, but could not feel or verify in any way whether the eye lid responded or not. I only knew that it remained dark on that side. This brought me to another conclusion and not a pessimistic one at that. I simply believed, in spite of the pain, that something had struck me in the eye and had closed it.

I did not know then, as I know now, that a bullet striking the ground immediately under my left cheek bone, had ricocheted upward, going completely through the left eye and then crashing out through my forehead, leaving the eyeball and upper eyelid completely halved, the lower eyelid torn away, and a compound fracture of the skull.

Further progress toward the Major was impossible. I must confess that I became so intensely interested in the weird sensations and subjective research, that I even neglected to call out and tell the wounded officer that I would not be able to continue to his assistance. But after a while, lying there with my left cheek flat on the ground, I saw him rise to his feet, and in a perfect hail of lead rush forward and out of my line of vision.

It was several days later in the hospital that I learned that he reached the shelter of the woods beyond without being hit again, and in that place, although suffering intense pain, was able to shout back orders which resulted in the subsequent wiping out of the machine gun nest that had been our undoing. For this supreme effort. General Pershing decorated him with the Distinguished Service Cross.

I began to make plans to get out of the exposed position in which I was lying. Whereas the field when I started across it had

Chicago Tribune war correspondent Floyd Gibbons charged into the fighting with the Marines at Belleau Wood. He received three wounds, including a shot to the eye. *Source:* Harris & Ewing Collection, Prints and Photographs Division, Library of Congress, LC-H261-29649.

seemed perfectly flat, now it impressed me as being convex, and I was further impressed with the belief that I was lying on the very uppermost and most exposed curvature of it. There is no doubt that the continued stream of machine-gun lead that swept the field super-induced this belief. I got as close to the ground as a piece of paper on top of a table. I remember regretting sincerely that the war had reached the stage of open movement, one consequence of which was that there wasn't a shell hole anywhere to crawl into.

This did not, however, eliminate the dangerous possibility of shelling. With the fatalism that one acquires along the fronts, I was ready to take my chances with the casual German shell that one might have expected, but I devoted much thought to a consideration of the French and American artillery some miles behind me. I considered the possibility of word having been sent back that our advancing waves at this point had been cut down by enemy machine gunners who were still in position preventing all progress at this place. I knew that such information if sent back would immediately be forwarded to our guns and then a devastating concentration of shells would be directed toward the location of the machine gun nests.

I knew that I was lying one hundred yards from one of those nests, and I knew that I was well within the fatal bursting radius of any shells our gunners might direct against that German target. My fear was that myself and other American wounded lying in that field would die by American guns. That is what would have happened if that information had reached our artillery, and it is what should have happened.

The lives of the wounded in that field were as nothing compared with the importance of wiping out that machine-gun nest on our left which was holding up the entire advance.

I wanted to see what time it was, and my watch was attached to my left wrist. In endeavouring to get a look at it, I found out that my left arm was stiff and racked with pain. Hartzell, I knew, had a watch, but I did not know where he was lying, so I called out.

He answered me from some distance away but I could not tell how far or in what direction. I could see dimly but only at the expense of great pain. When he answered I shouted back to him:

"Are you hit?"

"No, are you?" he asked.

"Yes, what time is it?" I said.

"Are you hit badly?" he asked in reply.

"No, I don't think so," I said. "I think I'm all right."

"Where are you hit?" he asked.

"In the head," I said; "I think something hit my eye."

"In the head, you damn fool!" he shouted louder with just a bit of anger and surprise in his voice. "How the hell can you be all right if you are hit in the head? Are you bleeding much?"

"No," I said. "What time is it?"

"I'm coming over to get you!" shouted Hartzell.

"Don't move!" I hastened to shout back. "If you start moving, don't move near me. I think they think I'm dead."

"Well you can't lie there and bleed to death," Hartzell replied. "We've got to do something to get to hell out of here."

"Tell me what time it is and how long it will be before it's dark," I asked.

"It's six o'clock now," Hartzell said, "and it won't be dark till nine—*this* is June. Can you stick it out?"

I told him that I thought I could, and we were silent for some time. Both of us had the feeling that other ears—ears working in conjunction with eyes trained along the barrels of those machine guns a hundred yards on our left—would be aroused to better marksmanship if we continued to talk.

I began to take stock of my condition. During my year or more along the fronts I had been through many hospitals, and from my observations in those institutions I had cultivated a keen distaste for one thing—gas gangrene. I had learned from doctors its fatal and horrible results, and I also had learned from them that it was caused by germs which exist in large quantities in any ground that has been under artificial cultivation for a long period.

Such was the character of the very field I was lying in, and I came to the realization that the wound in the left side of my face and head was resting flatly on the soil. With my right hand I drew up my British box respirator, or gas mask, and placed this under my head. Thus I rested with more confidence, although the machine-gun lead continued to pass in sheets through the tops of the oats not two or three inches above my head.

All of it was coming from the left, coming from the German nests located in the trees at the apex of the V-shaped field. Those guns were not a hundred yards away and they seemed to have an inexhaustible supply of ammunition. Twenty feet away on my left a wounded Marine was lying. Occasionally I would open my right eye for a painful look in his direction.

He was wounded and apparently unconscious. His pack, "the khaki doll," was still strapped between his shoulders. Unconsciously he was doing that which all wounded men do, that is, trying to assume the position that is the most comfortable. He was trying to roll over on his back.

But the pack was on his back, and every time he made the attempt would roll over on this it would elevate his body into full view of the German gunners. Then a withering hail of lead would sweep the field.

It so happened that I was lying immediately in line between those German guns and this unconscious moving target. As the Marine would roll over on top of the pack his chest would be exposed to the fire.

I could see the buttons fly from his tunic and one of the shoulder straps of the back pack part as the sprays of lead struck him. He would limply roll off the pack over on his side. I found myself wishing that he would lie still, as every movement of his brought those streams of bullets closer and closer to my head. I even considered the thickness of the box respirator on which I had elevated my head off the ground. It was about two inches thick.

I remembered my French gas mask hanging from my shoulder and recalled immediately that it was much flatter, being hardly half an inch in thickness. I forthwith drew up the French mask to my head, extracted the British one and rested my cheek closer to the ground on the French one. Thus, I lowered my head about an inch and a half—an inch and a half that represented worlds of satisfaction, and some optimism, to me.

Sometimes there were lulls in the firing. During those periods of comparative quiet I could hear the occasional moan of other wounded on that field. Very few of them cried out, and it seemed to me that those who did were unconscious when they did it. One man in particular had a long, low groan. I could not see him, yet I felt he was lying somewhere close to me.

In the quiet intervals, his unconscious expression of pain reminded me of the sound I had once heard made by a calf which had been tied by a short rope to a tree. The animal had strayed round and round the tree until its entanglement in the rope had left it a helpless prisoner. The groan of that unseen, unconscious wounded American who lay near me on the field that evening sounded exactly like the pitiful bawl of that calf.

Those three hours were long in passing. With the successive volleys that swept the field, I sometimes lost hope that I could ever survive it. It seemed to me that if three German bullets had found me within the space of fifteen minutes, I could hardly expect to spend three hours without receiving the fatal one. With such thoughts on my mind I reopened conversation with Hartzell.

"How's it coming, old man?" I shouted.

"They're coming damn close," he said. "How is it with you? Are you losing much blood?"

"No, I'm all right as far as that goes," I replied; "but I want you to communicate with my wife, in case it's west for me."

"What's her address?" asked Hartzell.

"It's a long one," I said. "Are you ready to take it?"

"Shoot," said Hartzell.

"'Mrs. Floyd Gibbons, No. 12 Bis, Rue de la Chevalier de la Barre, Dijon, Côte d'Or, France.'" I said slowly.

"Good lord!" said Hartzell. "Say it again."

Back and forth we repeated the address correctly and incorrectly some ten or twelve times until Hartzell informed me that he knew it well enough to sing it. He also gave me *his* wife's address. Then, just to make conversation, he would shout over, every fifteen minutes, and tell me that there was just that much less time that we would have to lie there.

I thought that hour between seven and eight o'clock dragged the most, but the one between eight and nine seemed interminable. The hours were so long, particularly when we considered that a German machine gun could fire three hundred shots a minute. Dusk approached slowly. Finally Hartzell called over:

"I don't think they can see us now," he said; "let's start to crawl back."

"Which way shall we crawl?" I asked.

"Into the woods," said Hartzell.

"Which woods?" I asked.

"The woods we came out of, you fool," he replied.

"Which direction are they in?" I said. "I've been moving around and I don't know which way I am heading. Are you on my left or on my right?"

"I can't tell whether I'm on your left or your right," he replied. "How are you lying? On your face or on your back?"

"On my face," I said, "and your voice sounds like it comes from in back of me and on the left."

"If that's the case," said Hartzell, "your head is lying toward the wrong woods. Work around in a half circle and you'll be facing the right direction."

I did so and then heard Hartzell's voice on my right. I started moving toward him. Against my better judgment and expressed wishes, he crawled out toward me and met me half way. His voice close in front of me surprised me.

'"Hold up your head a little," he said. '"I want to see where it hit you."

A German trench mortar captured during the Battle of Belleau Wood. *Source:* Kurt Kaestner Collection, United States Marine Corps Archives & Special Collections. Wikimedia Commons.

"I don't think it looks very nice," I replied, lifting my head. I wanted to know how it looked myself, so I painfully opened the right eye and looked through the oats eighteen inches into Hartzell's face. I saw the look of horror on it as he looked into mine.

Twenty minutes later, after crawling painfully through the interminable yards of young oats, we reached the edge of the woods and safety.

That's how it feels to be shot.

The First All-American Offensive

"All France buzzed with rumors of the forthcoming great American push."

Lincoln Eyre
"Story of Great Victory is Thrillingly Told in Cable to Evening World"
The Evening World (New York), September 13, 1918

With the First American Army in Lorraine, Sept. 13—The Germans are being thrown out of the St. Mihiel sector.

American troops, commanded by American Generals, led by American tanks, following a barrage laid down by American guns, and covered overhead by swarms of American airplanes, are doing the job.

All the American first objectives were reached on scheduled time.

The advance on a forty-mile front already has attained a depth of five miles, and the St. Mihiel sector is being obliterated to-day. Thus far it is officially reported 8,000 German prisoners have been sent to the rear, but unofficially it is believed the number is far in excess of 10,000.

Enemy Retires to his Second Defenses

The attack is being continued with violence everywhere, and the enemy is in full retreat to his second line of prepared defenses.

St. Mihiel itself has been passed on both sides by French troops, who, in smaller units, are with the Americans, under command of Gen. Pershing. Thiaucourt, five miles within German lines, Montsec, and more than a score of villages are in the hands of the Americans and French. Nine big German howitzers are known to have been captured, together with vast war depots.

St. Mihiel was captured on the fourth anniversary of its surrender to the Germans. The enemy is reported to be putting up a fierce resistance in parts of the city in the hope of holding Fort Romain, south of the city.

Is Purely an American Offensive

The entire operation is being commanded by Gen. Pershing personally, and the vast majority of troops engaged are Americans, comprising the American First Army. In previous operations in which Americans participated they were brigaded with French divisions, commanded by French officers. In this offensive, French units are brigaded with American divisions, commanded by American officers.

It is the first real American offensive, launched the day weather compelled a slowing down of the Anglo-French offensive in Picardy, and will keep the German High Command busy. American casualties have been remarkably light.

The great offensive began at one o'clock yesterday morning. At that moment, thousands of French and American guns abruptly ended the long era of tranquility that has hung over the "quiet sector" of the ancient battlefields of Lorraine, and a thunderous choir bade the boche begone out of the strongholds he has held since Sept. 12, 1914.

For four hours the Allied batteries, operating under the supreme command of Gen. Pershing as commander of the First Army, American Expeditionary Forces, smashed and tore asunder the scientifically-planned and powerfully-built trench systems along both sides of the Marne salient from the neighborhood of Les Eparges in the north to Pont-a-Mouson in the east.

Then our infantry swept forward along a front of ten miles along the southern side of the salient that so long "has pointed like an arrow at the heart of France."

In a couple of hours the "doughboys"[26] had penetrated the first and intermediate German positions, capturing numerous villages and much booty.

At 8 o'clock, three hours after the start of the drive from the south, American and French contingents pressed forward in an easterly direction from the sector around Les Eparges.

In the centre of the salient, immediately opposite the town of St. Mihiel itself, French troops maintained close contact with the foe, ready to follow him up the moment he fled before the pressure on his fortifications on the Meuse Heights, in Apremont Forest and at Montsec caused retirement. There was no direct onslaught in the centre, however, because of the "pincers" operations on both sides of the salient, which, if successful, would necessarily squeeze the Germans out of the St. Mihiel stronghold without a fight.

Americans in Tanks Lead the Fighting

A host of tanks, among which, for the first time, were included a large number piloted by Americans, rolled along with the infantry.

Supremacy in the air was assured by the greatest massing of airplanes ever beheld. The bulk of the aerial squadron engaged were French, but every available American flying unit was on the job.

All these forces were commanded by Gen. Pershing, who is the first American General in complete charge of so important and extensive an operation.

Many volumes of military history will be written about the battle that began yesterday morning. The difficulty of preparing and carrying through plans of the American General Staff which, from the first, had the complete approval of Marshal Foch, as the Allied Generalissimo, was tremendous.

American soldiers are talkative and, despite every precaution, news that our divisions were moving back to Lorraine from Soissons and the Marne country could not be wholly suppressed. All France buzzed with rumors of the forthcoming great American push. In Paris every barber and bartender pretended to have "inside information" as to the exact day and hour it would be launched,

26. Slang name for American soldiers.

and in shop windows maps appeared with the "American front" underlined, from Verdun to Switzerland.

Plans Made with all Possible Secrecy

But the weeks went by and nothing happened. All the amateur strategists' forecasts and dope proved to be wrong. The wiseacres began to be a bit apologetic and to hint that the offensive had been permanently abandoned.

Meanwhile, with all possible secrecy and despatch, preparations were proceeding all along the line. One seasoned division, holding quiet parts of the front or reposing in rest areas miles in the rear, suddenly began to move. They marched at night, and so efficiently unostentatious was their progress that not a soul, including the Kaiser's spies, was aware of their movements. Huge guns were spirited into hidden emplacements, invisible to the prying boche airman. Aircraft and tanks by the hundred were scattered all over Lorraine in inconspicuous nooks and crannies.

Vast supplies of munitions were so cleverly veiled that one passed within fifty yards of the dumps without noticing them.

The enemy was very much on the alert, but also very much in the dark. He dared not transfer the bulk of his reserves from Picardy and the Soissons sectors, where the British and French were shoving him backward far swifter than he desired to go. So be contented himself with sleepless vigilance and shifting to and fro the few reserves he felt obliged to maintain along his lines east of the Meuse.[27]

Only Wednesday did he reveal any particular concern for his positions in the St. Mihiel sector. At several places our patrols discovered that he had evacuated his advanced posts and fallen back on his centres of resistance. He even withdrew some of his batteries from the sinister slopes of Montsec, which for four years he has held and glowered down on the plains north of Toul.

Wednesday evening one of our airplanes flew over this height at a low altitude without being fired at. But the enemy could not have

---

27. The Meuse River flows through northeastern France into Belgium and the Netherlands, draining into the North Sea. St. Mihiel is situated on the Meuse.

had any definite knowledge of our plans. The proof of this is the paucity of the artillery fire with which he answered our preparatory cannonade.

Was America's Mightiest Barrage

From this high ground toward the eastern area of our attack I watched this mightiest bombardment the American gunners have ever hurled at a foe, and which is also the mightiest that's ever echoed (deleted).[28]

It was raining and the scarlet flickering of the shells gleamed liquid against the black heavens. The rain stopped, but the night was dismally cloudy, silhouetted against the growing background of the battle zone, ground across which our boys were moving to the fray, there seemed the most desolate slough of despond human being ever trod upon.

Among every road stepped among the hills and dales of Lorraine on my way to the front I passed blast furnaces, tossing flames sky high. The horizon, set alight by our bursting shells, was like a colossal blast furnace blazing aloft at one spot and dying away at another with the electric abruptness of lightning flashes.

Plodding through the mud came columns of men, "going up and in." They seemed gray phantoms in the mist, until, in the brief glare of a flare, pocket lamp or a match, one could glimpse the grins on their dirt and sweat stained faces.

Neither the clammy weather nor the frightful ordeal that lay ahead, where projectiles were leaping like ghastly fireworks, could rub out those grins.

"This time it's 'Black Jack' himself who is going to hand it to 'em," I heard one veteran mutter to a youngster alongside him, going into action for the first time. "You're in luck to be in on Pershing's 'First Show.'"

I talked with many of them, waiting there in the darkness for the "zero hour" to strike. All of them knew their commander in chief was "The Boss" of this affair, and all of them were mightily pleased over it.

---

28. Notations such as this occasionally appeared in news stories to indicate where a censor had deleted information thought to be militarily sensitive, such as the names of individuals, a location, or military unit.

American artillery in action at St. Mihiel. Note the one spent shell casing that is flying through the air, while a new shell is being thrust into the breech in the same fraction of a second. Library of Congress. *Source:* U.S. Army Signal Corps, Prints and Photographs Division, Library of Congress, LC-USZ62-37484.

Fighting Under the "Big Noise"

"We'll fight under the French or the British, if that's the best way to lick the Kaiser, but who would not rather be in a real American scrap under 'The Big Noise' himself!" one soldier asked me as I walked forward a way to get a better view of the barrage.

The American officer who shared my point of vantage informed me that he had just learned that the Boche counter-preparation fire, starting fifteen minutes after our guns gave tongue, had been all but smothered in thirty-five minutes.

The only German shells I clearly identified in the uproar of explosives were a few big calibre ones flung forth spasmodically by railroad artillery located miles behind the enemy front.

As the "zero hour" approached the blast furnace effect of the bombardment was enhanced by the glittering showers of sparks from the star shells that leaped high above the German trenches and by the multi-colored rockets, signaling frantically to the silenced Boche batteries for protection.

Then the sound of the exploding projectiles grew just a bit less thunderous and the rockets rose less high above the horizon.

"It's 6 o'clock," the officer beside me whispered, as one whispers in some sacred place.

Pershing's doughboys were on their way.

Argonne Fighting Breaks the German Army

"It was bitter fighting in the woods, brush, and ravines."

Associated Press
"Yankee Drive Deathblow to German Army"
Chicago Tribune, November 18, 1918

Paris, Nov. 17—[By the Associated Press]—Out of the confusion and daze of the crowding military events on the western battle line since late in September, when battle followed battle until, from Flanders to Verdun, there was ceaseless action, it is now permissible to outline, to a certain extent, the part played by the American armies in the final decisive battle of the war, which ended with the armistice on last Monday.

Military reasons heretofore have prevented accentuating the accomplishments of the Americans, except in a most general manner. The dispatches from the field have been necessarily fragmentary and possibly were overshadowed by the accounts of the more dramatic operations over the historic battlefronts of the west.

Used 750,000 Combat Troops

But it now may be stated that twenty-one American divisions, totaling more than 750,000 American combat troops, participated in the action beginning Sept. 26, known variously as the battle of the Argonne and the battle of the Meuse, but which history may call Sedan[29]—the battle that brought Germany to her knees and, as far as human foresight goes, ended the world's bloodiest and costliest war.

In order to understand the military situation which made the Argonne operations the crux of the war it is necessary to go back to the reduction of the St. Mihiel salient in the middle of September.

Bring Threat to Metz

This brilliant American accomplishment is still fresh in history. It cut off at one stroke a menacing enemy projection toward Verdun and weakened the enemy's defenses by threatening Metz, one of Germany's two greatest advance railway centres for distributing troops and supplies along the Montmedy-Sedan line.

Metz also was the pivot on which the enemy swung through Belgium and into France, and therefore, obviously, it was the pivot on which his retirement must hinge. The Argonne, the next step below here, threatened the great railway arteries running westward from Metz.

Decide on Broad Offensive

With the conclusion of the St. Mihiel action the steady inflow of American forces caused a displacement of power as between the allied and German armies. Thus it no longer was necessary to pursue a policy of reducing a salient or nibbling at it. The American troops had shown what they could do.

A broader policy of general attack along the entire line was then adopted, and the high command called upon Gen. Pershing to take the Argonne sector, admittedly one of the most, if not the most, difficult of the whole front. The broken terrain, the topography, and the lack of roads made the problem difficult to describe.

Germany had in four years fortified it to the last degree of military skill, with superb roads, both rail and motor, connecting up to the rear positions and the bases.

Physical Conditions Terrible

The outstanding feature of the Argonne forest is a long chain of hills running north and south, covered with a dense growth of trees,

---

29. The battle is most commonly known as the Meuse-Argonne. It encompassed the Argonne Forest and the Meuse River. One of its objectives was to capture the vital German rail center at Sedan.

and undergrowth, making an advance difficult and offering superb defensive qualities. Virtually no roads exist in the forest except for a few transversed passes running east and west. The soil is such that the least rain converts it into a slippery, miry mess.

In other words, the physical condition is such that the line of the attack for an advancing army is limited to valleys, chief among which is that of the Aise river.

From the edge of the forest, where the resistance was viciously strong, the enemy possessed innumerable flanking positions. But beyond this difficult region lay the Montmedy-Sedan line, which was recently captured. A German order described it as "our life artery." It represented one-half of the German rail supply on the western front. It meant death if cut.

The allied command told Pershing to cut it. The American First army was put in motion from St. Mihiel. In nine days it was on the Argonne line ready for an attempt, the failure of which might mean disaster and the success of which would give untold results. This quick movement of an enormous body of men, the establishment of a new line of supply and all the complicated military preparations, was regarded with pride by the American commanders.

The Americans knew what confronted them. They realized that this was no second St. Mihiel, but an enterprise at which other armies had balked for four years. They knew that here was to be fought a fight to rank with the first battle of the Marne, with Verdun, with the Somme and the Chemin-Des-Dames;[30] and they knew that on them depended the fate of the great attack on the rest of the front. If forced back here, the enemy must give way to the west. If he held he could hold elsewhere.

Use Up Enemy Reserves

It was at daybreak of Sept. 26 when the Americans went in. Using nine divisions for the preliminary attack, and under vigorous artillery support, they advanced five kilometers the first day. But the enemy was not taken wholly by surprise. The second day he threw into the line five counter attack divisions he had held in close reserve. They were his best troops, but they failed not only to push

---

30. Four of the largest, most important battles on the Western Front. The Chemin des Dames was a strategic ridge to the north of Paris that had been held by the Germans since November 1914. Three battles had been fought for it, all named the Battle of the Aisne, for the nearby Aisne River.

the Americans back but they failed to check the gradual advance of the Americans over the difficult terrain.

The first phase of the action ended Oct. 31, during which the American gains were not large, but they compelled the enemy to use a large number of divisions, which became slowly exhausted and thus were unable to parry the hammering he was receiving from the French and British on the west.

It was bitter fighting in the woods, brush, and ravines, over a region perfectly registered and plotted by the enemy, where his guns, big and little, could be used with the greatest efficiency. The original nine American divisions in some cases were kept in the lines over three consecutive weeks. The American reserves then were thrown in until every division not engaged on another part of the line had been put into action.

Many Green Troops Used

It is a fact commented upon with pride by the American commanders and complimented by the allies that seven of these divisions that drove their way through the hard action never before had been in an active sector, while green troops, fresh from home, were poured in as replacements.[31]

The Associated Press dispatches from day to day told what these men did; how the enemy was slowly pushed back from his strongest and most vital positions, through one defense system after another, using his finest selected troops, which had been withdrawn in many instances from other portions of the line, in an effort to hold an enemy which he derisively said last spring could not be brought to Europe and if so could not fight, and even if he tried to fight would not know how to do so.

Opening of Second Phase

The attack delivered the morning of Nov. 1, which began the second phase of the Argonne battle, was the death blow to the German army. Between Sept 26 and Oct. 31 enemy divisions to the number of thirty-six were identified as being opposed to the Americans in

---

31. Some historians have been critical of the use of so many green troops in this offensive, suggesting that it resulted in unnecessarily high casualties.

Fighting during the Meuse-Argonne offensive. Library of Congress. *Source:* U.S. Army Signal Corps, Prints and Photographs Division, Library of Congress, LC-USZ62-3783.

this sector. Between Nov. 1 and Nov. 6 the enemy threw in fourteen fresh divisions, but all in vain.

Fighting every foot of the way, the American advance averaged five kilometers daily over terrain constantly growing more difficult, with lines of communications and supply daily lengthening and attenuating, while roadmakers for the transport and other supply organizations worked day and night at their tasks.

Day by day the official communications and the telephones, even to the farthest advance line, told the Americans that for every mile the Germans gave way before them they were yielding another mile to the British and French on the left; that the American pressure was felt like an electric current throughout the line.

Germans Admit Break Through

On the morning of Nov. 2 the German official communication told Americans they had won, because, for the first time in the war, the enemy officially admitted that the American attack had effected a break through. The Americans knew that what finally happened on the morning of Nov. 11, when the armistice was signed, was only a question of days.

Last Monday morning the general commanding a certain division was called to the telephone in a far advanced position and asked if he had understood that hostilities were to have ceased at 11 o'clock in the morning.

"Yes," replied the general, "I did. But at 10:58 we were going like hell."

Chapter 9

✦

✦

✦

✦

✦

Wounded Warriors

Introduction

For nearly three years, the American public viewed the advent of modern warfare, including the introduction of machine guns, gas, and prolonged artillery bombardment, from the safety of its distant neutrality. Even after the United States entered the war, its soldiers did not see serious combat for the better part of a year, a time during which the AEF built up its medical corps and hospitals.

The flood of American wounded began in May 1918, with the battle of Cantigny and fighting along the Marne River. The larger campaigns of the summer and fall maintained a steady flow of casualties. Their care began when stretcher bearers carried them off the battlefield. Ambulances rushed them to dressing stations and field hospitals for initial care, where wounded and dying often overflowed wards, hallways, and outside courtyards, waiting their turn in surgery. Ambulances or hospital trains transported the more serious cases and those needing convalescence to base hospitals farther behind the lines.

For journalists, it was yet another face of war that had to be described to their readers. Some wounds were so terrible or unfamiliar that they required explanation. Readers had to be introduced to the mutilating effect of shrapnel, what poison gas did to the lungs, and the mysteries of "shell shock" that could reduce otherwise healthy men to fits of shaking, incoherence, or acute panic. But reporters always took care to balance the pathos of suffering, broken bodies, and death with positive themes. They found a unique American character in the resolute courage and good will of the wounded, stressed the nobleness of their sacrifice, and noted how compassionate was their care.

This chapter offers three contrasting views of the wounded, one by a YMCA volunteer on a hospital train transporting wounded, one by a chaplain who finds an uplifting religious theme in his experience with wounded soldiers, and one an impressionistic account of a nurse's aide and Red Cross "searcher," who tried to locate missing soldiers and reconnect the wounded to their families. It is that third article, "Down from Château-Thierry," that hints at the enormous service rendered by the thousands of American women who served as nurses in France, either with the U.S. Army Nurse Corps or the Red Cross. Both groups rendered care to allied soldiers, and, in the war zone, to civilians as well.

The article "Makes New Faces for Mutilated Soldiers" tells about the unique contribution made by American sculptor Anna Coleman Ladd that allowed soldiers with horrible facial wounds to resume some measure of a normal life.

A network of hospitals and rehabilitation facilities waited the post-war return to America of wounded and rehabilitating soldiers. Still the U.S. scrambled to accommodate the vast numbers who required care in the months following the Armistice. To the extent possible medical science and vocational training prepared them to resume their civilian lives. But these physically and emotionally damaged men were fated to be the most visible and lingering legacy of America's role in the war.

The First Flood of Wounded

"One comes away from such scenes too deeply affected for descriptive details."

Charles H. Grasty
"Rush Wounded to Paris"
New York Times, June 10, 1918

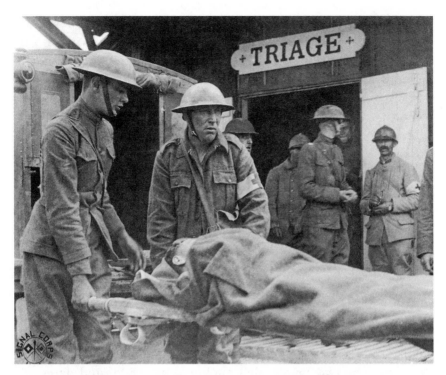

Sorting the wounded at a triage station to determine the urgency of their condition. Some receive immediate treatment, and others are rushed to hospitals in the rear. *Source:* Otis Historical Archives National Museum of Health & Medicine. Wikimedia Commons.

Paris, June 9—Although I have been at all fronts and in many of the first-line trenches, I feel that I have seen real war today for the first time. I made a round of visits to the Red Cross hospitals, to which have been rushed the casualties from the various fronts where the American troops are engaged.

Paris is headquarters now for taking care of our wounded. At all the surgical hospitals today the facilities were taxed to the utmost. I found wards filled with American casualty cases, halls filled with men lying on cots, in courtyards, and even outside in the streets, waiting until the surgeons, working forty-eight hours straight without sleep, could take them into the operating room.

The largest hospital is American No. 1, at Neuilly,[1] and during the last two days there had been a stream of camions bringing

1. The American Hospital at Neuilly was founded in 1906 by the American community in Paris. At the outbreak of war, it offered its service to the French government as a military hospital. By the time the United States entered the war, the hospital was treating 1,600 wounded soldiers daily and ran a fleet of thirty-five ambulances.

our wounded from the Marne. I went there primarily to see Floyd Gibbons,[2] the details of whose experience with the Marines northwest of Château-Thierry already have been cabled. The surgeons had taken out what a machine-gun bullet had left of his eye, and nurses were dressing a wound in his left shoulder and another which went through the same arm between the shoulder and the elbows, fortunately missing the bone. He was serene and philosophical over his misfortune, thanking his lucky star that it was no worse. He was more concerned over the gap his absence would leave in the service of his newspaper than in personal consequences to himself. He was confident he would be back at work within a few days. He was saved from death by his helmet, which the bullet penetrated before putting out his eye. He brought the helmet away as a souvenir.

Are Anxious to Fight Again

Mr. Gibbons was with a conducting officer, and ambitiously approached the firing line, where he was caught under machine gun fire. The two found what shelter they could, and dared not move for two hours, when they went back to a dressing station, and Mr. Gibbons got first aid. Then he rode all Thursday in an ambulance to Paris, and was operated upon soon after his arrival. Mrs. Gibbons, who is in France, was with him and witnessed the operation.

Next to Mr. Gibbons's cot was a red-haired private with a leg wound, who listened intently to our conversation. When Mr. Gibbons said the place where he was wounded was a few miles northwest of Château-Thierry, his neighbor broke in with a question.

"How far have we got to go before we drive those Germans across the Rhine?"

I afterward learned that the poor boy would have a long road to go before he could have any part again in the drive, for he has a bad infection in his wound. But his question illustrates the spirit that prevails among all the wounded. They are eager to get back in the game. Their fighting blood is up. I encountered the same spirit in

---

2. Gibbons was a war correspondent for the *Chicago Tribune*. He was injured at the Battle of Belleau Wood, losing sight in one eye. Chapter 8 includes an article in which he describes the experience of getting shot.

man after man, lying helpless on the cots but looking ahead to the day when they could have revenge on the boche.

In the same room was a chap whose leg had been amputated above the knee several weeks ago. The stump was dressed while I was there. Before and afterward the boy was writing a letter home. He was so emaciated that I wondered at his energy, but there was no shadow of depression on his pale face.

Three cots away was a big fellow with a German name from a Western state. He had been in the Cantigny show.

"Scratch" Twelve Inches Long

"My wound is only a scratch," he said, "but it is just below the back of my neck where the nerves all cross, and it gives me a bad quarter of an hour when the sisters dress it. I was in a hand-to-hand fight when a second boche came up behind and jabbed me with his bayonet. Luckily for me the wound was across my back, and did not touch a vital part."

Presently, the sisters came and took the dressing off, and the wound looked so terrible that I was obliged to look away. The "scratch" was nearly twelve inches long and very deep.

I walked through the crowded halls, stopping and talking with men classified as not seriously wounded. One was a boy from New York, without a sign of a beard on his lip. He scarcely looked 14, although he doubtless is older. He had a piece of shrapnel in his thigh. He was a dispatch rider at Cantigny.[3] Another was a husky lad who enlisted in Idaho in April last year and went over the top at Cantigny.

In one ward I saw a woman who lives at the Ritz[4] wheeling around a dressing table, and she stopped at a cot to which a 19-year-old private was just being brought. His right forearm had been shot off and he had a bad shrapnel wound in his left thigh. When they lay him down on the cot he laughed out loud and said: "Gee, but this bed feels good!"

When I looked a little closer I found that he had also a gunshot wound in his left palm. His war days are over, poor lad.

---

3. The first American battle of the war.
4. The Hôtel Ritz in Paris catered to the rich and famous, including royalty, politicians, and film stars.

The sister told me of a remarkable case. A young chap was brought in two days ago, badly gashed. He died, and when they looked him up they found that his father was an officer in the German Army, although the son was a naturalized American. The address of his nearest relative was in Germany. He was wrapped in an American flag and buried in Paris.

Dr. Blake's Hospital Filled

This hospital has provided hundreds of extra beds, although the rush of yesterday and last night is probably now over. A few squares away I visited Red Cross Hospital No. 2—Dr. Blake's, with 500 beds—where similar conditions existed. There were lines of camions and ambulances in the street filled with wounded Americans waiting for room on the operating tables. Great work is being done here. In all there are five hospitals under the American Red Cross in Paris.

Mr. Morrow of Morgan & Co. and I drove to see No. 5, which was completed this morning and has plenty of spare beds for convalescents and walking cases which do not require surgical attention. It has a thousand beds and was constructed in thirty days. The material used is Bessoneau tents,[5] of which there are fifty-one. In addition to its Paris hospital plants, accommodating 2,500, the Red Cross has several near the front line, and is opening others.

500 Beds in Whitney Hospital

An existing hospital, Mrs. Payne Whitney's,[6] has been like special Providence in the recent emergency. She opened it in 1914, and it has been used by the French, but its 500 beds were ready when needed for Americans. It is situated near the Meaux, and served as a casualty clearing station where urgent operations were performed. Two other hospitals are being opened today in the same vicinity.

One comes away from such scenes too deeply affected for descriptive details. Everybody who has given a dollar for this work of mercy for our own may feel fully rewarded for his generosity.

5. A Bessonneau "tent" was actually a temporary building. It was delivered as a kit, with pre-made parts that could be assembled and disassembled quickly. The correct spelling is "Bessonneau."

6. Wealthy New York socialite Mrs. Harry Payne Whitney actively supported the American Hospital in Paris and established her own hospital there as well.

How much more can be said for those who are giving their personal service! I saw a woman working today whose presence in Paris many had previously been inclined to criticize—a rich woman who might have come here looking for excitement. But the emergency came, and they are doing the greatest work that can be given to human hands to do.

I hear that 20,000 military nurses have been called for from America, and after seeing what I have today, I hope that American women who are in a position to do so will not miss this unequaled opportunity for the noblest service it has ever been in the power of human beings to render. Nurses and surgeons should come quickly.

What the percentage of efficiency in the American Red Cross organization is I am unable to estimate, but I have no hesitation in saying that it has done work in these last few days that would justify its existence and the support given to it if it never did anything else. The Red Cross has been getting ready. It has been collecting money and spending it, filling warehouses and accumulating medical and other supplies for months past. It had 6,000,000 surgical dressings in stock in Paris alone. It had 600 or 700 camions and motor vehicles, 300 of them in Paris. Its personnel in France numbers 2,700.

Many people have looked askance at these huge preparations. In the early operations in Lorraine the Red Cross furnished considerable supplies, but the army could have got along any way. Then came Cantigny, and the Red Cross was at hand with a hospital. And now the organization is ready at Paris to take the wounded American heroes of the second Marne battle.

Evacuating the Wounded on a Hospital Train

"Blood-stained hands fumbling at their bandages, and the excited talk of battle and death."

Roger Gilman
"With the Wounded from the Marne"
The Outlook, October 16, 1918

"Here you are, fellers, what'll you have? New York 'Herald' or Chicago 'Tribune'?"

"Say, man, what's that? Sure, a New York one for mine."

What wouldn't you give to be handing these out to those boys in pajamas, with heads or hands wrapped in bandages, sitting in the door of a French box car? So I thought yesterday as I walked along the train or clambered into other cars where there were no grinning boys in the doorway, only quiet figures on stretchers, each with the inevitable big white bandage.

It was July 17, the third day of the great drive on the Americans at the Marne, and our first big fight. All the night before in [deleted by Censor] ambulances had rolled through the starlit streets from the front, huge hospital supply trucks had stopped me at two in the morning to ask the way, and the courtyard of the Army hospital had been filled with a steady stream of limping figures and groping stretcher-bearers. No lights showed anywhere for the hospital [deleted by Censor] at Jouy had just been heavily bombed.

Then came a blazing day in the freight yards, where a superb Red Cross train had loaded and pulled out in the early morning. From ten o'clock on, the ambulances were busy filling a French hospital train, on which I had been asked by the anxious doctor to act as interpreter.

By four the cars were furnaces; everybody was begging me to take his blanket off, and the gas cases in the doorways were rolling up their pajamas and dangling their bare feet. The French doctor in charge came up with his coat unbuttoned and even his hat on the back of his head.

"You go to Paris, monsieur? You can assist us much! It is very painful to have no one with us who can speak their language. Yes, we go to Paris. It will take four hours."

Of course I did not have the safe-conduct so much insisted on for moving about in the war zone—only strict instructions not to leave my post; and there was every prospect of losing days in Paris when the battle was on. But here were over two hundred wounded Americans, many just off the operating-table, a French medical staff, and in this first great rush no one but myself to speak for them. Well, naturally, there was nothing else to do, and I never climbed on a train more gladly.

Finally the last four litters were gently lifted out of the ambulances; for ambulance men, even after two nights and two days of driving and unloading, are as gentle as ever you mothers could be; and the train, with the pitiful burden, moved out.

Immediately the blessed breeze began to blow through the open door and sift in through the vestibules between the cars, and the whole train sighed its relief. The country, seen in great pictures, looked almost like "God's own;" whiffs of hay blew in from the broad meadows; white clouds drifted by in the sun. War seemed impossible. And yet here were these stiff figures, swollen eyes that could not open, blood-stained hands fumbling at their bandages, and the excited talk of battle and death.

"My captain, he died right in my arms, all shot to pieces."

"Say, I don't mind seeing men killed—men like ourselves; but when I saw in that village little children with their heads blown clean off by shells—God, it's awful!"

"Gee, I won't be worth a damn back home like I am now! I hope I don't go."

And what could one do for them so? Oh, just the littlest things that seemed so futile, but were accepted with such pathetic thanks. For instance, you got a huge tin pitcher of water and a little hospital cup with a spout—a "chick beak," the French orderly called it—and went down the line. Everybody took it, and everybody said, carefully, "I thank you," or, better still, just smiled.

"Say, Y.M.C.A. man, I don't suppose you've got a cigarette?"

You say, "I'm sorry, old man," but tell him that you'll "bum" one for him, and two beds away you ask a boy with some color left under his three days beard.

"Sure, there's some 'Lucky Strikes.' Aw, take him some more."

"What's your name and outfit? I'll tell him who it is."

"Naw, naw; just Sixth Artillery, that's all."

Next there is a big boy with bandages who has to be propped up with blankets and turned just a trifle, so slowly. And again a poor head has lost its pillow and is tipping away back, till you find the pillow on the floor and softly put it right again. And another wants you to look for a little map knotted up with all his worldly goods in a wet bath towel.

About half-way down the train you suddenly see in the narrow passage between the litter frames a huge perspiring face grinning delightedly under its cropped hair. It's the gassed man who offered to go into the town, just before we started, to get some fruit.

"Say, I got 'em, but I had to run for it. The first woman, she wanted too much, and I went clear to that kind of a market they have at the other end of the place. But they're good little plums, all right."

And so "Doc," as kind-hearted as a father and as merry as only a red-headed American private can be, went through the train with his big basket. No Apostle curing a lame man at the gate of the Temple was ever more happy than he.

But what sort of cases were they? And how did they stand it, poor boys?

The gas cases ran all the way from simple weakness and burns, slight or terrible, to those who had got the gas into their throats and could not drink or speak. The wounds were mostly from shrapnel or shell, sometimes two or three or five, and some were from machine-gun bullets. There were scarcely any gunshot wounds, and not one from a bayonet.

And stand it? I can't tell you how fine they were! Not one moaned, only two asked for help. From the young captain whose head and neck were strapped with bandages, lying with set face and hands crossed, like a marble image, to the tousled-haired boy who spoke with an Italian accent, they just lay still and stood it. At first I could hardly realize what they were going through, but a clear-skinned fellow whom I started to jolly a little answered with such a piteous crumpled-up smile that I knew once for all. After that one I was very careful.

But the two who did ask for help? Well, I'll tell you about them. One was so swathed in bandages from his hips up that I had asked if he ought to go with us, but the doctors thought he might. He kept saying that he couldn't breathe. When I was away, he got up twice, somehow, till the others put him back. So I told him he mustn't move, and he said, "Just stay with me." We tried to talk about Brooklyn and Coney,[7] but he was always putting his arm around my neck to lift himself and saying, "Oh, please, mister, please let me sit up!"

Well, he had two drainage tubes, so he couldn't, but finally neither the French soldier-orderly nor I could stand it any longer. So the broad-backed little *poilu* lifted him slowly on his feet and we steadied him along to the car door and laid him in the draught on a fresh stretcher, and somehow his poor body felt better and his moaning stopped. All the farther end of the car asked in awestruck tones, "Is he dead?" No, thank Heaven, he wasn't. Just content.

---

7. Coney Island was a popular amusement park and seaside resort in Brooklyn, NY.

Presently we stopped at a junction where some of our newly arrived men looked in, and then there was real interest. No veterans ever regaled their listeners with more easy confidence than did these boys of five days on the line. And they got it across. Wonder and envy were in every open mouth on that platform.

And then, although the train had merely crept on its way, the long four hours of jolting began to tell. They asked more often what time it was, they wanted more water but drank less at a time, the white bandages began to show spots, and the air grew heavier.

At this time the one other complaint began. It came from a little fellow with anxious, white face. "Couldn't you give me something to relieve my pain? Just to relieve my pain."

So I picked out a man who could move around and told him to reassure the sufferer and stay there right by him, so that I could find him again. Then I went off and hunted up the doctor. When we returned, the boy said little, but his eyes were full of tears. The kind old Frenchman gave one look and said he should have an injection, but before he could return the train grew suddenly dark, and we rolled into an immense barn-like station. In the confusion I lost the patient for a little, but presently found him again, and got the stretcher bearers to take him out among the first. Then an ambulance man stayed by him and talked to him while we hunted up the station doctor and a nurse, and then they hunted up some tubes and needles. It all took a long, long time, but there was only the same anxious whisper: "Oh, give me something to relieve my pain!"

The next time I passed it had been done. He was even smiling a bit, and he answered, "Oh, yes, I feel just fine."

Then there came along a dark young fellow, painfully hobbling down the platform. As he put a heavy arm over my shoulder he began to talk:

"Glad I'm here, all right. They had me prisoner for a while the first afternoon. There were three of us wounded in a shell hole, and the squareheads[8] came along and pinched us and put us in a barn. And they had a little machine gun, and every time one of the boys would come along they'd get him and put him in there. And then they went off and left us for a little, and I said, 'Come on, fellers,

---

8. Add Squarehead to the list of nicknames used for German soldiers.

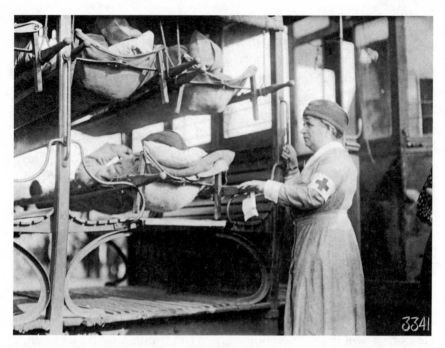

An American Red Cross nurse at the railroad station at St. Etienne, France, helping wounded soldiers on to the tram cars which are being used as ambulances, July 1918. *Source:* Prints and Photographs Division, Library of Congress, LC-DIG-ppmsca-40772.

let's beat it, and I got another one that was wounded on my back, and so we did. Me? I'm from Louisiana. Good-night."

In the station everything seemed dim and huge under the blue-shaded arc lights—vast spaces filled with little frames, long canteen counters, endless ambulances rolling in, army doctors, shouting traffic officers, and a group of kind-faced Red Cross women. The wheels had scarcely stopped turning before they were in among the boys, fanning some, taking addresses for others, offering them cool milk.

In the midst of it all I came upon a figure in a damp flannel shirt, hunched up in the door of the car. It was "Doc," all in from his trudging to and fro with his basket of plums and the heat. So a limping boy still wearing a helmet and a gassed man and I got him off to a cool corner of the baggage platform. The last I saw of him he was lying on his back with his legs crossed in the air, half asleep, but smoking a Fatima.[9]

9. A brand of American cigarettes.

An hour later, rolling along on the front seat of an ambulance in the blackness of the outer boulevards, the driver and I got to talking. He told me a story of a boy in a field hospital just coming out of the chloroform. The boy thought he was a prisoner in German hands, and he began to fight. It took eight men to hold him. Then he gradually heard their voices, but he couldn't see. So he reached up and got hold of their caps, and pulled them down to him one by one. And when his fingers touched the American rank insignia, he smiled and just said,

"Thank God!"

Somewhere in France,[10] August 12, 1918.

Bringing Religion to the Gas Ward

"O thou Christ who stilled the waves of Galilee, come thou into the hearts of these boys."

William L. Stidger
"Gas, Shell-Shock and Souls"
The Outlook, October 9, 1918

It was the gas ward. I had held a vesper service that evening and had had a strange experience. Just before the service I had been introduced to a lad who said to the chaplain who introduced me that he was a member of my denomination.

The boy could not speak above a whisper. He was gassed horribly, and, in addition to his lungs and his throat being burned out, his face and neck were scarred.[11]

"I have as many scars on my lungs as I have on my face," he said, quite simply: I had to bend close to hear him. He could not talk loud enough to have awakened a sleeping child.

He said to me: "I used to be leader of the choir at home. At college I was in the Glee Club, and whenever we had any singin' at the fraternity house they always expected me to lead it.

---

10. War correspondents, who were often prevented from identifying their location by censorship restrictions, would instead use the generic term "Somewhere in France." It became the title of a popular song in 1918.

11. The effects of mustard gas.

"Since I came into the Army the boys in my outfit have depended upon me for all the music.

"In camp back home I led the singing. Even the Y.M.C.A. always counted on me to lead the singing in the religious meetings. Many's the time I have cheered the boys comin' over on the transport and in camp by singin' when they were blue. But I can't sing any more. Sometimes I get pretty blue over that. But I'll be at your meeting this evening, anyway, and I'll be right down on the front seat as near the piano as I can get. Watch for me."

And, sure enough, that night when the vesper service started he was right there. I smiled at him, and he smiled back.

I announced the first hymn. The crowd started to sing. Suddenly I looked toward him. We were singing "Softly now the light of day fades upon my sight away." His book was up, his lips were moving, but no sound was coming. That sight all but broke my heart. To see that boy, whose whole passion in the past had been to sing, whose voice the cruel gas had burned out, started emotions throbbing in me that blurred my eyes. I couldn't sing another note myself. My voice was choked at the sight. A lump came every time I looked at him there with that book up in front of him—a lump that I could not get out of my throat. I got so I dared not look in his direction.

After the service was over I went up to him. I knew that he needed a bit of laughter now. I knew that I did too. So I said to him, "Lad, I don't know what I would have done if you hadn't helped us out on the singing this evening."

He looked at me with infinite patience and sorrow in his eyes. Then a look of triumph came into them, and he looked up and whispered through his rasped voice: "I may not be able to make much noise any more, and I may never be able to lead the choir again, but I'll always have singing in my soul, sir! I'll always have singing in my soul!"

And so it is with the whole American Army in France; it always has singing in its soul, and courage, and manliness, and daring, and hope. That kind of an army can never be defeated. And no army in the world and no power can stand long before that kind of an army.

That kind of an army doesn't have to be sent into battle with a barrage of shells in front of it and a barrage of shells back of it to force it in, as the Germans have been doing during the last big offensive, according to stories that boys at Château-Thierry have been telling me. The kind of an army that, in spite of wounds and gas, "still has singing in its soul" will conquer all hell on earth before it gets through.

Then there is the memory of the boys in the shell-shock ward at this same hospital. I had a long visit with them. They were not to come to the vesper service for fear something would happen to upset their nerves. But they made a request that I come to visit them in their ward. After the service I went. I reached their ward about nine, and they rose to greet me.

The nurse told me that they were more at ease on their feet than lying down, and so for two hours we stood and talked on our feet.

"How did you get yours?" I asked a little black-eyed New Yorker.

"I was in a front-line trench with my outfit down near Amiens," he said. "We were having a pretty warm scrap. I was handling a machine gun so fast that it was red-hot. I was afraid it would melt down and I would be up against it. They were coming over in droves and we were mowing them down so fast that out in front of our company they looked like stacks of hay, the dead Germans piled up everywhere. I was so busy firing my gun and watching it so carefully because it was so hot that I didn't hear the shell that suddenly burst behind me. If had heard it coming, it would never have shocked me."

"If you hear them coming, you're all right?" I asked.

"Yes. It's the ones that surprise you that give you shell-shock. If you hear the whine, you're ready for them; but if your mind is on something else, as mine was that day, and the thing bursts close, it either kills you or gives you shell-shock, so it gets you both going and coming." He laughed at this.

"I was all right for a while after the thing fell, for I was unconscious for a half hour. When I came to, I began to shake, and I've been shaking ever since."

"How'd you get yours?" I asked another lad from Kansas, for I saw at once that it eased them to talk about it.

"I was in a trench when a big Jack Johnson[12] burst right behind me. It killed six of the boys, all my friends, and buried

12. A "Jack Johnson" was the nickname used to describe a shell from the German 15-cm heavy artillery. The name is taken from Jack Johnson, the U.S. heavyweight boxing champion from 1908–1915.

me under the dirt that fell from the parapet back of me. I had sense and strength enough to dig myself out. When I got out, I was kind of dazed. The captain told me to go back to the rear. I started back through the communication trench[13] and got lost. The next thing I knew I was wandering around in the darkness shakin' like a leaf."

Then there was the California boy. I had known him before. It was he who almost gave me a case of shell-shock. The last time I saw him he was standing on a platform addressing a crowd of young church people in California. And there he was, his six foot three shaking from head to foot like an old man with palsy and stuttering every word he spoke. He had been sent to the hospital at Amiens with a case of acute appendicitis. The first night he was in the hospital the Germans bombed it and destroyed it. He was taken out and put on a train for Paris. This train had only got a few miles out of Amiens when the Germans shelled it and destroyed two cars.

"No wonder, man; who wouldn't shake after that?" I said. Then I asked him if he had had his operation yet.

"It can't be done until I quit shaking."

"When will you quit?" I asked, with a smile.

"Oh, we're all getting better, much better; we'll be out of here in a few months; they all get better; ninety per cent of us get back in the trenches."

And that is the silver lining to this silhouette spiritual. The doctors say that a very large percentage of them get back.

"We call ourselves the 'First American Shock Troops,'" my friend from the West said, with a grin.

"I guess you are shock troops all right. I know one thing and that is that you would give your folks back home a good shock if they saw you."

Then we all laughed. Laughter was in the air. I have never met anywhere in France such a happy, hopeful, cheerful crowd as that bunch of shell-shocked boys. It was contagious. I went there to cheer them up, and I got cheered up. I went there to give them strength, and came away stronger than when I went in. It would cheer the hearts of all Americans to take a peep into that room,

---

13. Trench systems consisted of three rows of trenches: front-line, support, and reserve. Communication trenches were dug at an angle to those trenches and used to transport men, ammunition, equipment, and food.

if they could see the souls back of the trembling bodies, if they could get beyond the first shock of those trembling bodies and stuttering tongues. And, after all, that is what America must learn to do, to get to see beyond the wounds into the soul of the boy; to see beyond the blinded eyes, the scarred faces, the legless and armless lads, into the glory of their new-born souls, for no boy goes through the hell of fire and suffering and wounds that he does not come out new born. The old man is gone from him, and a new man is born in him. That is the great eternal compensation of war and suffering.

I have seen boys come out of battles made new men. I have seen them go into the line sixteen-year-old lads and come out of the trenches men. I saw a lad who had been through the fighting in Belleau Woods. I talked with him in the hospital at Paris. His face was terribly wounded. He was ugly to look at, but when I talked with him I found a soul as white as a lily and as courageous as granite.

"I may look awful," he said, "but I'm a new man inside. What I saw out there in the woods made me different somehow. I saw a friend stand by his machine gun with a whole platoon of Germans sweeping down on him, and he never flinched. He fired that old gun until every bullet was gone and his gun was red-hot. I was lying on the grass, where I could see it all. I saw them bayonet him. He fought to the last against fifty men; but, thank God, he died a man; he died an American! I lay there and cried to see them kill him; but every time I think of that fellow it makes me want to be more of a man. When I get back home, I'm going to give up my life to some kind of Christian service. I'm going to do it because I saw that man die so bravely. If he can die like that, in spite of my face I can live like a man."

The boys in the trenches live a year in a month, a month in a week, a week in a day, a day in an hour, and sometimes an eternity in a second. No wonder it makes men of them overnight. No wonder they come out of it all with that "high look" that John Oxenham[14] writes about. They have been reborn.

---

14. The popular British writer William Arthur Dunkerley wrote poetry under the pseudonym John Oxenham. His 1917 poem "What Did You See Out There?" ends with these lines: "You've a right to your deep, high look, my lad / You have met God in the ways, / And no man looks into His face / But he feels it all his days. / You've a right to your deep, high look, my lad, / And we thank Him for His grace." Like the writer of this article, Oxenham found an uplifting religious theme in the war.

"How do the Americans stand dressing their wounds and the suffering in the hospital?" a friend of mine asked a prominent surgeon.

"They bear their suffering like French men. That is the highest compliment I can pay them," he replied.

And so back of their wounds are their immortal, undying, unflinching souls.

That night I said, just before I left, "Boys, it's Sunday evening and they wouldn't let you come to my meeting; would you like me to have a little prayer with you?"

"Yes! Sure! That's just what we want!" were the stammered words that followed.

"All right; we'll just stand if it's easier for you."

Then I prayed the prayer that had been burning in my heart every minute as we had been standing there in that dimly lit ward talking of home and battle and the folks we all love across the seas. All that time there had been hovering in the background of my mind a picture of a cool body of water named Galilee and of a Christ who had been sleeping in a boat on that water with some of his friends when a storm came up. I had been thinking of how frightened those friends had been of the storm, of the tossing, tumbling, turbulent waves. I had thought of how they had trembled with fear, and then of how they had appealed to the Master. I told the boys simply that story and then I prayed:

"O thou Christ who stilled the waves of Galilee, come thou into the hearts of these boys just now and still their trembling limbs and tongues and bring a great sense of peace and quiet into their hearts."

"O ye of little faith!" When I looked up from that prayer, much to my own astonishment and to the astonishment of the friend who was with me, the tremblings of those fine American boys had perceptibly ceased. There was a great sense of quiet and peace in the ward.

The nurse told me the next day that after I had gone the boys went quietly to bed, that there was little tossing that night and no walking the floors as there had been before. A doctor friend said to me: "After all, maybe your medicine is best, for while we are more or less groping in the dark as to our treatment of shell-shock, we do know that the only cure will be that something comes into their souls to give them quiet of mind and peace within."

"I know what that medicine is," I told him. "I have seen it work."

"What is it?" he asked.

Then I told him of my experience. "You may be right."

And so it is all over France. As I have worked in some twenty hospitals, from the first-aid dressing stations back through the evacuation hospitals to the base hospitals, I have found that the reaction of wounds and suffering is always a spiritual reaction, and I know, as I know no other thing, that the boys of America are to come back wounded or otherwise, a better crowd of men than they went away. They are men reborn.

Working as a Nurse's Aide and Red Cross "Searcher"

"I think we'll leave you in charge for the rest of the night."

Shirley Putnam
"Down from Château-Thierry"
The Bellman, October 19, 1918

Ten o'clock—a full moon. Orderly, dark windows ranged above the street. Yes—it must be the same regulated hospital that I knew in the winter: duty at eight in the morning, food wagon at eleven-thirty and five, temperatures at four, movies for some patients, appetites for all. No sentry challenges; I leave my coat in Marie's vestiaire,[15] and present myself, and my winter's experience, to a new night nurse.

Instead of the cold, "Oh no, it's too late now, we have all the help we need, thank you," that I expect, I am greeted with a fagged but welcoming: "Indeed we can use you. Go right down to the tents and find Mrs. Warren."

Tents—but where? Through what used to be the offices and the nurses' building; out where the ambulances were. I feel in my pocket for my bandage scissors and extra safety pins, pat my Dutch cap, and hurry through the swing doors. But what corridors! Along the tiled floors I rub against knee-high alleys of brown, hummocky cots, with a white splotch at one end screwed down among the blankets. Scrubby chins, rough coverings, pillows without pillow

---

15. A locker room, changing room.

slips, and sleep—sodden and long overdue—weighing down pale
foreheads. An arm flung out, a muddy hobnailed boot blocking
one's passage: the arms, the boots and the mud, of our victory!
Château-Thierry[16]—the night after! A sudden lump comes in my
throat; I hurry faster to offer my every inch of strength to make
this night of payment a little less dear to those who have given
of their very blood.

Mrs. Warren, at the door of a long, dim tent, looks up from the
ether case she is watching. She shows no surprise at seeing me
again after five months.

"Good evening, Miss Putnam; I'm glad you've come to help us.
You'll find plenty to do. There are three tents, about forty-five
patients in each; here is Miss D—, who can stay all night, and there
are three or four men, too, volunteers. They're men who've been
working in Paris all day, in aviation, and other things, and who'll
work again tomorrow. They'll do anything you ask. I've got to go off
now. There'll be other ether cases coming along. You'll find extra
blankets, pillows and pajamas in that basket. There's some drinking water; here's cough medicine for that third bed from the end,
if he starts again. Keep an eye on the bandages; if there's anything
like a hemorrhage you'll find the doctor in the operating room, or
call up the night nurse. I think we'll leave you in charge for the rest
of the night."

The "in charge" loses its apprehension as the night wears on,
and I realize—as I might have known at first—that tent cases mean
no abdominal or amputation cases, nothing that couldn't have
lived without me or any other "lady in charge" until morning. But
would I have missed the rest of that night! Not for all the parades
and mass meetings and war crosses in patriotism! A night among
heroes; when the "something of divine in every man" comes radi-
ating out through the grimy surface, through the crooked speech
of our mongrel army, through the red and brown, the blood and
the blankets.

I want you to see them there, so prostrate and twisted along
the low tent walls, blotched under the one electric bulb, that
some one has muffled in a page from the Saturday Evening Post.
The bare foot or bare shoulder escaped from the cover, the hand

16. Château-Thierry, one of the first battles involving the AEF, was fought on
July 18, 1918.

clutching the blanket, the parched mouth begging for water—will pain you intolerably at first, as they did me. "Is this the most we can do for our men," you will say, "in one of the best equipped and longest established hospitals in France?" Why, there's one man who says he hasn't felt water on his face for six days—two going to the front, three there, one getting away. You bring it—warm. He sighs: "First warm water I've felt in France." How little to offer! But think again. The man "got his" only yesterday, was carried back by German prisoners to a dressing station an hour later; was operated on last night at the fine hospital behind the lines, and shipped down here on a capacious hospital train. Now he's under a roof, on a mattress, with doctors and nurses within call, who will "see to him" again when the day comes. Don't ask the super human of your thousand-bed hospital, that is now sometimes sheltering two thousand a night; of doctors who operate in steady shifts, of day nurses who stay on half the night, of "corps men" who haven't slept for thirty hours. Hurry back, now that you've tucked in the knee case near you, and brushed the sand out of his bed, and help Mrs. Warren tear herself away from her rapidly emerging ether patient. He has tousled red hair and blacksmith arms. He bursts into speech:

"Are you a Red Cross nurse?"

"Why yes, son," answers Mrs. Warren's motherly, jolly voice.

"Oh, God bless you! God bless you! God bless you!" sobs the blacksmith, flinging his arms around her waist, and drawing her toward him.

Elbows prop up along the three dim rows, a chuckle with a catch in it runs down the tent. I hear a very big catch just behind me, where I see one of the volunteers from the aviation, on the first lap of his medical career, trying to keep his face from working. Such a stand-by he proves, later on in that long brief night—an attorney from California—who pats the boys, turns their heads from the light, rubs the aching spots, and says: "Now go to sleep, Buddy; that's right." That's all I can tell you about him, except that we stood still once, for a second, about three o'clock, in the moonlight between the tents, and said how we'd never forget to be grateful for the chance of this night.

Mrs. Warren is gone, and when some one calls, "Nurse," it means me. How often the question: "Do we go on from here tonight?"

Whereat I, all indignant and unknowing, scold them: "What a question! Of course not; forget about it!"

"Nurse, please come here. I want you to tell me something. Now look. My foot is off, isn't it? They took it off, I know they did. You can't make me believe they didn't."

You do your best to prove to him that the bandaged thing in a wire splint way off at the foot of the bed is what he's looking for; and you get the aviation man to swear to your statement. You bring a swallow of cough medicine to the American "poilu" in bed three. (They're so far from a shave, most of them, that they look like some strange foreign legion.)

Another voice, as foreign as the scrubby chins, a voice foggy with ether:

"Oh, I do hope dat Doctor didn't go an' pinch my vatch an' chain, vot my sister give me! Oi, Oi! How my leg pain me! But vot iss dat to me! Let me haf just von half de ether dan vot dat doctor gif me, an' I'll finish de damn Kaiser, an' his baby Crown Prince, an' all his damn family! Vot's he got ofer me! mebbe a little college ejication, him an' his silly son; but vot's college ejication—br-r-ou, but I'm cold—ven it comes to a vight?"

I dig another blanket out of the basket and push a pillow under his head, just in time to answer a moan from the far end:

"God, I'm all in! Please, lady nurse, aren't you ever coming near me? I want a pillow under my foot; it's all crooked, and the blanket's all scrooged into my back. Yes, I was at Soissons"[17]— Soisson-nes, every letter pronounced. "You know which division, I guess." I ought to, if I have any right to be called the Red Cross searcher[18] I've been for the past months.

And now the oval face, with curly dark hair, a face very white under the bleary electric light, is tossing on the pillow. He's another who's not yet out from under—by a long shot. What's that he's saying?

"Nurse! Lady! Listen to me. I want to tell you something. You won't go away right off, will you? Do you know—it's a very

17. American troops assisted the French Army at the Battle of Soissons (July 18–22, 1918).
18. A "Searcher" was part of the Red Cross Home Communication Service, charged with keeping relatives at home informed about the welfare of soldiers, particularly those in hospitals. They also gathered information about those reported dead, and attempted to trace those reported missing or taken prisoner.

wonderful thing—all around the world—yes, all around the world" (he chants it in a rapt child's voice). "With the marines you do it. And anywhere in the world you go, you'll never find anything like the marines. They're the best—the very best, in the whole world. But" (he tells you in secret) "I'll tell you. I've just been through this European war. And I wish my girl was here! Ah! I feel a kind hand; yes, a very—kind—hand. Girlie—when I look at you, and they tell me you're a marine—why, d'you know? I'll believe them. Because why, girl? Because you're blue!" His vague eyes rest for a moment on my blue Auxiliary dress.

"Now boys! All together. Got your grenades? Over the top! Now's the time! What do you say? Over the top! Here goes!" Another redhead sits bolt upright, blinks about, and brandishes an armload of bandages. You and the aviation man finally have to stop the offensive by holding the blankets down with those safety pins, and tying a draw-sheet across the heaving Irish-American chest.

"Mamma mia! Mamma mia!" moans the little East Sider, near the door; and you put up a screen between his bandaged shoulder and the chill night wind. A sudden proclamation from the very center of the sleepers:

"I'm goin' to get that Kaiser, if I have to go all the way to Berlin. You just watch me!"

"Aren't you goin' to let us in on the party?" asks Joe, a big chap in the next bed, who's been smoking cigarettes, and staring all night, by preference, straight at the light, because, as he says, "Thank you—there's nothing you can do—only my back hurts too much to sleep."

"No! Don't you dare come in on it. I want to get that Kaiser all *my-self*!" His voice breaks with indignation, as if he were a child being robbed of his dearest toy. The arch enemy of the Americans is neither "Fritzie" nor "Jerry" nor the "sâle Boche,"[19] but "Bill the Kaiser," every time.

At last they all simmer down; Miss D—[20] reports her tent quite quiet, since we were so bold as to loosen one bandage a millimeter, and to tighten another. We drink in the stillness, the serene sky, the quiet walls of the building above us, where the breath of pain

19. "Dirty German."
20. The author used the same censorship guides required of the military of not identifying individuals.

seems to have relaxed for the moment. Suddenly—stabbing the peace, shrieks a wail of warning from the city: up, up, up—hurrying your heart up with it—into your mouth. The siren! Then, once more, the comforting hum-burr-hum of guardian motors, spinning a shelter over our heads, as they have been doing since twilight. We listen, as to something very far away—the echo of wars on some other planet; but we turn quickly at the rattle of stretcher wheels coming down the gangplank from the receiving ward.

Another ether case! And every bed heavily slept in! This is the hardest task of the whole night, hurrying along the beds, turning back blankets in search of a man that looks walkable. Here is one with one sock on, one off; all his clothes on, only his arm in a sling. "Wake up, son—it's too bad; but you'll have to go into a bed in the receiving ward—and give yours to an' ether case."

He staggers out of his dream, gropes for his Red Cross bag. You help him fumble on his shoes. The orderlies slip the new man off the stretcher, and are away again. Back stumbles the original occupant:

"Sister, didn't see my puttees, did you? Had 'em since the Border, or I wouldn't care."

When I thank him for giving up his bed so-ungrudgingly, he says, with a fine, wan smile:

"Why, what else could a fellow do? He's sicker than me, isn't he? That's what we expect."

And so it was with every one of the eight or so that we had to rout out, to make room for the "one sicker"—never a grumble!

"Sister," yes, they call you that—one in ten of them; they've caught it from the Tommies, perhaps, or it just comes natural. It's a profitable form of address, somehow; you can't help wanting to spoil a patient that "Sisters" you. I hadn't, to be sure, thought of the American for Sister, as Sammy is to Tommy, till I accused the above tent-dweller of being English.

"Well, s'pose I call yer Sis. Ain't nothin' English 'bout Sis, is there?"

So it may be as "Sammy" and "Sis" that we'll push through the war in our own un-euphonious Yankee way.

At four, as dawn is lifting curtains at the ends of our tents, a white-coated doctor walks in.

"Are you in charge of these tents?"

"I seem to be, until a nurse comes."

"Will you please tell me how many of your cases can go out lying and how many sitting?"

"Go out!" I gasp.

"Why, yes; we begin evacuating all the tents at half-past five, and I want them all dressed for the journey."

I laugh to myself, rather desperately. So I had lied to them, after all. We grope down the aisles, throwing back blankets and noting "nature of wounds." They sleep druggedly; I feel a betrayer. Then I pull myself short again. Of course they must go out, on another hospital train; one more journey, not too long, and well padded at that; and they'll be in some spacious base hospital in a watering-place, or by the sea; baths and pillow slips for all, without the asking—in comfort at last, their wounds only two days old.

At four-thirty a giggling group of French maids invades us with hot, hot coffee and bread and butter. "Wake them, yes, but do head that girl off quick, from the last ether patient; he'd eat the whole bread basket if you'd let him."

Then comes the rummage by Miss D— and me for armfuls of socks and flannel pajamas, bath robes, caps—an endless to and fro till every foot is shod, and every shorn head wears at least a knitted nightcap. Slings for the sitting arm cases; and they are ready to prop themselves on benches outside to await the ambulances.

The few cigarettes I had brought warm ten minutes of the wait.

"I want to take a good look at you, and shake hands, if you don't mind," say I, "because I'm going to America."

"To America!" Such a wistful lingering over the syllables. "Say, say that again, lady! Back to God's country! Well, wave to the Statue of Liberty for us. Can't you hide us in your trunk?"

"Would you really want to be coming back now?"

"Well, no; can't say I would. You know we'd kind of hate not to see the thing through, now we're here."

"And I hope to get back, and see it too. But right now I'm going straight to New York, and stand on top of the Woolworth Building, and shout: 'Do you know where I've been? I've been shaking hands with the men who fought at Château-Thierry!' And they'll rush out and drag me in triumph up Fifth Avenue on top of a bus! What shall I tell them? That you're—still grinning?"

"You bet!" shout the benches.

The more serious cases are being trundled out from the wards and fitted carefully into the ambulances, four to each. Two stretchers pause for a moment on the ground.

"What's yours, Buddy?"

"Left leg gone."

"You don't say! And it's my right. Well, kid, have you decided yet which it's to be, shoe-strings or chewing gum?"

"No," chortles the freckled Buddy; "can't quite make up my mind. But if you tell me I'm lucky—I'll say I am! Was a mechanic before the war, and can go right back to it. Then it isn't as if I hadn't got the folks. They'll make everything all right. Why! my leg—I don't even think about it!"

At five a nurse comes out to take charge; but there is more than enough to keep us all three on our feet till the last car drives out the gate at nine-thirty.

How much longer we seem to have lived than the fresh morning people who stand about in groups; a few officers—the two "godmothers" of the hospital—to watch the evacuation. we take a last look at the four or five most recent ether cases, who will be moved into the wards later in the day; and a first look at our hands, and once white aprons and shoes! Only twelve hours, after all, of work at top notch; how little to be allowed to do, in a world where the top notch is being exacted for days at a stretch—and given gladly—"still grinning."

A French officer steps up:

"Mademoiselle, pardon, are you English, American? Ah! I must tell you. I must shake your hand. These are your soldiers who were at Château-Thierry. They were fighting beside my own regiment. How they get on together—the French and the Americans! And I tell you, mademoiselle, I do not say this because you are American—but they are magnificent. Nothing can stand against them. There is not one who is not the equal of our bravest French soldier!"

Masking the Disfigurements of War

"Hundreds and thousands of fine men have been torn and mutilated until they scarce resemble human beings."

"Makes New Faces for Mutilated Soldiers"
Daily Capital Journal (Salem, OR), December 19, 1918

When Aladdin gave new lamps for old he did nothing very wonderful. But when humanity, sympathizing with the misfortunes of others, replaces war-torn, seared faces with new—when it hides honorable disfigurations gained in the defense of liberty—then there is story worthwhile the telling.

This, then, is the story of "Old Faces For New." It is a recital pathetic and pitiable; it is a tale of men's glory and woman's devotion; it is a song of sympathy and humanity—of practical Christianity—of materialized altruism.

Since time began wounds received in battle were considered badges of honor. Men gloried in them; women admired. But that was before the coming of modern armament—of shell and shrapnel—of mines and poison gas. In those other, more humane days, scars of battle wounds were considered sacred. As the late William Shakespeare—or was it Bacon?—said: "He laughs at scars who never felt a wound."

But things have changed since then. Not that scars are not marks of respect, but some mutilations are so repulsive as to evoke horror mixed with pity. Wounds in the face and head leave the ugliest marks. In the present war hundreds and thousands of fine men have been torn and mutilated until they scarce resemble human beings. Photographs received in this country show men with their lower jaws shot away, with their lips torn off, with half their face gone.

It is these men who were a problem for their fellow men. They—mutilé as the French call them most aptly—had the sympathy of their friends—of the grateful public. But something more tangible than sympathy was needed—something which would hide their awful scars and disfigurations. To replace a missing arm or leg or hand or foot is easy enough. But to replace a face or the part of one that was a real problem.

And a woman solved that problem! It is true that a mere man, Captain Derwent Wood, an English sculptor, conceived the idea of making masks for the mutilés, but it remained for Mrs. Maynard Ladd,[21] an American sculptor, living in Paris, to perfect the work and to materialize masks which would replace torn and missing tissue so naturally that the wearer would be able to live out his life in comparative happiness.

---

21. Anna Coleman Ladd.

Mrs. Ladd is an artist of international repute. Born in Philadelphia, she was educated in private schools, going to Paris and Rome, where for more than twenty years she worked with Professors Ferrari and Gallori. She exhibited in the Paris salon, in this country and in London. In 1913 she exhibited forty bronzes at Gorham's in New York and at the Corcoran Art Gallery in Washington. She received an honorable mention for her work at the Panama Exposition. Incidentally she is an author, having published several novels.

Captain Wood's original conception was to make a mask to fit those portions of the face missing. If the chin was missing then the mask would extend only over the chin. If the cheek was missing then the scarred portion would be covered. The question to be solved by Mrs. Ladd was in the manufacture of the masks. They had to be light, yet strong, of some composition which would not tarnish and would retain the color placed upon its exterior surface.

After considerable experimentation Mrs. Ladd hit upon thin copper as having sufficient strength. Then she decided to have the base plated with silver to give it a better finish. Next came the method to be employed in fitting the masks. Consultations with surgeons brought to light the fact that nothing could be done with mutilés until several months after their wounds had healed completely, as tissues contracted even after complete cicatrization[22] had taken place.

Eventually a perfected method was evolved. When the mutilé has been nursed back to health and the tissue and muscles have done contracting Mrs. Ladd takes a plaster cast of the torn face. If possible she obtains a photograph of the mutilé taken before he received the wounds.

From the photograph and the plaster cast Mrs. Ladd, guided by her sculptor's art, reconstructs another plaster cast of only those parts which are mutilated. Then a copper mask is made of an inch thick. Then comes the first fitting.

If the mask so far as finished fits properly then it is silver plated. Next comes the question of making the mask appear natural. If eyebrows are needed they are inserted hair by hair; if eyelids are

---

22. The process of a wound healing to form a scar.

missing artificial eyelids adorn the mask, with a hole through them that the wearer may see; if eyes are missing altogether then artificial eyes are placed in the mask.

When the mask is complete the mutilé goes for a final fitting. Mrs. Ladd adjusts the mask or has one of her expert assistants attend to the task. The mask is held in place by "fake" eye glasses and strings or by a wig, the attaching mechanism being camouflaged as to be practically invisible.

But the work is not yet done. One of the most important operations in its manufacture is in the coloring. Mrs. Ladd takes her palette and with specially prepared pigments colors the mask to match the complexion of the mutilated part of the face. Then the work and labor of love is done.

Then the mutilé walks out of Mrs. Ladd's studio a new man. He is no longer a mutilé—an object of horror mingled with pity. He is a human being again, self confident, happy. He no longer dreads to be seen in public. People no longer gaze on him in pity,

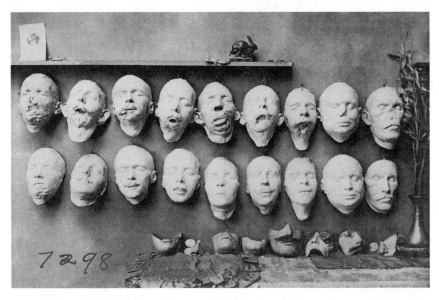

Photograph shows casts taken from soldiers' mutilated faces; the lower row shows the faces which Mrs. Ladd modelled on the foundation of the life mask with help of photographs taken before the wound was received. On the table are some of the final masks made to fit over the disfigured part of the face. *Source:* Prints and Photographs Division, Library of Congress, LC-USZ62-137189.

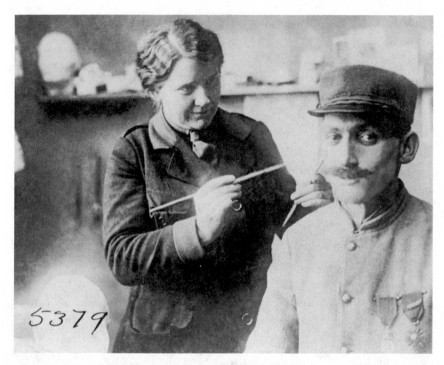

When Mrs. Ladd has completed the molded resemblance, a copper reproduc-
tion is made, which is first silvered and coated with enamel, and finally painted
in flesh colors. *Source:* Prints and Photographs Division, Library of Congress,
LC-USZ62-137180.

scarcely able to disguise their aversion. The transformation is
complete—at a cost of $20 supplied by the American people and
the devotion of an American woman.

The accompanying pictures [of mutilés wearing masks] were
taken especially for the American Red Cross that the people of the
United States might know of her splendid work in saving human
beings for society. Mrs. Ladd may be seen in one painting the mask
worn by M. Caudron, who was mutilated early in the war. The man
wearing the glasses was a fine, healthy man, whose lower face was
completely shot away. Without the mask he would have been an
object of intense horror despite his patriotic sacrifice. The third
picture shows an assistant fitting a mask on a mutilé the left side of
whose face was torn to shreds. The fourth picture shows the shape
of various masks.

The Nation Prepares to Welcome Home 190,000 Wounded

"Their cases are studied and assignments made to reconstruction or convalescent hospitals."

Associated Press
"Wounded Return from Battlefront"
The Sunday Star, (Washington, DC), December 15, 1918

New York, December 14—November's swing of the pendulum of history from war to peace, which reversed the eastward flow of America's fighting millions—the greatest transoceanic troop movement ever known—brought the American people face to face with the tragedy of the casualty lists.

Gen. Pershing's announcement that more than 58,000 of the expeditionary forces had given their lives in the nation's cause, and that 14,000 others, exclusive of prisoners, were missing, created a profound impression, but the human touch of almost 190,000 wounded, 16.000 of whom already have been returned in various stages of helplessness to their native shores, promises to give the country its first real appreciation of the sacrifices of its sons who followed the flag on foreign soil.

Solicitous Care Observed

The method of their debarkation denies to the homecoming wounded the popular honors paid their comrades in full health. But the War Department, operating along lines intended to give the lie to the "ingratitude of government" has arranged for medical, recreational and educational attention, whose aim is to restore these maimed heroes, as fully as possible, to physical comfort and financial independence. From the day of their arrival at New York or Newport News, the ports of debarkation, to their re-entrance into civilian life, a host of Good Samaritans—Army doctors, nurses and orderlies and workers of the American Red Cross—will minister to these sufferers from a ruthless enemy's engines of war. Harbor hospital boats, debarkation hospitals, hospital trains and general hospitals for reconstruction or convalescence form a chain of service linking the westward-bound fleets of transports with the homes of the wounded. And in this service the Medical Debarkation Corps,[23] suddenly thrust into the foreground of publicity by the collapse of the central powers, plays an important picturesque.

Big System Put in Readiness

The end of the war found the port medical authorities prepared to shoulder the heavy burden laid upon them. During nineteen months of American participation in the conflict they had maintained an embarkation hospital service, treating the comparatively rare cases of illness among the troops ready to go overseas.

When American forces entered the trenches small groups of wounded, evacuated from hospitals in France, began to filter through the service on this side of the Atlantic. With this experience, accentuated by the lessons of the allied governments in repatriating their wounded, the debarkation system was put in readiness for the reception of injured men at the rate of 10,000 to 15,000 a month.

During the war and a five-week period following the signing of the armistice approximately 11.500 wounded had been received at New York and 4,500 at Newport News. And the authorities were prepared, on official advices from Washington, to handle 50,000 cases in the next four months.

Majority to Debark at New York

The Army embarkation service at New York, which sent three-fourths of the nation's 2,000,000 men overseas, is expected to debark a majority of the returning forces, and the westward flow of wounded also will be directed here, with some diversion to Newport News and possibly, later on, to Boston. To carry on the work at this port the medical department has a personnel of 7,306—greater than the entire Army Medical Corps when the United States entered the war. On this staff, headed by Col. J. M. Kennedy, veteran of twenty-five years' service as an Army surgeon, 950 are medical officers, 983 nurses (men and women). 5.184 enlisted men and 189 civilian employees.

---

23. The Medical Debarkation Corps transferred wounded and convalescing soldiers from ship to hospital and then from hospital to home.

The operating faculties include eight debarkation hospitals with an aggregate capacity of 16,900 beds, two base hospitals with 4,290 beds, reconstruction hospital at Columbia University for cases too serious to he moved to interior institutions, five harbor hospital boats with 300 beds each, seventy-five ambulances, with fifty additional held in reserve by the Red Cross and four hospital trains, each accommodating upward to 200 patients.

To Clear Charges in a Week

The base hospitals are at Camps Merritt and Mills,[24] former embarkation, now debarkation, cantonments for the overseas Army. The debarkation hospitals are strategically located on or near the harbor front.

The port medical authorities, responsible for soldier patients from the time of their arrival from Europe to their delivery at general hospitals nearest their home communities, aim to clear their charges from the hospitals within a week. The work begins at the port quarantine station. Here medical officers board incoming transports and assist the doctors aboard in preparing the men for landing. In practically all cases the wounded are taken directly from the ship to the harbor hospital boat, which conveys them to a pier near one of the debarkation hospitals, where ambulances are in waiting.

While the men get their "shore bearings" their cases are studied and assignments made to reconstruction or convalescent hospitals.

Medical Officer for Group

The next process is the attachment of a medical liaison officer to the group he is to conduct to an interior station. When he has become familiar with his charges he applies for a hospital car or train, according to the size of his party, and for an escort of doctors, nurses and orderlies. If a train is assigned, the journey, even across the continent, is simple, but if the wounded fill only one car, which must be attached to regular trains, the feeding problem becomes acute. Here the Red Cross lends its aid, arranging by telegraph with its auxiliaries along the way for meals for the travelers at

---

24. Camp Merritt was located in Cresskill, NJ. Camp Mills was on Long Island, NY.

points where neither dining car service nor station restaurants are available.

The hospital trains, equipped with specially constructed Pullman sleeping and kitchen cars, have accommodations both for "walking cases" and for men so severely injured that they must remain abed both day and night. In anticipation of their use on an extensive scale, officers and 200 men are in training here and a smaller company at Newport News, as escort detachments.

Chapter 10

+

+

+

+

+

Heroes

Introduction

W hen the former war correspondent and aid to General Pershing, Lt. Col. Frederick Palmer, hurried out a book in 1919 to describe America's final battle of the war, *Our Greatest Battle (The Meuse-Argonne)*, he made a conscious decision not to mention the name of any individual soldier below the rank of division commander or to single out any recipient of the Medal of Honor or the Distinguished Service Cross.[1] "I like to think that our men didn't fight for Crosses; that they fought for their cause and their manhood."

Such attitude—and censorship restrictions—limited reporting on the heroic actions of American fighters during the war. Many soldiers who distinguished themselves during the fighting would not have their bravery officially acknowledged until after the war concluded. Pilots were the exception to this restriction. (See the articles on Raoul Lufbery and Eddie Rickenbacker in Chapter 8.)

Medals of Honor were awarded to 119 soldiers, sailors, airmen, and Marines for action in WWI. Any of them might have been

---

1. The second highest award for bravery in combat that can be awarded by the U.S. Army.

featured in this chapter. The heroism of many went virtually unnoticed by the press, but a few earned headlines not only for their brave deeds but because their actions carried symbolic value. They represented something about the American experience or spirit.

Henry Johnson was the first American soldier to receive the French *Croix de guerre* medal with palm and the last American soldier to receive the Medal of Honor for his role in World War I. That Medal of Honor presentation occurred in June 2015. Johnson's heroism was significant for two reasons. For one, it occurred in May 1918, when other U.S. soldiers still waited impatiently to fight the Germans. And two, because he was black.

The same discrimination faced by African-American soldiers at home followed them into the U.S. army. Over 200,000 black soldiers served with the AEF in France. Considered unsuitable for combat, most were used instead in labor battalions, unloading ships, transporting supplies, working construction projects, digging latrines, burying bodies, etc. However, two black divisions, the 92nd and the 93rd, did see combat, on "loan" to the French army. This put them into combat before any other soldiers of the AEF.

When two soldiers from the 93[rd2] became the first U.S. fighters to win the French medal for bravery, it drew positive attention to the prowess of the black fighters. This chapter includes an article about those black heroes—Henry Johnson and Needham Roberts—that was published in one of the largest circulation African-American newspapers, the *Chicago Defender*. Since the *Defender* did not have its own correspondent in the war zone, it reprinted an article on the heroes that had appeared in the *Chicago Daily News*. Although Johnson became the most famous African-American soldier of the war, his accomplishment was not officially recognized by the Army. Johnson did not receive the Purple Heart for his twenty-one wounds until 1996 (posthumously), followed by the Distinguished Service Cross in 2002, and the Medal of Honor in 2015.

The exploits of prisoner of war Navy lieutenant Edouard Isaacs (aka Isac) and army Major Charles W. Whittlesey both demonstrated the admired never-say-die, never-surrender mentality that played well with the American public.

---

2. Johnson was with the 369th Infantry Regiment, a converted National Guard unit, nicknamed the "Harlem Hellfighters."

Whittlesey garnered the biggest headlines during the war, for both what he did and what he did not do. While leading a unit that was completely cut off and surrounded by the enemy, the "Lost Battalion," he held out for several days under fierce assault, with little food or ammunition. He truly endeared himself to America however, when it was reported that in response to a German call to surrender, Whittlesey had answered with "Go to hell." Whittlesey did not actually say that, but the public took such pleasure in the attitude it reflected that the quote became permanently enshrined as one of the signature phrases that would define the war.

Tennessee mountaineer Sergeant Alvin York's fame did not materialize until five months after the war ended, when an article about his valor during fighting in the Argonne Forest appeared in the two-million circulation *Saturday Evening Post*. His extraordinary actions, combined with his homespun background and deep religious faith cast him as a symbol for America itself, forced to fight against its deep conviction but then eager and wildly proficient at the war game.

A subsequent biography and the 1941 movie about his life, *Sergeant York*, starring Gary Cooper, enshrined York as the best-known American hero of the Great War.

Black Fighters Earn First Honors

"... worthy of the best traditions of the American army."

Junius B. Wood[3]
"Beat Back Force of 25 Germans, Winning French War Cross"
Chicago Defender, May 25, 1918

(This story is published in the Chicago Defender with special permission of the Chicago Daily News, as we have no correspondent at the front.)

With the American Army on the French Front, May 20.—This story of the gallantry of two American Negro soldiers who attacked

3. In December 1916, *Chicago Daily News* reporter Junius B. Wood wrote a series of articles on African-Americans that proved so popular that they were published as the booklet *The Negro in Chicago*.

a party of 25 Germans early last Thursday morning and completely routed and beat off the enemy, killing or wounding five men, although themselves wounded, carries with it the announcement that Negro troops for about a month have been holding a part of the front line trenches in the St. Menehould region west of Verdun. These troops, acting in close association with the French,[4] have discharged their duties in the most excellent fashion, the Thursday night fight being typical of their conduct. It is described by military observers as worthy of the best traditions of the American army.

Names of the Two Heroes

Early Thursday morning five Negroes occupied an advance post jutting out into "No Man's Land." Three were asleep in a dugout and the two others were on guard. These two men, whose names should always be remembered, were Henry Johnson of 25 Monroe street, Albany, N. Y, and Needham Roberts of Trenton, N. J. About 2 o'clock, when it was still dark, Johnson thought he heard a voice and called out, "Here they come!" A sergeant back of the post shot off a flare, disclosing the figures of a squad of Germans trying out the barbed wire surrounding the post. Later it ascertained that they had entered an abandoned trench to the right of the post about 2 o'clock with the intention of gobbling up the occupants.

Just as soon as the flare lighted up the surroundings the Germans threw grenades, which wounded Johnson and Roberts, felling both. But the two men while lying on the ground threw hand grenades at the Germans who were now forcing an entrance. As the first German came in Johnson regained his feet and shot the man through the chest, but his rifle jammed and so he used it as a club, knocking down a second German with a blow on the head.

Bolo Knife Effective Weapon

Three other Germans had slipped by and one was trying to choke the prostrate Roberts, while two others tried to carry him off. His rifle was broken, but Johnson drew a long trench knife, which the Colored men call a "bolo knife," and brought it down upon the skull of one of the Germans. Later it was found that the

4. They actually wore French uniforms.

knife was stained with blood, as was a German cap picked up nearby. Another German leaped at Roberts, who lunged forward with his knife, almost disemboweling the man. Both Johnson and Roberts swear that the German cried out in English: "The son of a ----- got me."

Johnson all this time was shouting, "Turn out the guard," but another German fired at him with a revolver, the bullet striking him in the arm. As the intrepid Negro fell he managed to hurl a single grenade, which from the signs found in the morning blew the German to pieces. Then Johnson fainted.

But the Germans had had enough and they scuttled off in the darkness, bearing away their killed and wounded and leaving behind stretchers, wire cutters, grenades and revolvers. Strong patrols searched for them, but they were unable to find them.

Both Get French War Cross

Both the Colored men were awarded the French croix de guerre with palms, accompanied by army order citations reciting their deed. The Johnson citation read: "Johnson gave a magnificent example of courage and energy." Roberts was described as a "good and brave soldier."

Negroes previously took part in a raid in which they entered the German trenches and brought back three prisoners after finding slight resistance. This operation was executed with the French. They go out patrolling "No Man's Land" every night and have been shelled frequently. Their sector is a veritable snipers' nest and German bullets whistle about constantly, but they are full of enthusiasm in their new surroundings. They had not had a casualty until Thursday's fight. Both Johnson and Roberts will recover, though wounded in many places by grenade splinters.

Most of these troops are from Now York and their commander is a former New York official. After several months spent in construction work at the ports the Negroes were given a fairly brief period of training in consideration of the work they had already done in the United States. They entered the trenches on a small scale at first, but their line was rapidly extended. They have adapted themselves to life in the trenches so well that they are making jokes about it, one Colored soldier asking permission to be sent on a "dangerous"

Henry Johnson and Needham Roberts, of the 369th Harlem Hellfighters Regiment, became the first American soldiers awarded the prestigious French Croix de Guerre medal. Ironically, their unit was not allowed to serve in the U.S. army, but was fighting with the French army at the time. *Source:* U.S. Army.

mission. They are cheered up by the music of their famous jazz band,[5] which has won many prizes.

Kidnapped by a U-Boat

"Soon we sighted two of our own destroyers and depth charges began to fly."

Ralph Courtney
"Out of the Jaws of Death and Hundom—A Yank's Escape,"
New York Tribune, November 24, 1918

After the most thrilling series of adventures yet recorded in this war Lieutenant Isaacs,[6] of the torpedoed *President Lincoln*,[7] has arrived in England. He swam the Rhine and finally got free on October 13 last. Lieutenant Isaacs spent some days aboard a German submarine and had American destroyers dropping depth charges so close that the vessel shook as though struck by an earthquake; he made four attempts to escape in spite of threats that he would be shot if he did so again; he was nearly starved and nearly shot and once nearly clubbed and kicked to death.

Lieutenant Isaacs, who comes from Cresco, Iowa, told his story to the *Tribune*, as follows:

Under a Salvo of Depth Charges

"When the *President Lincoln* was torpedoed going west at 9 o'clock in the morning of May 31, I stepped off on a raft with about fifteen other men. After forty minutes we were taken aboard a lifeboat. Then the submarine, U-90, cruised about looking for the captain, of whose whereabouts we all professed to know nothing. Finally it came along side our boat, where I was hiding my uniform stripes. The commander asked me where the captain was

5. The 369th regimental band became famous during the war, introducing the previously unknown music called "jazz" to French and British audiences.
6. Lieutenant Edouard V. M. Isaacs.
7. The USS *President Lincoln* was a troop transport ship. Formerly belonging to the German-owned Hamburg-American Line, the ship was seized in New York harbor when the United States entered the war.

and said he had orders to take prisoner the captains of all torpedoed ships and shouted questions to several other boats about
the captain, and they replied in the same way. After a while the
submarine commander said that if the captain couldn't be found
I would do instead. I was hauled on board the submarine and the
commander said: 'Go below; I'll have to take you to Germany.'
Afterward we immediately submerged.

"Soon we sighted two of our own destroyers and depth charges
began to fly. About twenty were dropped altogether. Every German
stood at his post and as the terrific thuds of concussion struck
us the petty officer at the bow in charge of the listening devices
shouted to the captain his estimate of the direction from which
the bombs were coming and how far away they were. The vessel
shook from stem to stern and everything loose on board jumped
and rattled. Five of the explosions were very close. Not a word
was spoken by the crew at their posts until finally the explosions
became fainter and fainter. When they could no longer be heard we
came to the top.

"There was absolutely no animosity shown toward me on board
the submarine, and I dined at the officer's mess. We lived on the
best food Germany could provide. We had sausages, sauerkraut,
fresh eggs and real coffee, among other things. We had four meals
a day and all the men on board were strong and husky. Captain
Remy was courteous to me, and said he couldn't understand why
America came into the war.

"While we were cruising about we sighted another American
destroyer flotilla looking for us and as the captain thought things
were likely to get too hot for him in these parts we steered for
the Kiel Canal[8] via the Skagerrak and Cattegat. During the trip to
Germany we were once submerged eleven hours, while, presumably, avoiding or going through a mine field.

"While passing through Dutch waters I made my first attempt
to escape. We were on the submarine deck and I determined to
jump overboard as soon as it became dark enough to give me some
chance of escaping. We were about four miles from land and I had
a life-belt on. I waited till 12:30 a.m., but it was still light in these
northern latitudes. I saw there was no hope of its getting darker,

8. Germany's Kiel Canal passes through the Jutland Peninsula, shortening the passage
between the North Sea and the Baltic Sea.

so I maneuvered to jump over the side and was about to do so when the captain seized me. I had no other chance of getting away before reaching Wilhelmshaven.[9] The captain sent me below, but said very little about my trying to jump overboard.

In Germany's Most Secret Port

"At Wilhelmshaven I was put on board the submarine's mother ship,[10] where my only food was sour black bread and colored water which was called coffee. Wilhelmshaven is the most secret of all German ports, and it is difficult even for officers in uniform to get in and out. After a few days in the mother ship with a sentry outside my barred window and another outside my barred door, I was transferred to a similar land gaol, being still fed on the same bread and coffee, which I found out afterward was made from acorns and roasted barley. After another three days of the land gaol they shipped me off to Karlsruhe. To my joy, I discovered while in the mother ship a $5 bill which had been overlooked, and which came in useful later. I got the captain of the submarine to change it when he came to see me and asked him to purchase me a toothbrush, which also helped me when I finally got away. While at Wilhelmshaven I was also taken on board the flagship, and interrogated by the chief of staff of the high seas fleet. He began in a very friendly way to talk to me. He also inquired why America had cast her lot in with England and said he was surprised at America's entry into the war. I asked him in return whether he thought America was the kind of country which could forget the *Lusitania*,[11] and whether he considered America could be friends with the nation that invented the 'Hymn of Hate.'[12]

---

9. An important German naval base on the North Sea.

10. A submarine's "mother ship" or "tender" supports a submarine by carrying fuel, food, torpedoes and other supplies. It either rendezvous with the submarine at sea to replenish it or does so while the submarine is in port.

11. On May 7, 1915, a German submarine torpedoed the British passenger liner RMS *Lusitania*, taking 1,193 lives, 128 of them American. It roused considerable anti-German feelings in the U.S. and made the submarine one of the most despised and feared weapons of the war.

12. A popular German nationalistic poem aimed at England, which included these final lines: "You shall we hate with enduring hate; We shall not forbear from our hate; Hate on water and hate on land, Hate of the head and hate of the hand, Hate of the hammer and hate of the crown, Hate of seventy million pressing down. We love as one; we hate as one; We have one foe, and one alone—ENGLAND!" The hymn was distributed to the army, taught to school children, and played in concerts. Both sides used propaganda to instill hate, but the "Hymn of Hate" enculturated it.

Our conversation ended in a less friendly tone, and I could see I had made his ears burn.

"On the way to Karlsruhe I only saw one herd of cattle and that was one which was reserved for the fleet. We went to Karlsruhe via Hanover, Frankfurt, and Manheim. I was in charge of a naval officer and two men.

In a "Listening Hotel"

"At Karlsruhe I was put immediately into the 'listening hotel,' where it is hoped prisoners will give away information, which is overheard through microphones. They put me in a room by myself for the first day, then on the second day, presumably because I spoke French, I was put with eight French officers. We found and tore up four Dictaphones[13] in that room. On the third day I was placed with three British officers. I was also questioned by an intelligence officer. I told him we were building an immense navy and were sending so many troops to France that the German line couldn't possibly hold. On my fourth day in Karlsruhe I was transferred to the Zoological Gardens, the general distributing centre of prisoners of all nationalities. There were Serbs, Italians, Russians, and representatives of almost all the countries fighting Germany. Here I met two English generals who were real live wires. I confirmed information I had obtained by talks with other prisoners, and decided I must endeavor to get away. I led two plans of escape from the camp, but both were betrayed. I also joined a French attempt, which went wrong through a letter to a woman in Karlsruhe, who was to help us, falling into the hands of the commandant. Usually we never knew by whom we were betrayed, but suddenly found our plans circumvented by additional wire being put up or something of the kind. We also planned to get away in blankets wrapped around us to look like German officers' cloaks, but the Germans had become suspicious and decided to clear the camp of officer prisoners. I was told I would be sent to Villengen in Baden.

Another Fruitless Dash for Freedom

"On the way to Villengen I decided to try again to escape. A sentry was sitting on either side of me in the train, so there was little hope of success. Nevertheless, I waited till the train had gone pretty far

13. An early sound recording device.

south and then when one of my guards was dozing and the other was looking away I dived through the narrow window before they could grab me and fell on the line. The train must have been going at about forty miles an hour, so I was dazed by the fall. My head was hurt, but this would not have stopped me if I hadn't hit my knee in falling. Nevertheless, I tried to run. My guards must have stopped the train immediately, for I soon heard them shouting 'Halt!' and bullets came whizzing by me. When they were only about 75 yards away I saw it was no use, so turned and put up my hands. When they reached me they turned their rifles and beat me over the head and body and finished me off by kicks. One man hit me so hard over the head that the stock of his rifle broke. I was taken to Villengen, about five miles away, where I collapsed completely and had to be bandaged from head to foot. I suffered terribly and the vermin made things worse. At the end of a few days I could move sufficiently to keep the vermin off the top part of my body, which was some relief.

"After about a week I was court-martialed for trying to escape and given two weeks solitary confinement. I was also told that if I tried to escape again I should be shot. Some American officers in the same camp sent me some books, so I was not so badly off.

Revived by Red Cross Food

"I soon began to regain strength on Red Cross food[14] and started to plan to get away again. There were twenty-five non-combatants and officers from the raider Wolff[15] in the Villengen camp and a number of Russians. Several plans to escape failed through treachery. The Russians in the camp were starving and would do almost anything for food. There were a few guards who were not unfriendly, and the Russians managed to obtain some wire-clippers from them for us. We made another pair and had three before the final attempt to escape was made.

"The escaping party was divided into four groups, who were to make the attempt at different points of the camp in order to divide the attention of the guards. Three groups were to use the wire-clippers and my own was to crawl over the obstacles by means

---

14. The Red Cross provided packages of food and comfort items to prisoners of war.

15. The *Wolf* was an armed merchant raider in the Imperial German navy. On a 451-day voyage, the ship raided commercial vessels and planted mines, mostly in the Indian Ocean. It returned to its base at Kiel on February 24, 1918, with 467 prisoners of war, some of which were imprisoned with Lt. Isaacs.

of a bridge which I had invented. Aviator Willis, of Boston, one of the Lafayette Escadrille,[16] was to try to get out the front gate in the confusion. I had made a rendezvous with him at a point about two miles from the camp in case we made good our escape.

"The escape of my party was to be over about 15 feet of barbed wire from our window sill. We had to get through a barred window, then over a ditch about 7 feet wide filled with barbed wire and finally over a barbed wire fence about 8 to 10 feet high. We had filed the minor bars of the window, but dared not file the large centre bar for fear of making too much noise. We had, however, prepared it for being wrenched out.

"An essential part of the plan was the short-circuiting of all electric lights of the camp at a given moment. We had thoroughly investigated the lighting and made sure of our work. Meanwhile I had everything ready for my party. Ever since coming to the camp I had collected all the screws I could find and had about a hundred by the time the escape was to be attempted. We had also collected slats of wood suitable for making the steps of a ladder and these with our tools we hid in odd places till the time came. The two uprights of my ladder were to be two sets of light double boards about 18 feet long which were used to mark the tennis court. We calculated that 15 feet would take us over the last wire fence, leaving three feet inside the window on which our friends could hang while we crawled to the end and dropped off.

"We had to work feverishly the night of our escape suddenly to assemble all our preparations during the only short time when this could be done. I used my toothbrush and shoe-blacking to paint the tennis court markers so that they could not be seen in the dark and it seems to me my hands are still sore from screwing on the slats to our ladder.

An Exciting Getaway

"When all was ready the lights suddenly went out. I leaped at the remaining solid bar of the window and it came out with a crash. The alarm was raised instantly, but in the darkness and confusion

16. The aviator referred to here was Harold Buckley Willis. The Lafayette Escadrille was a squadron within the French Air Service, composed mostly of American volunteer pilots, that was created before the United States entered the war. The unit was disbanded in February 1918, and some of the pilots joined the U.S. Air Service.

we managed to put out our ladder and first the lightest man crawled over. As we went over the ladder we heard the sentries between the wire rushing about and shouting, but they evidently hadn't thought any one could escape over their heads. Outside the last fence there was a sentry every 30 yards, but all three of us managed to get over the wire and drop to the ground. The guards shouted in the darkness and fired. We scattered immediately. I dashed for the hill about 400 yards away, while bullets buzzed in all directions. When I jumped clear of the wire there was a guard not more than 10 feet away on the one side and another not much further on the other. I was probably ten yards away before they could do anything. When I got to the rendezvous I found Willis had also got away. I know some of the others got out of the camp, but I never knew exactly what became of them. One passed me at right angles as I was going up the hill. Willis and I did 25 miles that night.

"During the first three days I think Willis and I made 75 miles. We slept in fir brush during the day and lay under trees in the rain trying to keep ourselves warm. We had little food, but during the nights we managed to get some cabbage or some potatoes from the fields. We had a compass and a fairly good map.

"On the seventh day after our escape we arrived at the bank of the Rhine and were faced with a new probem. Most of the bank was sheer cliff and at other places where the descent was possible there were sentries. From 10 p.m. till midnight we explored up and down the bank trying to find an opening, but failed. Then we hit upon another plan which saved us. We found a mountain stream flowing into the Rhine and decided to go down the bed of this. It took us about two hours to get to the mouth of the creek. We went on our hands and knees, feeling every stone before putting our weight on it, for fear it would overturn and rouse the sentries. While we were creeping down the stream Willis whispered to me to be sure and take off my trousers, and when I turned to whisper back he was no longer there. The current of the Rhine had suddenly swept him away, and while I was thinking about his disappearance it swept me away, too.

"The Rhine where we swam it is very fast and full of whirlpools. I got to the middle of the river and found I couldn't get any further. The water was icy cold, so cold that when I put the back of my head in it to float on my back it felt as if I had been struck a violent blow. I shipped some water in mid-stream and just as I was about to collapse I realized I was beginning to progress a little out of the centre of the current. I must have swum the rest of the way almost unconsciously, for a few seconds later, as it seemed to me, my foot struck a rock. I tried to rise but couldn't and lay there for a while in a state of collapse. One of the difficulties of swimming the Rhine was to swim so noiselessly as not to be heard and be shot at from the bank.

"Finally I managed to stagger to my feet. I walked about till I found a farmhouse and knocked. When the Swiss[17] farmer and his wife found that I was an American they couldn't do enough for me. I was tucked in bed with hot-water bottles and fed, and was given the care that I certainly needed. I sent the farmer out to look for Willis and he met another farmer who had been sent out by Willis to look for me. Willis has gone back to France and I am on my way to America."

Story of the Lost Battalion

"Few braver deeds of the war are on record than these attempts at rescue."

Frazer Hunt
"Here's Story of He-Man Yanks of 'Lost Battalion'"
Chicago Tribune, October 16, 1918

In France with the American army. Oct 14—Seated tailor fashion in a "funk hole"[18] scooped out from the slope of a steep wooded hillside, two or three kilometers from the front line, Maj. Charles W. Whittlesey recited last night for the first time the complete story of the gallant stand of his battalion of the Seventy-seventh division. For five days and nights this battalion was cut off in the heart of the forest of the Argonne.[19]

---

17. Switzerland maintained a status of "armed neutrality" during the war. In addition to being a hotbed of espionage, diplomacy, and commerce, it also served as a haven for refugees.

18. A dugout.

19. The Argonne Forest was the scene of America's final battle of the war, the Meuse-Argonne Offensive, September 26–November 11, 1918.

Tall, slender, and smooth shaven, wearing thick lensed spectacles, this man, who when surrounded beaten and cut up, had answered the German demand for his surrender with a polite invitation to "go to hell" told in low pitched voice what is probably one of the greatest stories of the war. His uniform was ragged and dirty and he was wrapped in an ill-flitting private's overcoat and wore an old winter cap that had been issued long ago at Camp Upton.[20]

Although three days before on the field of battle he had been made a lieutenant colonel, there was no mark of rank about him. And the tale he told was as simple and as honest as the clothes he wore. Across the bridge of his nose was a deep cut made by a shell—a scar that he will always wear.

Real Beefsteak Brings Cheers

Shells were whining overhead—answers, it seemed to the German peace proposals—and the dusk of early evening was adding to the unutterable mystery of this great forest, that in American history memories will rank with Belleau Wood.[21] Supper was being brought up from the rolling kitchens tucked far below in the gulley and when these men who had been through the terrible strain saw real beefsteak they awoke the whole woods with their cheers.

It was their first real meal since they started fighting their way through the black unknown forest seventeen days before. Many of them had grubby week old beards, their clothes were torn and dirty, but they were joking and laughing.

Already, it seemed, they had forgotten the five long terrible nights, the days of thirst and hunger and suffering when even hope was gone and only dogged determination remained. Romance and wonder of war had gripped them—it had brought them rescue and now was bringing them rumors of peace and hot food.

Tells of Argonne Battle

For hours we had ridden by motor over the slippery, muddy forest roads, now swept along by a great tide of moving guns, marching troops, camions. wagons, and all the paraphernalia of war,

20. An army training camp on Long Island, NY.
21. The Battle of Belleau Wood, June 1–26, 1918

now swept back by the undertow bound to the rear. Finally we left the car in one supertraffic jam and tramped miles through these tragic, majestic woods, searching for this man who some day will have a place alongside Custer.

First he traced briefly his story of the battle in the Argonne up to the night when his command was cut off and surrounded. At 2 o'clock on the morning of September 26, the bombardment started. Four hours later these New York City boys went over the top. On the first day they advanced four kilometers.

Than night came on mysteriously and slowly, with darkness dropping over the woods like some great bowl. Night sounds, always so intense and dramatic, were made more terrible by the knowledge of what great unknown tasks lay ahead.

One of War's Great Tasks

Hun machine guns swept the woods, spitting like giant angry cats and promising certain death to any who might move. The Yankees could only lay low in their holes and await dawn.

Then they started again, reaching forward through the tangle of underbrush and virgin trees like blind men feeling their way through strange streets. At times they could not see fifty feet ahead through the screen of brush. Always there were machine guns ahead firing upon them.

This was one of the great tasks of the war—to clean out this woods, roughly three miles wide and three miles long.

Sixty thousand gallant Frenchmen, thousands upon thousands of the enemy had gone down here. The night ghosts of these seemed to roam through the deathless tracts uttering sobbing entreaties amid the cries of the wounded and the moaning of the winds.

This was work for men of the outdoors, but these boys, whose feet had traveled only the great White Way,[22] now traced machine guns by their sound, battling with all the cunning wood-craft and bravery of old Indian fighters. On the second day they made three kilometers, the third and fourth days a little less. The enemy's resistance was strong now. Only by pushing one group forward with heavy sacrifices and sending others to flank

---

22. The Great White Way refers to Broadway, in New York City. Most of the men in the battalion were from New York City.

the enemy positions was it possible to gain at all. All day long they fought. When night dropped down they could only stop and wait for dawn.

Ordered to Dig In

On the morning of Oct. 2 our forces were approximately two-thirds through the woods. Maj. Whittlesey's men had been fighting continuously. They were now ordered to advance to a certain road that ran alongside a high slope and about halfway up. They made this advance across a deep, narrow valley, getting into a position on the hillside just below the road.

On the other side of this deep gully rose a great wooded slope on the crest of which was an old boche trench. They had fought their way through it.

With Maj. Whittlesey at this time were 550 men, parts of two battalions of the Three Hundred and Seventh regiments and two platoons from machine gun companies, with heavy guns.

Immediately upon gaining the position Maj. Whittlesey ordered his men to dig "funk holes," which were only large enough to get their bodies below the level of the ground, and prepare to spend the night there.

Fighting against numberless machine guns, when one unit had advanced as far as it could and with the whole movement like a checker game, liaison had been very difficult, and while there was a system of runner posts established back to regimental headquarters there was no connection with the units on the flanks.

At dawn on the morning of Oct. 3 things began to look bad for the little command here by itself, not knowing just where friend or foe was. At 8:50 clock Maj. Whittlesey sent his first message by carrier pigeon: "Being shelled by German artillery. Can we not have artillery support? Fire coming from northwest."

Much concerned because he was receiving no orders and no food, ammunition, or details of troops were coming, Maj. Whittlesey received his first definite assurance two hours later that he was actually cut off.

"One of the runners from the post across the valley came up frightened and shaking and reported his post had been attacked and one man killed and another one wounded, while he escaped only by luck." Maj. Whittlesey went on, talking slowly, with no effort at the dramatic. "This man said he knew the post next him had been attacked at the same time and the runners probably had been killed.

"I knew that this meant only one thing—the Germans had filtered through from our left flank and occupied the hill across the valley behind us, taking over their old line trenches there. Immediately I sent a strong patrol to the right to see if they could get through. When they returned and reported a stiff fight I saw we were completely out off.

Bullets from All Sides

"All this time the machine guns from the hill across the valley were firing at us, and I sent E company to clean it out if possible. They tried desperately, but met heavy resistance.

At 4 o'clock on this first evening they opened up on us with a mortar hidden behind a hump in the slope. This gun did a lot of damage. We tried to capture it, but the boche enfilading[23] machine gun fire made it impossible.

"Then just at dusk they sent over their first attack, coming into us from practically all sides. You see our position was a road cut along a hill. Above this, after a sharp rise of ten feet, ran the hill, which the boche claimed except for our patrols.

"They charged down this hill, lobbing 'potato mashers' on us while others attacked our flanks from across the valley below us.

Fight for Four Hours

"For four hours we fought. Finally the Germans retired to their position. It was dark now, and the firing died down except when they swept our whole position with machine guns.

"Then the protecting night came. Darkness was never more welcome to these men crouched in their tiny holes on hillsides. For a distance of 300 yards and almost down to the bottom of the gully they had dug themselves in now. Those who were uninjured went from one hole to another helping the wounded, dividing their iron rations in their packs and fetching water.

---

23. Enemy fire directed at the flank of a military formation.

"Other groups dug shallow graves and buried the men who had been killed. At the bottom of the gulley ran a little stream, and the men went down to this and filled their canteens. At intervals some boche machine gun would sweep the valley and rake the hillside. Every now and then some man would cry out that he was wounded.

"In the meantime Maj. Whittlesey was trying desperately to fight his way out. Again and again he sent patrols to find a way. Always they came back—their wounds offering ample evidence of the desperate position they were in. On the second morning another precious carrier pigeon was sent with a message.

"Huns still around us, but in smaller numbers. We have been heavily shelled by mortar this morning. Present effective strength about 235. Cover bad if we attempt advance up hill. Very difficult to move wounded if we attempt to change our position. Situation is cutting into our strength badly. Men are suffering from hunger, exposure, and wounds. In very bad condition. Cannot support be sent at once?"

This pathetic appeal for support was unnecessary, for a whole brigade was trying desperately to cut through the Germans, now heavily entrenched, and get to the trapped Americans. Time after time these men, surrounded on the hillside, could hear heavy firing across the valley and identified it as attempts at rescue.

Rescuers Fight Gallantly

Few braver deeds of the war are on record than these attempts at rescue. Brig. Gen. Evan M. Johnson personally led two attacks. In one of them a machine gun bullet cut through his puttee,[24] missing his leg by a fraction of an inch.

While the gallant attempts to rescue them were going on by land, aeroplanes were attempting to drop boxes of food and ammunition from the air. So heavy, however, was the screen of trees over the unknown terrain that all fell into boche hands.

On the fourth day, when the desperate strain of hunger was gripping the men one box was seen to drop a few hundred yards away. Immediately eight men volunteered to reach it. Five were killed and the remaining three were injured and captured.

---

24. A puttee was a narrow piece of cloth wrapped around the lower leg, a standard part of the uniform.

A few hours later one of these three injured men came in with a letter demanding that the Americans surrender.

"Tell Them to Go to Hell"

"I guess we will just tell them to go to hell," Maj. Whittlesey remarked when the message was brought to him. A little later the words of the major spread about the hillside and the men sent up a defiant cheer.

That night another attack was beaten off in the same way as all the others had been. Day came on this last and fifth morning with one-third of the men able to handle their rifles. Only a little ammunition remained. This was carefully hoarded. The machine guns had used practically all their ammunition. In every third funk hole lay a wounded man.

The artillery, mortar, and machine gun fire had broken down much of the protection which the trees and underbrush had afforded, but still the men moved about helping the wounded. A score had lost their lives getting these wounded water. Long ago the last drop of food and tobacco had been used up—still no help came.

That night at 7 o'clock shouts came from the right of the thin line. Then there came calls for Maj. Whittlesey. Hurrying along the slope he found the rescuers had come. The advance guard had broken through to the left. He knew this meant the withdrawal of Germans from his rear.

Weak, worn out, but happy now, the beleaguered men gathered about their rescuers. Then these men who had fought their way through turned over their own reserve rations and their cigarets were divided among the wounded.

Promoted on the Field

Toward morning plenty of food and a big relief with ambulances and doctors came. A divisional general arrived, too, and when he saw the man who had fought back so bravely and so long he gripped his hand and told him that from that moment he was a lieutenant colonel.

That morning they removed the wounded. Yesterday they carefully took out the bodies of the dead from the shallow graves and carried them to the heart of a valley below, where they buried them in a consecrated spot.

In the center rises a rough hewn wooden cross, and it will mark for all time where American heroes died rather than surrender.[25]

Alvin York Hero of the Meuse-Argonne

"Nine hundred and ninety-nine thousand nine hundred and ninety-nine men out of a million would have considered the situation hopeless."

George Pattullo
"The Second Elder Gives Battle"
Saturday Evening Post, April 26, 1919

Alvin C. York comes from Pall Mall, Tennessee, and is second elder in the Church of Christ and Christian Union. The sect is opposed to any form of fighting; they are conscientious objectors. But York refused to ask exemption,[26] went to war, and as Corporal York of Company G, 328th Infantry, killed twenty Germans on October eighth, captured one hundred and thirty-two prisoners, including a major and three lieutenants, put thirty-five machine guns out of business, and thereby broke-up an entire battalion which was about to counterattack against the Americans on Hill 223 in the Argonne sector near Chatel-Chehery.

He outfought the machine-gun battalion with his rifle and automatic pistol. There were seven other Americans present at the fight, but it was York's battle and only York's. But for him not a man of them would have come out alive except as prisoners. In my estimation it stands out as the greatest individual feat of the war, not only because of the amazing things he did that day but because of the man's deep religious convictions and scruples. For though York joined the army when drafted he remained troubled for months, and it was only after his captain had laid his doubts

25. The 2002 movie *The Lost Battalion* celebrated this episode in the war. On October 7, 2008, the town of Binarville, France erected a monument to the Lost Battalion.
26. The truth is a bit more nuanced than this. When York registered for the draft, he wrote on his draft card "Don't want to fight," interpreted as a request for conscientious objector status. However, his request was denied because his church was not a recognized Christian denomination.

Humble, religious, from the backwoods of Tennessee, Alvin York became the most famous American soldier of the war for his actions during the Meuse-Argonne offensive. *Source:* U.S. Army Signal Corps. Wikimedia Commons.

by quoting biblical authority for taking up the sword that he saw his duty clearly. Once his conscience was at ease the second elder went in for fighting in earnest—and he surely did one fine job.

Which is not to say that he has no regrets over the necessity which compelled him to kill so many of the enemy, but he is fortified by the knowledge that he was fighting in a sanctified cause and so his soul is at peace.

"What do you suppose Pastor Pile will say when he hears of your exploit?" I asked him there on the scene of his achievement.

"What can he say? What can any of them say?" he replied earnestly. "'Blessed is the peacemaker,' isn't he? Well, there was sure some stir-up in this country!"

York is now a sergeant and has been decorated with the Distinguished Service Cross. He has also been recommended for the Congressional Medal of Honor. To him said Maj. Gen. C.P. Summerall, in front of all the officers of the 82d Division—and "Honest John" is some soldier himself: "Corporal York, your division commander has reported to me your exceedingly gallant conduct during the operations of your division in the Meuse-Argonne Battle. I desire to express to you my pleasure and commendation for the courage, skill and gallantry which you displayed on that occasion. It is an honor to command such soldiers as you. Your conduct reflects great credit not only upon the American Army, but upon the American people. Your deeds will be recorded in the history of this great war and they will live as an inspiration not only to your comrades but to the generations that will come after us. I wish to commend you publicly and in the presence of the officers of your division."

York stood there, unflustered, looking him straight in the eye as one man to another. To him had been given the honor of carrying the colors that day. Never once did he do the wrong thing, though he was several times in situations about which he had received no instruction. This Tennessee mountaineer seems to do everything correctly by intuition; army officers who have been over the ground where he fought assert that no amount of military training could have improved his tactics, yet with York it was entirely the working of instinct, for until November 14, 1917, he was living on a small farm on Wolf River, five miles from the Kentucky border. On that day he joined the army at Camp Gordon, Georgia, and became No. 1,910,421.

He has always farmed or worked at blacksmithing. Possibly that is where he gets his physique, for York is a whale of a man, standing six feet, and tipping the scales at two hundred and five pounds. Once he wore a shock of red hair; now it is clipped close, as becomes a soldier, but it still flames like a headlight. His features are not rugged, but clear cut, and his habitual expression is one of kindly humor; but whenever he is stirred to resentment his eyes contract and take on the peculiar high and piercing quality of the hawk's. I suspect that the second elder would be a bad hombre in a mix-up.

Have you ever seen a gunman of the old Southwest? A real gunman, not the loud, quarrelsome, spurious saloon hero? Well, that's York. The same rather gentle voice in ordinary conversation, with a vibrant note when he is stirred that fairly trumpets danger; he has the same gray eyes, flecked with brown which can harden to pin points. And he has the same unhurried, half-indolent confidence of manner. In his steady gaze is absolute sureness of self.

Somehow he didn't suggest timber for a conscientious objector, so after sizing him up a while I asked a question: "York, you didn't always belong to the Church of Christ and Christian Union? Haven't you raised a little excitement now and again in your day?"

He was slow in replying, but the answer was as I expected. "Yes. I used to drink and gamble some. I went all the gaits. But when I got to drinking I was kind of liable to fight, and it was like to get me into a right smart of trouble." He was silent a moment; then countered with: "A feller does a heap of things he's ashamed of later, don't he?"

I admitted it—no use in arguing facts.

"And now you neither drink nor gamble? You don't even swear?"

The answer came like the crack of a whip. "No, sir; I play the game straight."

That was like him too. He added: "A man can't do any of those things and belong to our church. He can't just be a Christian on Sundays. He's got to live up to it all the time."

Now we were standing on the spot where he had crouched amid the brush, with machine-gun bullets showering down twigs on his head as he shot it out against an entire battalion; and it seemed impossible to me—it seemed impossible to me that—

"Man, didn't you cuss a little during the fight? Not just a teeny bit?! Didn't the old Adam crop out during that inferno?"

"Not a single cuss," he replied, "because I wasn't excited. I was no more excited than I am now. My daddy used to tell me that, if I ever got into trouble all I had to do was to keep cool and I'd come out."

Lieutenant Woods, who counted the prisoners a few minutes after their capture, confirmed the statement.

"They came out of the brush down the side of the hill, and I began to think he had brought the whole boche army with him," he remarked.

Let me say here and now that York's story is genuine from start to finish. It has been thoroughly sifted by headquarters of the 82d Division; by Maj. G. Edward Buxton, Jr. of Providence, Rhode Island, who formerly commanded the battalion of the 328th to which York belongs; by Major Tillman, now commanding it; and by York's captain, E.C.B. Danforth, Jr., of Augusta, Georgia. On top of this I questioned every soldier in the detachment with York, checked up every detail with the official reports and information, and went over every step of the ground while he told his story. In telling it he was far more prone to leave out than to amplify; men who do big things seldom like to talk about them, and are never fluent. This would be a useful fact to remember when next you listen to the outpourings of alleged war heroes. So many are newspaper made; the soldiers over here could explode many a bubble reputation at home.

York's Life in Tennessee

The end of a week's investigation left me convinced that Corporal York had performed the most remarkable individual feat of fighting to the credit of the American Expeditionary Force. And the weapons he used were peculiarly American weapons—a rifle and a pistol. The big redhead is sure death with either. Back in the Tennessee mountains he used to carry off the money at most of the turkey shoots round Pall Mall and adjacent territory. You know the kind of matches I mean—the contestants crack down on a turkey, whose head only is showing. The object is to shoot it off. Usually a .32 is employed, but each entry can use whatever rifle he fancies.

Once, years ago, in a tavern row close to the Kentucky state line, York averted bloodshed by suddenly clipping the head off a tree lizard with his six-shooter as the lizard was running up the bole of a persimmon across the road. They just naturally quieted down after that. He is the crack shot of his battalion with the rifle, and in a contest with the automatic pistol against Major Tillman the corporal hit a penny match box every shot at forty paces.

He was born at Pall Mall on December 13, 1887, and is one of eleven children. He has a squad of brothers—seven—and three small sisters. The family has lived in Tennessee for generations. York's father was a blacksmith and had a small farm on which they raised corn and wheat and oats and other grains. Living is simple in that region; a farmer raises most of what his family consumes and trades his produce at the store for the rest. It isn't a country where money circulates abundantly.

The Pall Mall people do not belong, however, to the class of mountaineers known as moonshiners. Neither are they feudists, though living close to the mountainous districts where feuds flourish. They won't stand for moonshiners or lawlessness in Pall Mall; they are a devout population.

York, however, strayed far from the paths of grace in the days of his youth. He frankly admits it. Until four years ago he never missed a bet, but went blithely along the road so many red-blooded youngsters have traveled, he had many a bout with John Barleycorn, settled many an argument after the fashion of mountain men—and he was no slouch at stud poker, either. In short, he was then as far removed from the tenets and spirit of the Church of Christ and Christian Union as any roisterer in those parts.

Then his father, William York, died. That occurred in November 1911, and it left him provider for and protector of his mother, one brother and three small sisters; the other brothers had married or moved away. For a long time he took care of them, running the smithy which his father had left, and the farm on which the family lived. Still he did not change his habits, but went out from time to time with his old cronies, which was like to land him in a right smart of trouble more than once.

"My mother used to beg me to quit drinking," he said. "Often she would follow me out to the gate and beg me not to drink any more. So one day when she cried I told her I was through. And I haven't touched a drop since."

He came to this resolution in the fall of 1914. Shortly after that a girl of very fine character whom York expects to marry began urging him to join the church. This he was slow to do, being no backslider of sudden impulses, but a man who plays every game "straight." He would not embrace religion until he felt its promptings.

Finally he saw the light and joined the Church of Christ and Christian Union in February, 1915. From that day to this he has lived up faithfully to the rules of his sect. They are very strict. None but a man of deep convictions could adhere to their teachings; you cannot meet York without feeling a profound respect for his sincerity and the rugged strength of his faith.

His church is against fighting in any form, so when the draft came along and reached out for York he was in a difficult dilemma. For not only was he a member of the church, but second elder; often he led the services. He took a leading part in the singing, and several Sunday schools in the county owed their origin to him. What should he do?

The congregation were unanimous on the point: York must ask for exemption as a conscientious objector. Pastor R.C. Pile urged it long and eloquently. His mother, faced with the prospect of losing the head of the household at a time when her health was not robust, and with three small children on her hands, backed up his arguments.

But York refused. He belonged to the Church of Christ and Christian Union and subscribed to its doctrines, but he was not going to back out of serving his country when it was drawn into war. As with a great many other courageous men patriotism was stronger in the Tennessee mountaineer than any other impulse.

"They saw I wouldn't ask for exemption and so they used to plead with me," he remarked. "I remember one day especially. A man had been arguing quite a while, so I said to him: 'If some feller was to come along and bust into your house and mistreat your wife and murder your children maybe, you'd just stand for it? You wouldn't fight?'"

"And what did he say to that?"

"Well, he looked down at the ground and kind of studied a while, and then he says: 'No—I believe I'd kill him!'"

So York let the draft take its course with him. He was the only one of the family of eight boys to go; the others were all married or had other grounds for exemption. He reported at Camp Gordon, Georgia, and started in to learn soldiering.

Captain Danforth tells me that he made a good soldier, being willing and quick to pick up the work, and obeying all orders. But he was still troubled in regard to war; his conscience was not at ease; his religious convictions gave him many hours of worry. It was due to this that York was not made a noncommissioned officer earlier. The captain could not see his way to promoting a man with his ideas.

Often they discussed the question. York had read a fair share of war literature, but he remained dubious concerning some of the stories of atrocities. It was on the religious side, however, and not the justice of the cause, that his scruples lay. He could not reconcile killing his fellowmen with the teachings of the Savior.

A Soldier by Scriptural Warrant

Just before the 82d Division sailed for France York came to see the captain again; and once more they threshed out the whole matter. Danforth and Major Buxton had frequently quoted biblical authority for the employment of force, citing the incident of Christ expelling the money changers from the Temple. How much more consistent would it be, they argued, to use physical force to insure the safety and honor of women and children; did York think that he would be criticized for protecting the helpless and the pure?

On this night Captain Danforth and the Tennessee mountaineer talked late. The captain was as thoroughly in earnest as York was. He quoted texts from the Bible, such as the thirty-sixth verse of the twenty-second chapter of St. Luke; "Then said he unto them, But now, he that hath a purse, let him take it, and likewise his scrip: and he that hath no sword, let him sell his garment, and buy one." Or St. Matthew x, 34; "Think not that I am come to send peace on earth: I came not to send peace, but a sword." Or again, St. John xviii, 3: "Jesus answered, My kingdom is not of this world: if my kingdom were of this world, then would my servants fight."

Such were the influences brought to bear. Ezekiel delivered the finishing stroke. Captain Danforth read from chapter thirty-three: "Son of man, speak to the children of thy people, and say unto them. When I bring the sword upon a land, if the people of the land take a man of their coasts, and set him for their watchman: If when he seeth the sword come upon the land, he blow the trumpet, and warn the people; Then whosoever hearth the sound of the trumpet and taketh no warning, if the sword come, and take him away, then his blood should be on his own head ... But if the watchman see the sword come, and blow not the trumpet, and the people be not warned; if the sword come and take any person from among them, he is taken in his iniquity; but his blood will I require at the watchman's hand."

"All right," said York at last; "I'm satisfied." From that night all his doubts seem to have been laid: from that night he plunged whole-heartedly into the duties of a soldier.

The 82d Division was originally a Southern division—nearly all its officers hail from the South. But various shifts and changes resulted in every state of the Union being represented in the 82d in considerable numbers. For instance, one regiment can boast that thirty-five training camps have contributed men to its ranks. Therefore the 82d wears AA on its insignia—All America; and they are almost as proud of it as the veteran First Division is of the red numeral on the left shoulder. The men of the First think that means more than a Croix de Guerre; and I am inclined to agree with them.

York was soon promoted to corporal in Company G, 328th Infantry, 82d Division. And he was with his company when the 2d Battalion of the 328th jumped off from Hill 223, just north of Chatel-Chehery, at six o'clock on the morning of the eighth of October. Their objective was the Docauville railroad, two kilometers due west and by the way, they got it. They got it despite the sheer ridges they had to climb under artillery and machine-gun fire; and the boches were obliged to pull out of a sector of the Argonne Forest, their communications having been cut.

The battalion had to cross a valley several hundred yards in width. On the left rose a considerable hill from which the boches sprayed them with machine-gun fire; straight ahead towered the elevation known as 167, a steep high ridge, from which came a withering fire; Cornay Ridge, on their right, sounded like a thousand steel hammers at work. In other words the Americans were caught by fire from three directions.

York was on the extreme left of the advance, his platoon being the support platoon of the left assault company.

"We were losing a lot of men," he said. "See that little rise just where the slope of the hill comes down? Well, it looked like we couldn't get beyond that. The line just seemed to melt away when it reached there."

Under Cross Fire

This was due to the fact that boche machine guns on the hill—now known as York's Hill—had the Americans enfiladed. Therefore Sgt. Harry M. Parsons, formerly an actor, who was in command of the platoon, was ordered to advance with his men and cover the left flank. The fire was too hot in the valley, so they skirted the foot of the hill in order to gain some protection.

Parsons ordered Acting Sgt. Bernard Early to take two squads and put the enemy machine guns out of action. That was when the real business began.

Early had under him sixteen men—Corporal York, Corp. William B. Cutting, Corp. Murray Savage, Pvts. Maryan E. Dymowski, Ralph E. Weiler, Fred Wareing, William Wine, Carl Swanson, Mario Muzzi, Percy Beardsley, Joe Konotski, Feodor Sak, Thomas G. Johnson, Michael A. Sacina, Patrick Donahue and George W. Wills. Of these Corporal Savage and Privates Dymowski, Weiler, Wareing, Wine and Swanson were killed early in the fight, practically by the first blasts from the machine-gun emplacements. Sergeant Early, Corporal Cutting and Private Muzzi were wounded at the same time, the first-named being shot three times through the body. That left Corporal York and seven privates to turn the trick.

It was a clear day. There had been mists in the valley and shrouding the hills just after dawn, but they had lifted, so that the movements of the Americans were perfectly visible to the enemy along the ridges. As the little party started up the hill which they proposed to clear of boches, machine guns peppered them from the Cornay Ridge at their backs; but the trees and brush were very thick and they escaped beyond observation without losing a man. The nests they were after lay on the other side of a slope; the boches were firing at the infantry in the valley, and were wholly uncon-scious of the detachment bent on circling round behind them.

The Americans went stumbling upward through the leafy jungle, bullets whipping the branches above and round them. None were hit, however, and soon they gained above the fire. It was a stiff climb. I went up that hill later without a pack and free from anxiety, and found it hard going. What must it have been with full equipment, machine guns blazing at them, and the enemy ahead in unknown strength!

About two-thirds of the way up they came upon an old wide trench, probably built by the French early in the war. They entered this and followed it. The clamor of the fight on the other side of the hill now grew less.

The trench led over the crest. Going warily in single file, now stopping to listen and make sure that no enemy lurked near, now moving with painful caution lest they be heard, the detachment penetrated upward through the dense woods and began to descend the other slope. Sergeant Early was in the lead. Until wounded he directed all the operations; his behavior throughout the entire affair was of the highest order.

A Shrieking Bedlam

Still they saw no Germans. They could hear firing off at their right; they could hear it ahead; but not a sign of the enemy did they see. Finally they debouched upon a path, and there in the wet earth were fresh footprints.

They crossed the path and continued the descent, veering to the left to make sure they should get behind the enemy. A few minutes, and they entered another path well worn, full of new footprints.

"Which way had we better take?" whispered Sergeant Early to Corporal York.

"Let's right-oblique," answered the mountaineer; and they right-obliqued and went downward along the path.

It dipped steeply to a cuplike valley amid the hills. A puny stream flowed through this valley; everywhere were trees and bushes and tangles of undergrowth.

Suddenly they espied two Germans ahead of them in the path. Both wore the Red Cross brassard, and both started to run at the first glimpse of the Americans. Some shots were fired, and one stopped. He surrendered; the other disappeared.

"It looked like a battle was coming," said York, "so we went into skirmish order."

They scattered out amid the riot of brush and pushed forward. Presently the leaders of the party arrived at the stream, and there on the other side were about twenty or thirty Germans, gathered near a small hut that was evidently some kind of P.C. At any rate several officers were holding a conference and a number of the men were squatted on the ground apparently about to eat.

The Americans instantly let fly. A few of the enemy returned the shots, but the majority dropped guns and equipment and threw up their hands, shouting "Kamerad!"

What had happened? How came the enemy behind them?

"Don't shoot!" ordered Sergeant Early. "They're going to surrender."

Surrender they did, the whole outfit, including the major in command of the battalion.

"What are you? English?" he asked.

"Americans," answered York.

"Good Lord!" said the major.

Early's detachment now made preparations to take them out. But before they could move all hell broke loose. Along the steep slope of the hill facing them, not thirty yards away, was machine gun after machine gun, snugly placed in fox holes, but pointing in the other direction. The boches manning them swung these guns round and opened up a fusillade on the attackers. The valley became a chattering, shrieking bedlam. Some Heinies on a hill far to the rear of the Americans sensed a new menace and opened up wildly against their own position, but their fire was many yards high and merely seared the tops of the trees.

At the first blast of fire every Heinie prisoner dropped flat on his stomach and hugged the ground. The Americans followed their example. Some took refuge behind trees, others burrowed amid the underbrush; but six were killed. Sergeant Early was shot through the body; Corporal Cutting had three bullets through the left arm; Private Muzzi had a wound in the shoulder; Private Beardsley, who had an automatic, and was crouched down near Corporal York when the trouble started, crept back to a big tree for protection. On one side of him lay Private Dymowski and on the other was Private Wareing. Both were riddled with bullets—shot all to pieces. Beardsley told me afterward that he considered the situation hopeless and could not operate his gun.

Nine hundred and ninety-nine thousand nine hundred and ninety-nine men out of a million would have considered the situation hopeless. The millionth man was Corp. Alvin C. York. The second elder was down on his haunches amid the brush picking off the boches as fast as he could shoot. From this moment the battle became all York's.

Six of the detachment were killed almost immediately after the machine guns opened up; three were wounded, including the sergeant in command. York and seven privates remained.

Of these, Private Beardsley could do nothing from his position while the enemy fire kept up, for it raked both sides of his tree from close to the ground to a height of four feet.

Private Michael A. Sacina says in his statement: "I was guarding the prisoners with my rifle and bayonet on the right flank of the group of prisoners, so close to them that the machine gunners could not shoot at me without hitting their own men. This saved me. During the fighting I remained on guard, watching these prisoners and unable to turn round and fire myself, for this reason. From where I stood I could not see any of the other men in my detachment."

And Private Donahue, a game little Irishman: "During all this shooting I was guarding the mass of Germans taken prisoners and devoted my attention to watching them. When we first came in on the Germans I fired a shot at them before they surrendered. Afterward I was busy guarding the prisoners and did not shoot. From where I stood I could see only Privates Wills. Sacina and Sak. They were also guarding prisoners."

Never a Thought of Death

Pvt. George W. Wills: "When the heavy firing from machine guns commenced I was guarding some of the German prisoners. During this time I saw only Privates Donahue, Sacina, Beardsley and Muzzi. Private Swanson was right near me when he was shot. I closed up very close to the Germans with my bayonet on my rifle and prevented some of them who tried to leave the bunch and get into the bushes from leaving. I knew that my only chance, was to keep them together and also to keep them between me and the Germans who were shooting. I heard Corporal York several times shouting to the machine gunners on the hill to come down and surrender, but from where I stood I could not see Corporal York. I saw him, however, when the firing stopped and he told us to get along the sides of the column."

My purpose in quoting the statements of these men is to show by elimination what York did, in order to convince the skeptical. Every man except the second elder is now accounted for; we know from their own lips what the survivors of the first blasts did in the fight that ensued. But somebody killed more than twenty boches on the slopes of that hill and put thirty-five machine guns out of action. Who was it?

Capt. B. Cox, of Atlanta, Georgia, who later came over the hill frontally with his platoon, told me that he counted a dozen dead boches lying along a path, and saw the arms and legs of eight or ten more sticking out from behind bushes. His estimate placed the dead at twenty-five. I am putting the number at twenty, to be conservative and because the slaughter was the least part of the exploit. What counts is the fact that the second elder of a church opposed to fighting should have given battle to an entire machine-gun battalion—and got away with it.

He never thought of surrender. His problem was to make the enemy give up as quickly as possible, and he kept yelling to them to "Come down!"

Bang! Bang! "Come down!" York would shout, precisely as though the surrender of a battalion to an individual soldier were the usual thing—and I really believe he regards it that way, provided the soldier be an American.

"Somehow I knew I wouldn't be killed," he said. "I've never thought I would be—never once from the time we started over here."

At the first crack of the machine guns on the slope opposite him York dropped to earth. He was in a narrow path leading toward the emplacements. Directly in front lay the boche prisoners, groveling in fear of their comrades' fire. The machine guns were less than thirty yards away and were blazing straight down. Their stream of fire mowed off the tops of the bushes as though they had been cut with a scythe.

And then the second elder got going on his own account. Sighting as carefully as he was wont to do in the turkey matches at home in Tennessee he began potting the boches in their fox holes, and the boches who were hiding behind trees, and the boches who were firing at him from the shelter of logs. And with every shot he brought down an enemy. No, I am wrong; he showed me a crease on a tree bole later and confessed his belief that he had missed that one.

"You never heard such a clatter and racket in all your life," he said. "I couldn't see any of our boys. Early and Cutting had run along toward the left in front of me just before the battle started, but I didn't know where they were."

Shot the Whole Bunch

If I'd moved I'd have been killed in a second. The Germans were what saved me. I kept up close to them, and so the fellers on the hill had to fire a little high for fear of hitting their own men. The bullets were cracking just over my head and a lot of twigs fell down.

"Well, I fired a couple of clips or so—things were moving pretty lively, so I don't know how many I did shoot—and first thing I knew a boche got up and flung a little bomb at me about the size of a silver dollar. It missed and wounded one of the prisoners on the ground, and I got the boche—got him square.

"Next thing that happened, a lieutenant rose up from near one of them machine guns and he had seven men with him. The whole bunch came charging down the hill at me—like this. They held their guns like this.

"I had my automatic out by then, and let them have it. Got the lieutenant right through the stomach and he dropped and screamed a lot. All the boches who were hit squealed just like pigs. Then I shot the others."

"You killed the whole bunch?"

"Yes, sir. At that distance I couldn't miss." He killed this detachment before they could charge twenty yards downhill—eight men.

"As soon as the Germans saw the lieutenant drop, most of them quit firing their machine guns and the battle quieted down. I kept on shooting, but in a minute here come the major who had surrendered with the first bunch. I reckon he had done some shooting at us himself, because I heard firing from the prisoners and afterward I found out that his pistol was empty.

"He put his hand on my shoulder like this and said to me in English: 'Don't shoot any more, and I'll make them surrender.' So I said 'All right'; and he did so, and they did so."

As York himself would phrase it the battle now quieted down, and the boches descended from their positions on the hill. They came in droves; their arrival swelled the number of prisoners to ninety.

Meanwhile the enemy machine guns from the hills back of the Americans were still spitting wildly in their direction, and none of the little detachment knew at what moment other Germans might arrive or an undiscovered nest open on them. Their own dead lay about, and they had three wounded, but it became imperative that the detachment should return with their captures immediately. Accordingly Corporal York formed up the prisoners in column and placed his surviving comrades as escort.

To him came acting Sergeant Early and Corporal Cutting. The former said: "York, I'm shot, and shot bad. What'll I do? "You can come out in the rear of the column with the other boys." Private Donahue helped bring him in, for Early was seriously wounded. Corporal Cutting and Private Muzzi were able to walk out unassisted.

After the turmoil of fighting none but a woodsman could have found his way back. York's sense of direction was perfect, but though he knew whither he wanted to go he did not know the best way of getting there. The boche major decided for him.

"Go along this path," he suggested, pointing down the one which skirted the base of the hill.

Of course York went the other way; that was all he needed to determine him. He formed up his prisoners, placed the major in front of him as a screen, a couple of other officers behind him, and started up the side of the hill through the thick woods. The long line trudged behind, herded by the seven men left of the detachment, with Sergeant Early and the two other wounded bringing up the rear. All the boches had flung down their weapons and equipment on surrendering. The field of battle was littered with their stuff.

"Just as we started I passed the body of Corporal Murray Savage," York told me, strongly moved. "Him and I were cronies— he was my bunkie—but I had to leave him there. I didn't dare to take my eye off the mob of prisoners."

As they toiled up the hill the major tried to engage York in conversation.

"How many men have you got?" he inquired.

"I got aplenty," returned the second elder grimly, and made him step faster.

It was impossible to see where they were going, on account of the thick brush, but York knew that the direction was right to bring them out on the side of the hill where the Americans ought to have established a post of command by this time. A hundred yards or more, and they were challenged. They had stumbled upon another boche machine-gun nest. York thrust the major in front of him, covered the crew with his pistol and ordered them to surrender. They abandoned their weapons and equipment and joined the prisoners.

Back to Safety

During the journey back they flushed several more nests. In one the crew offered resistance.

"I had to shoot a man there," remarked Corporal York regretfully. "When we hit the next nest and I got ready to settle them if they didn't give up, the major tapped me on the shoulder and said: 'Don't kill any more and I'll make them surrender.' And he did."

The result of these operations was that York and his small detachment pretty well cleaned up that hill before they arrived on the other side. He says that somebody was shooting at them from behind as they went along, but without any damage.

Probably this firing came from a bunch of machine gunners whom Captain Danforth accounted for half an hour later. With Sergeant Olson and two runners he easily captured forty-four prisoners while going back for his support platoons.

On the far slope of the hill York heard a loud challenge of "Halt!" and perceived a bunch of doughboys about to fire. He shouted to them that he was bringing prisoners, and they permitted him to approach. The men were part of a detachment that had taken up position in the old abandoned trench York and his party had followed earlier in the day.

It was wearing on toward ten o'clock when York and his column emerged from the scrub at the foot of the hill and halted near a dugout in which the attacking Americans had just established a battalion P.C. The battalion was now well up on the ridges fighting its way toward the Decauville railroad.

"I certify that I personally counted the prisoners reported to the P.C. of the 2d Battalion, 328th Inf., by Corp. Alvin C. York,

Company G, 328th Inf., on Oct. 8, 1918, and found them to be 132 in number. Jos. A. Woods, 1st Lieut., Asst. Div. Inspector."

After reporting there York had to take his prisoners farther back. Their route lay through the valley for some distance, and a boche lookout on a knoll atop Cornay gave the range to his artillery. A few seconds, and shells began bursting close to the column. The prisoners yelled and squealed and some of them attempted to scatter. The Americans herded them back into line and York broke the whole column into a run, which was sustained until they got beyond the shelling.

Just a Plain Miracle

The German major was about the gloomiest officer on the continent of Europe that night; not even Ludendorff felt half so bad.[27] Here he had surrendered to a handful of the enemy; the rest of his command had been put out of action by one lone redhead!

They found an order on the major for his battalion to attack Hill 223 at ten o'clock in the morning. Later a doughboy brought in a boche runner as prisoner; he bore a report from this major to his commanding officer saying that the Americans had broken up his preparations for attack, and he could do nothing.

There on the scene of the fight at the foot of York's Hill are six graves where our dead lie buried. Simple wooden crosses mark them, and at the head repose the helmets, rifles and belts of the soldiers who gave their lives. Close beside their last resting place purls a tiny stream, and over the wooded hills broods a cathedral hush.

We stood long beside the graves in silence. At last I said: "I cannot understand, even now, how any of you came out alive."

York replied, simply but earnestly: "We know there were miracles, don't we? Well, this was one. I was taken care of—it's the only way I can figure it."

The last I saw of the big fellow he had only one worry that he might be late getting home for the April meeting. They have a week of revival every spring in Pall Mall and he wants to be on hand; but he was gassed and greatly fears that his voice will be ragged for singing.

---

27. German General Erich Ludendorff was the architect of the massive, last-ditch German spring offensive, failure of which signaled the end of German hopes for victory.

Chapter 11

♦

♦

♦

♦

♦

Armistice

Introduction

In early November 1918 all signs suggested that the end of the war was imminent. On November 7, when the United Press (UP) news service scooped the competition by being the first to report that an armistice had been signed, bringing the conflict to a close, a pandemonium of joyous celebration erupted across the country. But when no confirmation came from the State Department, allied governments, or other news sources, UP was forced to acknowledge that it had made a terrible mistake—the armistice had not yet been concluded. The *New York Times* called the UP error "the most flagrant and culpable act of public deception" in the history of journalism. The incident has gone down in history as the "False Armistice."

Four days later, the incident was overshadowed by the actual signing of the armistice cease fire. In his article "Dramatic Silence After Guns' Roar," Edwin L. James of the *New York Times* provides one of many stirring accounts of what transpired on the front lines the instant the fighting stopped.

The New York *Evening World* story included here, reports on the wild celebration reignited in America when official news broke in the press on November 11. For one euphoric day, Americans set aside all other business to rejoice.

On the day after the fighting stopped, UP correspondent Webb Miller put a postscript to the historic occasion when he took an airplane ride over the armistice line and witnessed the warring armies beginning to adjust to the new reality that the Great War had finally come to an end.

False Armistice

"The country was thrown into a delirium by these reports."

"Celebrations Are Premature"
El Paso Herald, November 8, 1918

New York, Nov. 8—Millions of Americans realized today that they had been hoaxed into celebrating the end of the war by publication of the United Press dispatches, declaring the armistice was signed and fighting ended.

Twenty-four hours have passed since the country was thrown into a delirium by these reports, which declared the armistice had been signed at 11 o'clock yesterday morning and that fighting had ceased at 2 o'clock yesterday afternoon.

People Are Fooled

Each hour brings added official evidence that reports were false and that the Americans were fooled. Not only have official communications from France to Washington denounced the reports as untrue, but the official statements of the French and British war offices show the fighting still going on.

Celebration Resumed

Thousands of ship workers threw down their tools in Staten Island yards today, crossed the harbor on ferry boats and began a march up Broadway, resuming their celebration of the false peace reports circulated yesterday. Apparently they had stripped the yards of most of the metal, which could be used as noise making devices.

15,000 In Parade

There were said to be 15,000 men in line which extended for half a mile. The parade leaders said they did not know where they were going but merely that they were out to celebrate.

Hoax Widely Circulated

The dispatch cabled to this country by the United Press was picked up here and circulated by another press association (not the Associated Press).

Below is a copy of the cablegram received by the United Press at its New York office:

"Unipress, New York:

"Paris: Armistice allies signed 11 morning; hostilities ceased 2 afternoon; Sedan taken morning by Americans. (Signed) 'Howard. Simms.'"

(Unipress is cable code address for United Press; Howard is Roy W. Howard, president of United Press, and Simms is William Philip Simms, Paris correspondent of the United Press.)[1]

Other Historical Hoaxes

The hoax recalled to the public mind others, which had fooled the country, if not the world. One was the alleged discovery of human beings on the moon and the other was Dr. Cook's claim of discovery of the northpole.[2]

A news hoax, however, more closely paralleling Thursday's was the one perpetrated on the country at the death of Pope Pius X. It was announced by the United Press some hours before it occurred, but as the dispatch did not specify the hour and minute a great achievement in giving the news to the world was claimed.

In the present instance, however, there will be abundant official evidence to guide the public. The armistice being a historical document will bear the hour and minute at which the signatures are set upon it, and the hour at which hostilities are to end likewise will be officially recorded and announced to the world.

No Agreement at Once

It never had been expected that the terms of the armistice on the western front might be accepted at one brief meeting. Many questions are involved now which were not involved when armistices

1. In the days following the false armistice story, the United Press scrambled to explain what happened and to vindicate itself. UP had gotten the false information from a U.S. Admiral, but in its haste to get a scoop, had failed to corroborate the story with other sources.
2. American explorer Frederick Cook claimed to have reached the North Pole in April 1908, a year prior to Robert Peary, the man credited with reaching it first. Cook's claim was initially believed, but lack of evidence from his polar expedition returned the honor to Peary.

were granted to Austria, Bulgaria and Turkey.[3] One of the principal points concerns the disposition of the German fleet, so vital to England.

Now that the fleet is in the hands of revolutionists,[4] it is not improbable that the German plenipotentiaries may not at once be enabled to give the assurances the allies will demand. It should be recalled in connection with this point that Great Britain insisted on having one of its admirals present with the commissioners and that Germany sent admiral von Hintze.[5]

Caught Europe Too

So far as is known the erroneous report was published in only two cities in Europe—in London and in Brest, France. The London newspaper later withdrew its edition and printed a retraction. The publication in Brest was by a newspaper which received the report from the United Press.

A question being asked by many is why the naval censors passed the dispatch for publication if it was not true. The answer is that censors do not pass upon the truth or falsity of dispatches: they are only concerned with whether they contain information likely to be of value to an enemy or damaging to the entente military forces.

The Instant the Fighting Stopped

"If one listened then, one heard just at 11 the great salvo from all our guns, and then silence."

Edwin L. James
"Dramatic Silence After Guns' Roar"
New York Times, November 14, 1918

---

3. These German allies had each left the war in the days leading up to the armistice. Their departures from the conflict did not raise the many issues that had to be resolved now that the armistice with Germany had brought an end to the war.

4. A revolt among sailors at the naval base at Wilhelmshaven on October 29–30, quickly spread across Germany. It led to the abdication of Emperor Wilhelm II and to the creation of a German republic on November 9.

5. Admiral Paul von Hintze served as Foreign Minister of Germany from July to October 1918.

With the American army in France, Nov. 11—They stopped fighting at 11 o'clock this morning. In a twinkling of the eye four years' killing and massacre stopped, as if God had swept His omnipotent finger across the scene of world carnage and cried, "Enough!"

In fact, it seemed as if some good spirit had helped set the stage for the ending of the great tragedy. They told me at the front today that never before had the telephones and wireless worked so well. All our divisions, all our regiments, all our companies, got the word to quit at 11, and quit they did.

History will record that the Americans fought to the last minute. Aye, more, they fought to the last second. I picked the sector northeast of historic Verdun in the scarred hills where were buried German hopes, to spend what may be the world's greatest day. On this front we attacked this morning at 9:30 o'clock, after heavy artillery preparation. Reaching the front this morning, expecting to find quiet reigning in view of the imminence of the cessation of hostilities, I found the attack in full swing, with every gun we had going at full speed, and roaring in a glorious chorus, singing the swan song of Prussianism.[6] It was a glorious chorus, drowning the discord of German shell fire. We were attacking.

Had Orders to Attack

Picture, if you will, that scene at 10:30 this morning. Back in the rear every one knew that the war was to stop at 11 o'clock, but in the front line no one knew, except the officers. The doughboys knew nothing except their orders were to attack. They had heard rumors, but at 10:30 they were chasing the Germans back from their last hold on the hills east of the Meuse. At 10:40, at 10:50, at 10:55 they were fighting on. What could be more dramatic than when at 11 the platoon leaders in the front line sharply called the order, "Cease firing!" and explained that hostilities had been called off?

If one listened then, one heard just at 11 the great salvo from all our guns, and then silence. They tell me that the lads from

6. The German Empire was established in 1871 under the leadership of Prussia. Prussian nobles held positions of power in the government and military. "Prussianism" here refers to militarism, a condition that exists when the military is glorified and the aims of the armed forces and the state join. The contrast made during the war was that a democratic government exists to serve the needs of the individual, whereas under Prussianism, the individual exists to serve the needs of the state.

"God's country" stood as if numbed with shock, and then smiles spread over their faces and they broke into laughs as they listened and learned the Germans, too, had called off the war.

Then through the fog across the ravine they saw the boches spring from their positions and shout and sing with joy. They saw white flags in the cold wind and they saw the boches waving their hands in invitation to come over. But strict orders had been issued to our men against fraternizing and the Germans, getting no encouragement, kept on their side of No Man's Land.

When all this happened, I was standing with a grizzled American General at Beaumont, just back of the line of one of our crack divisions.

"It's so big," said he, "that I cannot grasp it at all," and then he pulled from his pocket a paper, and handing it to me, said, "Here's the order that stopped the war."

What he handed me was a copy of the order written, I understand, by Marshal Foch, the self-same order being issued to all the allied troops this morning.

Pitted with Shell Holes

It was just after 11 o'clock when a General invited me to go from within the last front line. We started walking eastward from Beaumont. Over terrain torn so that there was not one inch that had not its shell hole, we climbed the heights of the Bois de Wavrille. Toiling through rack and ruin, stumps and wire and fallen tree, we came after an hour to the eastern edge of the Bois de Wavrille from which the Germans had been driven this morning.

Across a ravine lay the Bois Herbebois with St. André Farm, a mass of stones on the slopes nearest us. Half way up the hill toward the Bois Herbebois ran a road, and that road was the front line. Along it were doughboys ready if the boche changed his mind about stopping hostilities.

Right up the hill was the German line at the end of the woods. We could see Germans walking about. With a French Captain and an American Major, I started across, but the General called us back. Going up to the hill near St. André Farm, we got a good look at the boche lines, where the Germans appeared as unconcerned as if on a picnic. Out fifty yards ahead of our front line was a dugout from which curled smoke. In it were three boches cooking supper.

A platoon of our men wanted to go get them, but a Lieutenant ruled against it, so the Germans went on cooking supper.

Calm After the Storm

Over these hills, the scene of bloody warfare since the war started and the scene of perhaps the world's most bitter battle when the Crown Prince tried to take Verdun, an almost unearthly calm rested. Where the roar of a million and one shells had so often torn the air, one could have heard a sparrow twit had the ruthless war left a sparrow there.[7] Torn and twisted and tortured was that land. Of all the woods no tree was left whole. There were only blackened and stark sticks. Of pretty villages, there were only moss-covered and shattered stones, of roads not one trace was left. Over all were somber shadow and silence that would have seemed ominous had one not known that it was harmless. The war had stopped.

While we were there at the front Germans could be seen getting back, as if seeking sleeping quarters for more comfort. As we left the scene cold dusk was settling in a wet blanket over the landscape. As we reached the edge of the woods the General called my attention to hundreds of campfires lining the hills as far as the eye could see. It was the first time fire had burned on the front line since the days when the Kaiser ran amuck and started more than he and his misled people could finish. Germany stopped at the eleventh hour.

Cheering Americans Everywhere

As we came back along the roads the landscape seemed to be filled with cheering Americans. The news had spread everywhere and our men were behaving just as a victorious football team and its fans after the last game of the season. No Fourth of July in the United States ever saw such fireworks as tore their red, green, and blue streaks across the foggy sky.

---

7. One hundred years after the war there are official "Red Zones" around Verdun and other battlefields that are still too dangerous for humans. They overflow with unexploded shells and have soil contaminated with lead, chlorine, mercury, arsenic, and acids. Not to mention human and animal remains. The French agency Sécurité Civile has estimated that it will take 700 more years to completely clean these areas.

And what we saw at Verdun would stir the pulse of a dead man. Poor, torn, suffering Verdun! It had been suddenly changed to a place of glory. Gathering darkness hid its wounds, and what one saw was the French Tricolor and the Stars and Stripes flying from the housetops and parapets, searchlights showing their glory in all its splendor. At the top of the grizzled fortress walls a band, half French and half Yankee, was playing all the tunes it knew, while through the streets marched rejoicing Yankees and their allies, whom they love. What could be more fitting for allied victory than that immortal Verdun should celebrate it?

News of Armistice Flashed to New York

"Bugles sounded the news at the Battery, sirens took it up and the news went uptown in a wave of noise."

"Victory Day Celebrated by Millions in New York; All Nation Wild with Joy"
The Evening World (New York), November 11, 1918

Victory Day was celebrated throughout the United States in characteristic American fashion with New York leading in crowds and enthusiasm and variety of demonstration. The whole nation joined in the jubilation which, in one form or another rapidly spread all over the world—even into Germany where the people, although beaten in the war, expressed their thanksgiving over the downfall of the Hohenzollern.[8]

New York made a bluff at business as usual this morning, but there was no disposition on the part of anybody to attend to any business outside celebrating the end of the war.

The Stock Exchange and other exchanges closed. Schools were closed and factories and stores shut down when it became apparent that a holiday had been declared by the people themselves. All city departments were closed at noon and Mayor Hylan led the parade up Fifth Avenue. Such banks as continued to do business during the early hours of the morning closed their doors at noon.

---

8. The House of Hohenzollern was the royal dynasty of Germany, the last representative of which was Wilhelm II, Emperor of Germany until the end of the war, when a German republic was formed.

Celebrating the end of the war in New York City, the "most overwhelming attack of delirium New York ever witnessed." *Source: New York Times*. Wikimedia Commons.

The courts all suspended for the day and in minor courts judges and magistrates remitted fines and imposed only suspension of sentences. Judge Malone, in the Court of General Sessions, suspended sentence on thirteen first offenders who had pleaded guilty and sent them out to celebrate the world's rebirth of Liberty.

The celebration centered about mid-Manhattan this afternoon and Fifth Avenue, Broadway and other main avenues and the leading crosstown thoroughfares were all impassable. Soldiers, sailors, and college lads in uniform organized snake dances and defied the police. Street cars were stalled between crossings. The air was thick with slips of torn paper tossed from skyscrapers. Six million people in this vicinity went crazy with joy.

Long before noon celebrators of Victory Day began to pour into Manhattan from the other boroughs of the city, from Jersey City and Hoboken and Newark and Yonkers and White Plains and Mount Vernon and even Samford and Bridgeport and way stations. It appeared from the appearance of the visitors that the employees of every munitions factory and shipyard within one hundred miles had come in.

It would seem that the rehearsal of Thursday[9] taught New York a lot about how to celebrate Victory. That disturbance started spontaneously and was hampered by disquieting rumors before it was well under way. To-day's show grew of its own momentum until it became the greatest, most overwhelming attack of delirium New York ever witnessed. It is quite probable that never in history anywhere has there been so diversified an exhibition of joy. And it will keep up this evening, for Fuel Administrator Mercer P. Moody announced at noon that it is the desire of the administration that New York shall be illuminated to-night as she had never been illuminated—buildings and people, and everything.

"Let us," said the Fuel Administrator, in his order abolishing conservation of light, "give the Kaiser a wake so bright and gorgeous that the memory of all the fires his army started and all the guns his armies fired will be, for the moment, smothered and obscured."

When the news reached the theatrical and hotel district that the lightless night rule had been rescinded preparations were begun to entertain a great crowd. Every theatre was sold out this afternoon. Every seat at every table in the popular hotels and restaurants was engaged or, at least, the head waiters said they were engaged.

Probably all vehicular traffic will be barred from Broadway from Herald Square north to-night, and the street for miles, from building line to building line, will be turned over to pedestrians.

The parade which started from City Hall and moved uptown finally became the magnet about which the whole celebration centred. Under the direction of Henry MacDonald, director general of the Mayor's Committee on National Defense, that parade, as to spectacular features, grew like a snow ball rolling down hill. By the time formation was attempted in City Hall Park delegations of soldiers and sailors had arrived to head the column and give the affair a military aspect. The 22d Regiment band from Governor's Island, the Navy Yard band, the Police band, the Department of Street Cleaning band, other city department bands and numerous private bands furnished music.

The city, of course, was ablaze all through the day with the Stars and Stripes and the colors of the Allies. Everybody carried a flag of some kind or wore a patriotic button. The din of horns, which grew

9. Celebrations after the False Armistice.

gradually during the morning as merrymakers were released from their employments and thronged into the streets, grew to a deep, abiding roar this afternoon.

Every soldier and sailor in uniform of any of the Allies was a part owner of the town. The fighting men were smothered with kisses and caresses, especially along Broadway and Fifth Avenue, where girls formed in delegations of from twenty to fifty, swooped down on unsuspecting youths in uniform and embarrassed them exceedingly.

Not only in the city but in the harbor was the celebration effectively staged with the colors of the Allied Nations, for, with the coming of daylight, ships in the port were dressed. This was the first time such a display has been seen here since the beginning of the war. Fluttering flags, however, furnished about the only movement along the docks, for longshoremen were away celebrating.

The news that Germany signed the armistice naturally caused cessation of the work of raising the selective draft army. All entrainments for army camps and all inductions except for the navy and the marines have been cancelled. Probably about as earnest celebrators as the day furnished were the thousands of men who expected to be started for the training camps and now face the prospect that they will not be called for war. And as for their mothers and sweethearts and wives!

Effigies of the Kaiser were burned all over the city. Hundreds of thousands of hastily improvised signs were carried by enthusiastic revelers. Drivers of trucks—motor and horse—turned their vehicles into pleasure wagons and took friends and strangers for rides. The decorations on these trucks were characteristic. Everything on wheels carried everybody that could jam in.

In the shopping and light manufacturing districts uptown an effort was made to keep the wheels of industry humming but the effort died away at 10 o'clock. All the employees were at the windows. The manufacturers closed up and went out to take a hand in the celebration themselves.

Appropriately enough a bath of light thrown on the Statue of Liberty at 2:58 o'clock this morning was the first signal to New York that the armistice had been signed. Bugles sounded the news at the Battery, sirens took it up and the news went uptown in a wave of noise.

Aviators swept over the city during the day. Subways were caverns of deafening noise. It might be said therefore that New York celebrated underground, on the surface and overhead.

A great many statesmen made speeches during the day but nobody listened to them.

Aerial View of the End of the War

"A thousand and one different kinds of war materials were lying where they had been abandoned."

Webb Miller
"Front Line Scenes as Viewed from Plane"
The Daily Capital Journal, (Salem, OR), November 18, 1918

With the American armies in France Nov. 12 (Delayed)

With Lieutenant Jimmy Meissner[10] of Brooklyn, one of the premier aces, I flew over the furthermost American lines east of Verdun.

At a height of only 20 to 50 feet we skimmed along the line where the American drive had voluntarily halted. As we swooped down over the heads of the doughboys, they paused in their work of building temporary shelters and repairing roads to wave their hands and yell greetings.

With the exception of this digging, the front lines presented a strange scene of inactivity. Doughboys strolled idly over torn up fields and along roads without equipment or guns, smoking and gossiping. In tiny ruined villages which were taken just before the armistice became effective, crowds were sitting in the sunshine. In one field within a few yards of the line a group was playing base-ball, apparently "one old cat."[11]

Germans Watch Yanks

About 200 yards away 14 Germans stood at the edge of a wood, curiously watching the antics of the erstwhile "Amerikaner schwein."[12]

---

10. Flying ace, Major James Armand Meissner, credited with eight aerial victories.
11. An early form of baseball.
12. "American pig." A derogatory German term for American soldiers.

We circled over the ball game several times. The Germans waved their hands.

Near Fresnes, in the front line, was a blown up bridge. On the American side stood a Doughboy talking to a German opposite. Both waved their hands and pointed toward the airplane.

We followed the lines about ten miles northward. We saw groups walking about in the open. In one place, in the middle of a soggy, shell shattered field, a card or crap game was going on, while other men were digging a dug out. At another place the line ran thru a little valley. Not a soul was in sight but a small Ameircan flag was stuck in the ground to indicate the front line. At most points along the line we traversed, only a few Germans were visible. These evidently were privates. They were lounging in villages and along the roads, smoking and talking. Almost all of them waved a greeting at us. None carried a gun or equipment of any kind. So far as we could see no artillery or material remained.

Trucks Busy

At one point several miles in the rear of the German lines, we glimpsed a number of trucks hurrying toward Conflans. Farther back we saw huge fires smudging the skies with huge columns of black smoke. From one place we counted eight fires in the direction of Conflans, while over the region of Pinehuille we saw a great column of fire and white smoke shoot up and drift away with the wind.[13]

In little hamlets just behind the German lines, German soldiers were sitting in the sunshine, but no horses, trucks or other means of transportation were visible.

Once we saw six Germans in a village within the American lines, surrounded by a group of doughboys. Possibly they were recently taken priosners.

Bonfires in Fields

At many places in the lines the Americans were standing in the open fields around bonfires. Some were laundering and their clothes were laid on the ground to dry. We noticed one man

13. The Germans were blowing up their ammunition supplies.

washing himself in a brook. At another place a burial party was digging three graves on a knoll overlooking the lines. At the foot of the hill a unit evidently was preparing for inspection. All its quipment was neatly laid out in rows.

For several miles in one region we flew over a section that was pock-marked with shell holes that were literally rim to rim. There were clusters of farm houses which were mere heaps of stone. The whole region was a scene of unutterable desolation. The roads were cut up and there were smashed trucks and gun carriages in the ditches. Lying in the mud were dead horses, their legs sticking up at grotesque angles. A thousand and one different kinds of war materials were lying where they had been abandoned.

Villages Shattered

We looked down on three villages which were almost unbelievably shattered. Not a living thing was visible in them. Close by the lines was a forty acre wood. Every limb was stripped from the trees and the trunks were mangled. The whole landscape was criss-crossed with freshly made zig zag trenches. We saw two deserted German strong points on a hill. They were circular affairs, ringed with many lines of barbed wire and with sunken concrete pill boxes in the center. The entire field was churned up with shell holes, while lines of wire were smashed flat.

Turning back from the lines we circled over Verdun. The streets were alive with activity. But the only bit of color in the famous ruined French city was a Tri-color on the spire of the cathedral.

From Verdun we climbed to an altitude of 2000 feet. As we made our way back to the hangar we saw dozens of tiny, winding ribbons of road filled with lines of motor trucks carrying up supplies to the dormant war machine.

Bibliography

Chapter 1 – Mobilization

Carter, Hazel V. "Army 'Hello Girls,' Trained in New York, Will be a Picturesque Unit in France." *The Evening World* (NY), June 24, 1918, 8.

Collins, Nelson. "The First Convoy." *The Century Magazine*, September 1917, 790–796.

"Fighting Sisters of Fighting Men." *The Bourbon News* (Paris, KY), May 21, 1918, 7.

"My First Six Weeks with the Colors." *The Independent*, November 3, 1917, 216–217.

"Our War Preparations Lagging." *The Literary Digest*, May 19, 1917, 1487.

"Pershing Cool, Brave, Strong." *Aberdeen Herald* (WA), June 8, 1917, 2.

"Send Army to France for Moral Effect." *The Day Book* (Chicago), April 21, 1917, 1–2.

Chapter 2 – First American Troops Arrive in Europe

Associated Press. "Paris Wildly Enthusiastic Over Pershing." *Harrisburg Telegraph*, June 14, 1917, 1, 13.

Aumonier, Stacy. "Solemn-Looking Blokes." *The Century*, December 1917, 161–163.

Bazin, Henri. "France in Dire Need of U.S. Aid." *Evening Ledger* (Philadelphia, PA), July 6, 1917, 5.

Eyre, Lincoln. "U.S. Troops Quickly Landed on Arriving at French Port." *The Sunday Star* (Washington, DC), June 1, 1917, 16.

Chapter 3 – Learning to Fight

Associated Press. "American Guns on French Front." *The Ogden Standard*, September 14, 1917, 3.

Parke, Newton C. "Aggressive Spirit Instilled in Sammees." *Evening Ledger* (Philadelphia), October 17, 1917, 6.

"Teaching Our Soldiers the New Warfare." *The South Bend News-Times*, August 19, 1917, 11.

Williams, Wythe. "Stars and Stripes with Tri-Color Fly at Verdun Citadel." *The Sunday Star* (Washington, DC), July 29, 1917, 9.

Wood, Junius. "American Troops in France Want to Get to Firing Line." *Evening Star* (Washington, DC), August 17, 1917, 1.

Chapter 4 – American Firsts

Associated Press. "German Sub Is Sent to the Bottom by First Shot of Yankee Gunners." *The Rock Island Argus*, April 25, 1917, 1.

Associated Press. "Pershing's Troops Capture First Prisoner, Mortally Wounded by Patrol; Another Escapes." *New York Times*, October 30, 1917, 1.

Bazin, Henri. "Fired the First Shot for America in War." *Evening Ledger* (Philadelphia, PA) November 26, 1917, 4.

Ferguson, Fred S. "German Gas Attack Kills Five Americans, Poisoning Sixty-one." *The Daily Capital Journal* (Salem, OR), February 27, 1918, 1, 3.

Forrest, W. S. "Visit to Trenches of First Sammies Who Gave Up Lives." *The Daily Capital Journal* (Salem, OR), December 13, 1917, 1.

Holt, Hamilton. "The Shot Heard 'Round the World.'" *The Independent*, August 3, 1918, 148–149.

Lyon, C. C. "Sammies Demand Chance at Boche as Guns Roar." *The Washington Herald*, December 28, 1917, 4.

Williams, Wythe. "We're in the Line!" *Collier's Weekly*, March 23, 1918, 7–8.

Chapter 5 – At Sea

Bechtol, Howard Edwin. "Convoys Make Trip to Front Safe as a Church." *Bismarck Daily Tribune*, August 17, 1918, 3.

Cobb, Irvin S. "When the Sea-Asp Stings." *Saturday Evening Post*, March 9, 1918, 16, 41.

Shepherd, William G. "Chasing the Periscope." *Everybody's Magazine*, October 1918, 26–32, 82–83.

"The Foe's First Blow." *The Literary Digest*, November 3, 1917, 11.

Chapter 6 – In the Air

Associated Press. "Lufbery Killed by Leap from Flaming Plane." *New York Tribune*, May 28, 1918, 1.

Bazin, Henri, "France's Flying School." *Evening Ledger* (Philadelphia), July 26, 1917, 8.

Rickenbacker, Eddie. "Gab of the Gimper; Speed King of the Air." *The Daily Gate City* (Keokuk, IA), August 9, 1918, 6.

Seldes, George. "Modern Knights Who Ride to Battle in the Air." *The Sunday Star* (Washington, D.C.), July 21, 1918, 1, 16.

Winslow, Lieut. Alan F. "Tells How He 'Got' First Enemy Plane." *The Sun* (New York), June 16, 1917, 16.

Chapter 7 – In the Trenches

Corey, Herbert. "Meet the Tactics of Boche Veterans." *Evening Star* (Washington, DC), March 26, 1918, 23.

Corey, Herbert. "Uncle Sam's Boys Take Up Trench Life." *Evening Star* (Washington, DC), March 6, 1918, 10.

Green, Martin. "Eight Months at the Front with the American Army." *The Evening World* (New York), September 28, 1918, 9.

Hopper, James. "In the American Trenches." *Collier's Weekly*, June 8, 1918, 8–9, 22.

Chapter 8 – Battles

Associated Press. "Yankee Drive Deathblow to German Army." *Chicago Tribune*, November 18, 1918, 1.

Corey, Herbert. "When We Made Good." *Everybody's Magazine*, November 1918, 32–28.

Eyre, Lincoln, "Story of Great Victory is Thrillingly Told in Cable to Evening World." *The Evening World* (New York), September 13, 1918, 1–2.

Gibbons, Floyd. "The Hottest Four Hours I Ever Went Through." *The American Magazine*, March 1919, 34–35, 143–148.

Hatrick, Edgar B. "How Our Soldiers Turned the Tide at Chateau-Thierry." *Washington Times*, September 22, 1918, 5 and September 29, 1918, 5.

Chapter 9 – Wounded Warriors

Associated Press. "Wounded Return from Battlefront." *The Sunday Star* (Washington, DC), December 15, 1918, 4.

Gilman, Roger. "With the Wounded from the Marne." *The Outlook*, October 16, 1918, 253–256.

Grasty, Charles H. "Rush Wounded to Paris." *New York Times*, June 10, 1918, 1, 3.

"Makes New Faces for Mutilated Soldiers." *Daily Capital Journal* (Salem, OR), December 19, 1918, 6.

Putnam, Shirley. "Down from Château-Thierry." *The Bellman*, October 19, 1918, 431–434.

Stidger, William L. "Gas, Shell-Shock and Souls." *The Outlook*, October 9, 1918, 226–227.

Chapter 10 – Heroes

Courtney, Ralph. "Out of the Jaws of Death and Hundom—A Yank's Escape." *New York Tribune*, November 24, 1918, 9.

Hunt, Frazier. "Here's Story of He-Man Yanks of 'Lost Battalion.'" *Chicago Tribune*, October 16, 1918, 1, 4.

Pattullo, George. "The Second Elder Gives Battle." *Saturday Evening Post*, April 26, 1919, 3–4, 71, 73–75.

Wood, Junius B. "Beat Back Force of 25 Germans, Winning French War Cross." *Chicago Defender*, May 25, 1918, 1.

Chapter 11 – The Armistice

"Celebrations Are Premature." *El Paso Herald*, November 8, 1918, 3.

James, Edwin L. "Dramatic Silence After Guns' Roar." *New York Times*, November 14, 1918, 4.

Miller, Webb. "Front Line Scenes as Viewed from Plane." *The Daily Capital Journal* (Salem, OR), November 18, 1918, 1.

"Victory Day Celebrated by Millions in New York; All Nation Wild with Joy." *The Evening World* (New York), November 11, 1918, 1, 6.

Index

Page numbers in *italics* refer to illustrations.